श्रीमद्भगवद्गीता

The Song Divine
or, *Bhagavad-gītā*:
A Metrical Rendering

श्रीमद्भगवद्गीता

The Song Divine or, *Bhagavad-gītā*: A Metrical Rendering (with annotations)

by C. C. Caleb, M.B., M.S.

Edited and introduced

by

Morris Brand

and

Neal Delmonico

(Sanskrit)

Blazing Sapphire Press
715 E. McPherson
Kirksville, Missouri 63501
2011

ISBN 978-0-9817902-3-7 (0-9817902-3-2)

Library of Congress Control Number: 2011914624

Published by:
Blazing Sapphire Press
715 E. McPherson
Kirksville, Missouri 63501

Available at:
Nitai's Bookstore
715 E. McPherson
Kirksville, Missouri, 63501
Phone: (660) 665-0273
http://www.nitaisbookstore.com
http://www.blazingsapphirepress.com
Email: neal@blazingsapphirepress.com

Image Credits

Image on Front Cover:
The Fight between Arjuna and Karṇa (detail)
Indian. Rajasthani, about 1740
Object Place: Bundi or Kota, Rajasthan, Northern India
Opaque watercolor and gold on paper
Overall: 28.3 x 36.7 cm (11 1/8 x 14 7/16 in.)
Museum of Fine Arts, Boston
Marshall H. Gould Fund, Fredrick L. Jack Fund, and Mary S. and Edward Jackson Holmes Fund
1988.97

The Song Divine

Contents

Editors' Introduction ix
The Teachings of the *Gītā* xv
Bhakti in the Middle xx
The Translation xxiv
Editorial Practices xxv
Various Interpretations of the Gītā xxvi

Original Preface (1911) xxxi

Chapter One: Viewing the Armies (सैन्यदर्शनम्) 1

Chapter Two: The Yoga of the Reason-Method (साङ्ख्ययोगः) 21

Chapter Three: The Yoga of Action (कर्मयोगः) 53

Chapter Four: The Yoga of the Divisions of Knowledge (ज्ञानविभाग-योगः) 71

Chapter Five: The Yoga of Renunciation of Action (कर्मसन्न्यासयोगः) 91

Chapter Six: The Yoga of Meditation (ध्यानयोगः) 105

Chapter Seven: The Yoga of Discernment (विज्ञानयोगः) 123

Chapter Eight: The Yoga of Brahman the Savior (तारकब्रह्मयोगः) 135

Chapter Nine: The Yoga of the King of Secrets (राजगुह्ययोगः) 147

Chapter Ten: The Yoga of Expansion (विभूतियोगः) 161

Chapter Eleven: Seeing the Cosmic Form (विश्वरूपदर्शनयोगः) **179**

Chapter Twelve: The Yoga of Bhakti (भक्तियोगः) **213**

Chapter Thirteen: The Yoga of Nature and Self (प्रकृतिपुरुषविवेकयोगः) **223**

Chapter Fourteen: The Yoga of the Three Guṇa (गुणत्रयविभागयोगः) **237**

Chapter Fifteen: The Yoga of the Supreme Person (पुरुषोत्तमयोगः) **249**

Chapter Sixteen: The Yoga of Excellences (दैवासुरसम्पद्विभागयोगः) **259**

Chapter Seventeen: The Yoga of the Three Faiths (श्रद्धात्रयविभागयोगः) **269**

Chapter Eighteen: The Yoga of Liberation (मोक्षयोगः) **281**

Appendix: Traditional Summaries of the Gītā **311**
Gītā-bhāṣyopakramaṇikā of Śaṅkara 312
The Introduction of Śaṅkara's Commentary on the *Gītā* . . . 313
Gītārthasaṅgraha by Yamunā Muni 318
Collected Teachings of the *Gītā* 319
Introduction to the *Rāmānuja-bhāṣya* of Rāmānuja 326
Introduction of the Commentary on the *Gītā* 327
The *Gūḍhārtha-dīpikā* of Madhusūdana Sarasvatī 332
Lamp on the Hidden Meanings 333
The *Sārārtha-varṣiṇī* of Viśvanātha Cakravartin 342
Raincloud of Essential Meaning 343
The *Gītā-bhūṣaṇa-bhāṣya* of Baladeva Vidyābhūṣaṇa 352
The Ornament of the Gītā 353

Bibliography **363**

Editors' Introduction

The book presented here in a metrical English translation is hardly in need of an introduction in today's climate of widespread global cultural literacy. An ancient Sanskrit text more than two thousand years old, it has been translated hundreds of times into English alone, not to mention the many other languages of the world it has found expression in. It is one of those rare texts that belong to the most exclusive ingroup of religious texts, the "classics of world religion." There, too, it sits in a place of honor alongside the Bible, the Koran, the *Dhammapada* and *Lotus-sūtra*, the *Dao De Jing*, and the *Analects* of Confucius.

Millions of Hindus read and recite this book today and look to it for encouragement, reassurance, guidance and solace. It is read and studied as well by thousands outside that community who are interested in the practice of various kinds of *yoga*. Indeed, *yoga* is a central theme of the text. But, despite what many modern writers have claimed, the *yoga* of the Gītā does not mean "union" or "integration" or "yoking." It means primarily "discipline," "application" or "practice." Thus, *yoga* in the Gītā is the putting into practice or the application of the teachings of the Gītā.

The book's Sanskrit name, *Bhagavad-gītā*, has been variously translated as "the Song Divine," "the Song Celestial," "the Song of the Lord." The word *gīta*, "song," is peculiarly in the feminine grammatical gender, causing it to end in long "a" (ā). This is so, it has been suggested, because of another part of the name of the text that usually gets dropped. That part, *upaniṣat*, "secret or confidential teaching," is grammatically feminine and thus *gīta* as its modifier or adjective becomes grammatically feminine, too, according to the rules of Sanskrit grammar.[1] A full translation of the name

[1] Śaṅkara gives three different meanings for the word *upa-ni-ṣat*. He derives it from the root $\sqrt{sad}$ which means "destroy," "go" or "reach," or "mitigate." It thus means: "[that which] destroys the seeds of transmigratory existence," "makes seekers after final release go to the highest Brahman," and "mitigates multitudes of miseries such as living in the womb, birth, old age and disease." See Mayeda, *A Thousand Teachings: the Upadeśasāhasrī of Śaṅkara*, fn.

of the text, then, would be "the Secret Teaching Sung by the Lord."

Strictly speaking the *Bhagavad-gītā* is not an Upaniṣad, nor is it a song, though it can be sung or chanted. The texts called the Upaniṣads, another group of world religious classics from India, are texts that form the final or most recent parts of the Vedas. Thus, they are referred to as *Vedānta*, "final parts of the Vedas." They represent the final stage in the long period of literary production that began with the hymns that make up the Vedas (1500-800 BCE), hymns which were recited during the performance of the Vedic fire rites and sacrifices. By the time the Upaniṣads were composed (800-300 BCE), the focus of Vedic religion had shifted from a concern for the proper performance of the ritual actions of sacrifice and the proper application and pronunciation of the accompanying hymns or mantras—activities which were thought to lead to a prosperous life in this world and a good life after that in heaven—to a concern for gaining secret knowledge or *gnosis* of the deeper meanings and workings of the rites and the hymns that empowered them. The old goals began to seem shallow and impermanent, less worthy of striving for, and a new path emerged, a path thought to lead beyond the ephemeral pleasures and pains of both the earth and the heavens, a path to liberation from quotidian life which was then considered to be a repeating cycle of birth and death. That secret knowledge or wisdom was expressed in the Upaniṣads, or at least in the twelve earliest of them.

The *Bhagavad-gītā* comes at the end of that period, clearly in that same tradition, but it was not originally counted among the Upaniṣads. Since it draws so heavily from the Upaniṣads, quoting some passages verbatum, and reflects a similar system of beliefs, the *Bhagavad-gītā* has become recognized as an "honorary" Upaniṣad. Moreover, if the word *upaniṣat* (literally, "to sit down near") suggests a passing on of wisdom from a teacher (*guru*) to a disciple (*śiṣya*), then the *Bhagavad-gītā* is an epitome of that. Arjuna, in the second chapter of the *Gītā*, submits himself to Kṛṣṇa, accepting him as his teacher, and begins to learn the secrets not only of successful, nonbinding action in the world but also of the best way to gain ultimate freedom.

The word *bhagavat* or, in its masculine singular form, *bhagavān* is often translated "Lord" or "Fortunate One." It means literally the "possessor of fortune (*bhaga-vat*)" and refers to someone who is "glorious, illustrious, divine, adorable, or venerable." *Bhaga* means fortune because perhaps its fundamental meaning is "share." Someone who has a share in something, maybe a share of something to eat, is someone who is fortunate. Thus,

---

18, 106-107. These meanings can also be applied to the teachings of the *Gītā*.

bhagavat comes to mean "fortunate one" and by extension from that, the lord. *Bhaga* also has another interesting meaning. It also means womb or vagina. Thus, he who possesses a vagina or a womb is also *bhagavat*. One might say that to "possess" a vagina is either to be a woman or have a woman and to "possess" a woman is also to be immortal because women bear within them the secret power of creation through which, from the perspective of a man, one may recreate oneself or gain immortality through progeny. Women in India are often thought of and described as the *śakti* or power of their husbands. So to possess *bhaga* is to possess creative power and without that power one is nothing.

The word *bhagavat* later becomes a technical, theological term to describe one of the three ways in which the absolute was encountered in India. The three ways or terms for the absolute are Brahman, Paramātman, and Bhagavān. Brahman is the impersonal, all-pervading absolute conceived as pure consciousness without distinguishing traits or qualities. Paramātman is the indwelling witness and regulator of the living beings, the immanent presence of the absolute within the world. Bhagavān is the transcendent absolute understood as a supreme person, who though aloof from the world comes occasionally to reveal his divine sport or *līlā*.[2] Perhaps the most detailed exposition of the term is found in the work of Śrī Jīva Gosvāmin (16th century CE) called the *Bhagavat-sandarbha* ("The Treatise on Bhagavān"), one of his six theological treatises, the *Ṣaṭ-sandarbha* ("The Six Treatises"). There he draws on passages from earlier works in which the term had been defined or at least characterized. He cites and comments on a passage from the *Viṣṇu Purāṇa* (4th century CE),

[2]This triadic idea is based on an important verse from the *Bhāgavata Purāṇa*, 1.2.11: *vadanti tattattvavidastattvaṃ yajjñānamadvayam| brahmeti paramātmeti bhagavāniti śabdyate||*, "Those who know the truth say it is non-dual knowledge (consciousness) which is variously expressed by the words Brahman, Paramātmā, and Bhagavān." All three terms do appear in the *Gītā* with reference to the absolute. It is hard on the basis of the *Gītā* to distinguish them clearly. Śrī Jīva distinguishes them briefly in his *Bhakti-sandarbha* (para 5) in the following way: *śaktivargalakṣaṇataddharmātiriktaṃ kevalaṃ jñānaṃ brahmeti śabdyate| antaryāmitvamayamāyāśaktipracuracicchaktyaṃśaviśiṣṭaṃ paramātmeti| paripūrṇasarvaśaktiviśiṣṭaṃ bhagavāniti|*, "That which is simply knowledge or consciousness, without any traits or characteristics understood as powers, is called Brahman. That which consists of being the inner regulator of all things and which is qualified by the power of *māyā* and an immense number of particles of the power of consciousness (i.e., the living beings) is called Paramātman. That which is characterized by all of the powers at their fullest is Bhagavān." They are the same absolute, non-dual knowledge, perceived differently according to the degree to which its powers are manifested. In Brahman, no powers are manifest and it appears as only pure, unqualified consciousness. This is not to say that powers are not present in Brahman. They are fully present just not manifest. In Paramātman, two powers are manifest, the *māyā* power and the consciousness power in tiny particles which are known as the *jīvas* or living beings. In Bhagavān, all the powers are manifest.

for instance, in which each syllable of the word (*bha-ga-va*) is characterized in an effort to elucidate the whole meaning of the term after the method of the *Nirukta* of Yāska which does the same for Vedic gods and terms. In a passage which, broadly speaking, runs from 6.5.66 to 6.5.79 occurs a verse that has come to represent the accepted understanding of *bhagavat*. The verse was picked up by Śaṅkara and then was cited again and again by just about everyone who ever discoursed on the subject:

> *Bhaga* is the name of these six traits: complete sovereignty, complete valor, complete fame, complete wealth, complete knowledge and complete detachment.[3]

The possession of these six qualities together in their fullness indicate the stature of the one called Bhagavān. A few verses later in the same passage a slightly different set of six traits is mentioned:

> Knowledge, power, strength, sovereignty, valor, and splendor without limit are communicated by the word *bhagavat*, without any ignominious traits.[4]

Fame and fortune have been dropped in favor of different types of power and strength. *Tejas* translated here as splendor suggests a fiery urgency or energy. This group of traits implies something more along the lines of van der Leeuw's "*highly exceptional* and *extremely impressive* 'Other'" with its recognition of "the *Power* it generates."[5]

But who is this possessor of those *bhaga* or powers who "sang" the secret wisdom in the Song Divine? And, to whom did he sing? Though the word Bhagavān has been applied to many people in Indic literature, here Bhagavān refers to Śrī Kṛṣṇa who, according to the *Bhāgavata Purāṇa*, is the only one who can truly lay claim to that title.[6] Śrī Kṛṣṇa is the same

---

[3] *Viṣṇu Purāṇa*, 6.5.74:

ऐश्वर्यस्य समग्रस्य वीर्यस्य यशसः श्रियः।
ज्ञानवैराग्ययोश्चैव षराणां भग इतीङ्गना॥

The edition of the *Viṣṇu Purāṇa* edited by Thāneśacandra Upraiti has *dharma* instead of *vīrya*, complete righteousness instead of complete valor.

[4] ibid., 6.5.79:

ज्ञानशक्तिबलैश्वर्यवीर्यतेजांस्यशेषतः।
भगवच्छब्दवाच्यानि विना हेयैर्गुणादिभिः॥

[5] G. van der Leeuw, *Religion in Essence and Manifestation*, trans. by J. E. Turner, vol. 1, 23. (Gloucester, Mass,: Peter Smith, 1963)

[6] *Bhāg.*, 1.3.28: *kṛṣṇastu bhagavān svayam.*

as Śrī Viṣṇu, the ancient Vedic god who appears in several of the hymns of the oldest Veda, the Ṛg Veda. In the view of the great Vedic scholar, F. B. J. Kuiper, Śrī Viṣṇu represents completeness or the totality of reality.[7] "The same as" means different things in different periods of the development of the Vaiṣṇava sect of Hinduism. In the older texts like the *Harivaṃśa*, the *Viṣṇu Purāṇa*, and such (200 BCE. to 400 CE.), Kṛṣṇa is regarded as a descent (*avatāra*) of Viṣṇu into the world for the purpose of removing the burden created by demonic, that is, profoundly selfish, self-enamored, self-aggrandizing rulers and peoples of the world (the *asura* in the terms of Hinduism).[8] In the later texts (500 CE to 1400 CE.) like the *Bhāgavata Purāṇa*, the *Padma Purāṇa*, the *Brahma-vaivarta Purāṇa*, and such, Kṛṣṇa changes places with Viṣṇu and is recognized as the ultimate source of all descents. Indeed, Viṣṇu himself comes to be regarded as a mere partial aspect of him.

Kṛṣṇa begins his ascent to supremacy with India's great epic, the *Mahābhārata*, a tiny part of which makes up the *Bhagavad-gītā*. Certainly the seeds of Kṛṣṇa's ascent to ultimacy were planted in the *Gītā* itself. The majestic image of the all-powerful Kṛṣṇa on the battlefield revealing his cosmic form to his friend Arjuna, a form in which all the great warriors except Arjuna and his brothers perish into countless mouths, is gradually replaced over the centuries by the loving, threefold bending form of Kṛṣṇa, the lover of the cowherd girls (*Gopījanavallabha*). This newer Kṛṣṇa plays his enchanting flute and draws the love-struck girls, married and un-, out into the forest of an autumn night. Though the episode of the forest circle dance or Rāsa-līlā is mentioned briefly in the *Harivaṃśa* and *Viṣṇu Purāṇa*,

---

[7]F. B. J. Kuiper, "The Three Strides of Viṣṇu" in *Ancient Indian Cosmogony: Essays Selected and Introduced by John Irwin*, (Delhi: 1983): "Now it has long been clear that Viṣṇu's three strides are somehow connected with the totality of the universe, but it has never been expressly stated, what exactly is the mythical significance of the third step. Its explanation must be sought in the cosmogony, i.e., in the creation myth. In the beginning there was the undifferentiated primeval world consisting of the waters and the beginning of the primordial hill, which the cosmological boar had dug up out of the waters. Heaven still lay on the earth. By slaying Vṛtra, Indra rivets the hill, opens it, and 'props up' (*stabh*) the sky: thereby the dual organization of the cosmos is created. But at the same moment Viṣṇu 'strides out': his first step corresponds to the nether world (which includes the earth), his second step to the upper world, but his third step is a mystery, not perceptible to the human eye, for it corresponds to the totality of the opposed moieties, just as the thirteenth month stands for the totality of the preceding twelve months. All that exists is in the three steps, or in the third that represents them." (149) And, "In our opinion Viṣṇu, far from being a mere assistant [of Indra], must have been conceived mythologically as standing between the two parties in the Vṛtra fight, just as he stood in the ambiguous position between the Asuras and Devas in the *amṛtamanthana* [the churning of the ocean of milk to produce nectar], and to some extent also as Kṛṣṇa stood in the battle of the *Mahābhārata*." (150)

[8]In other words, something like the Ayn Rand crowd of today.

it occupies five central chapters in the Tenth *Skandha* of the *Bhāgavata*, about a tenth of the part of the text that describes Kṛṣṇa's life in Vṛndāvana. It became a source of literary and religious inspiration for numerous later generations of poets and *bhaktas*. There is very little of that erotic, heart-stealing Kṛṣṇa in the *Gītā*. Kṛṣṇa the charming, butter-stealing boy and heart-stealing lover of Vraja eventually superseded the cosmic Kṛṣṇa of the *Mahābhārata*, but the *Gītā* never lost its purchase on the hearts of the devotee.

Kṛṣṇa's partner in this great dialog is Arjuna, one of the five Pāṇḍava brothers, who are all sons of Kuntī and husbands of Draupadī. Kṛṣṇa and Arjuna are the best of friends and, in fact, brothers-in-law, since Arjuna is also married to Kṛṣṇa's younger sister, Subhadrā. Arjuna belongs to the *kṣatriya* or warrior class and though every effort has been made to avoid the internecine war about to occur, negotiations have failed and Arjuna finds himself on the brink of a massively destructive battle. Seeing his whole family gathered there to fight on one side or the other and knowing that many if not most of them are bound to die, Arjuna falls into a crisis of conscience and falters. Kṛṣṇa is there to guide him through it.[9]

Naturally, Arjuna represents everybody. We have all found ourselves in a crisis situation in which we have lost our will to act or our enthusiasm for the tasks facing us. We have been in situations in which we either fear or dislike the probable results of the actions we are epxected to take.

---

[9]Most traditional commentators, as well as many of today, believe that Kṛṣṇa actually spoke the words of the *Gītā* and that Sañjaya heard them, word for word, clairvoyently from the court of Dhṛtarāṣṭra. For them, the story told in the *Mahābhārata* of the events leading up to the great internecine war, of the war itself, and of its the devastating aftermath are history and occurred around 3000 BCE, or, according a more moderate view, around 1000 BCE. Surely, however, Śrī Krishna Prem's evaluation of the text in his *The Yoga of the Bhagavad-Gita* (10) is correct: "Though its author is unknown (for we can scarcely adopt the view that it was, as we have it, spoken by the historical Krishna on the battlefield of *Kurukshetra*) ... " Perhaps he is right, too, when he says later on: "To anyone who has eyes to see, the Gita is based on direct knowledge of Reality and the Path that leads to that Reality, and it is of little moment who wrote it or to what school he was outwardly affiliated." (11) However, those of us lacking those eyes must disagree. It is important to know who wrote it, when, for what purpose, and for whom. Although we are unable to say who wrote the *Gītā*, one useful way of viewing the text is as an early (300-200 BCE) response to Buddhism and perhaps Jainism from a defender of post-Vedic Hinduism. The caste system is justified and defended, as are the Vedas, though they are recognized as indeed mostly just "flowery words." Renunciation is redefined in ways that are compatible with the execution of caste duties and a theistic, Hindu view of reality. It is a powerful text, one that incorporates many of the insights and criticisms of the old Vedic sacrificial religion not only by Buddhists, but also by members of that very tradition who no longer found the Vedic worldview compelling, except, perhaps, in a sentimental way. It seems, at least in part, meant to keep Hindus from becoming Buddhists or joining other heretical groups by offering them an appealing and comparable Hindu option.

The situation facing Arjuna in the *Gītā* is without doubt one of the most dramatic examples of this, an example involving life and death and the survival of one's loved ones. Though our crises may not seem as great as Arjuna's, to us they can be earth-shattering and in those moments of deep vulnerability we wish for a guide like Arjuna's Kṛṣṇa.

The Teachings of the *Gītā*

So what does Kṛṣṇa teach Arjuna? The *Gītā* is full of instructions, not all of which are compatible with each other. However, one may say in general terms that the central message is an Indic version of the Greek oracular injunction of the Pythian priestess of Delphi: "Know thyself!" Kṛṣṇa, therefore, informs Arjuna that he is in essence not an impermanent being, but an immortal one like Kṛṣṇa himself and that he has had many births in the past, all of which Kṛṣṇa remembers, but none of which Arjuna recalls:

> The Blessed Lord said:
>
> O Arjun, know both thou and I
> Have left unnumbered births behind;
> I know them all, O Parantap,
> But they have faded from thy mind.[10]

The true self of Arjuna and all the soldiers gathered there on the battlefield ready to fight is immortal and therefore not subject to death, but only to repeated births.

> For verily I ne'er was not,
> Nor thou, nor any of these lords,
> And none of us who live this day
> Hereafter ever cease to be.
>
> Just as the dweller[11] in these frames
> Puts on his childhood, youth and age,
> So doth he clothe himself afresh;
> At this the wise are not perplexed.[12]

The death of the immortal self or soul is impossible:

[10] *Gītā*, 4.5.
[11] i.e., the embodied Self.
[12] ibid., 2.12-13.

Know him as indestructible
By whom pervaded is the world,
And none can bring about the death
Of him, the undecaying self.[13]

Kṛṣṇa provides an interesting example of the phenomenon of transmigration:

Like to the man who casts off garments old,
And clothes himself in other raiment new,
So too doth he, the dweller in these frames,
Discard the old to live in bodies fresh.[14]

One who knows this, however, is freed from the endless (and beginningless) cycle of repeated birth.

The sages who have wisdom gained
Renounce the fruit which action brings,
And from the bonds of re-birth freed,
Achieve the state which knows no pain.[15]

Theoretical knowledge of the self, however, is not enough. So, several paths are recommended for people of different dispositions. The three main paths are: detached action (*niṣkāma-karma*), that is, action performed without desire for or attachment to the results of that action; the cultivation of direct knowledge (*jñāna* of the true nature of the self, generally achieved through study of the revealed texts and the meditative practices of classical yoga); and *bhakti* or a loving, emotional engagement with, or, participation in, the being believed to comprise or be the source of the whole show, Śrī Kṛṣṇa himself. Traditionally, the first six chapters of the *Gītā* are said to expound detached action, the middle six *bhakti*, and the final six knowledge, but discussions of the various paths often appear outside their assigned sections.

In favor of detached action, we find:

Therefore, without attachment, thou
E'er do that work which should be done;
Work done without attachment is
Man's passport sure to the supreme.[16]

[13] ibid., 2.17.
[14] ibid., 2.22
[15] ibid., 2.51.
[16] ibid., 3.19.

On behalf of *bhakti* we also hear:

To those who ever are attuned,
And worship me with love,
That knowledge[17] do I freely give,
Whereby they come to me.

And all for love of them,
Indwelling in their very hearts,
With wisdom's light resplendent I
Their darkness[18] do dispel.[19]

And,

But I may yet be known like this,
By love on me alone bestowed,
And known and seen too as I am,
And entered into, Parantap.[20] 54

Who works for me, his highest goal,
Who loveth me, attachments freed,
Who hateth none, O Pṛthā's son,
He comes to me assuredly.[21]

On the path of knowledge we hear:

Yet they who th'eternal seek,
The undefined, the unrevealed,
Th'omnipresent, th'unthinkable,
Th'ineffable, th'immutable;

Restraining all their senses well,
And equal minded in all things,
Rejoicing in the good of all,
These also surely come to me.[22]

Kṛṣṇa warns, however, that the path of knowledge is very hard:

---

[17] *Buddhi-yoga*, discriminating knowledge.
[18] In the original, darkness born of ignorance.
[19] ibid., 10.10-11.
[20] Parantap, tormentor of one's foes, is another name of Arjuna.
[21] ibid., 11.54-55.
[22] ibid., 12.3-4.

The travail greater is of those
With minds set on the unrevealed,[23]
For such a goal[24] is hard to reach
By man in his embodied state.[25]

Thus, while recognizing all paths and indeed all gods (they are all really Kṛṣṇa incompletely understood),[26] the path of *bhakti* or surrender to Kṛṣṇa is reckoned easier and more direct. It is difficult for living beings who are used to dealing with forms, both physical and linguistic, to try to grasp and then focus their attention on a formless, undefined, ineffable absolute. It takes a good deal of deprogramming and the result, according to the three-manifestation theory (Brahman, Paramātman, and Bhagavān) is incomplete since it only discovers Brahman. That the path of *bhakti* is more direct is made clear in a verse that is often considered the summary verse of the *Gītā* since it occurs in the last chapter as Kṛṣṇa's last bit of advice:

Renouncing every duty then,
Seek shelter thou in me alone,
For I will truly set thee free
From all thy sins; hence, do not grieve.[27]

At such a reassurance from such a powerful being as Kṛṣṇa, believed to be fully capable of keeping his word, who would not rejoice? And how do we know that Kṛṣṇa is powerful enough to keep his word? That has surely been demonstrated in the climax of the text which occurs in the eleventh chapter with Kṛṣṇa's revelation to Arjuna of his cosmic or universal form:

Thus having spoken forthwith, king,

[23]The unmanifested.
[24]I.e., the goal of the unmanifested.
[25]Lit. by the embodied. ibid., 12.5.
[26]As we see in verses 9.23-4:

The devotees of other gods,
Who worship them in faith sincere,
These also, know, O Kuntī's son,
Though wrongly, yet they worship me.

Of every sacrifice I am
The lord and the enjoyer both,
But me they know not as I am,
And for this reason do they fail.

[27]ibid., 18.66.

Hari, the mighty lord of yoga
Revealed himself to Pṛthā's son,
In his supreme and sov'ran form.

Of countless mouths and countless eyes,
Of countless wondrous sights possessed,
Of countless heavenly ornaments,
Of countless heavenly weapons raised;

Bedecked with heavenly wreaths and robes,
Anointed with unguents divine,
All-wonderful and splendor-clothed,
Unbounded, facing every side.

The splendor of a thousand suns,
If all at once could light the sky,
It then perchance may shadow forth
The splendor of that mighty one.

There in the body of the god
Of gods, the son of Pāṇḍu saw
The whole world gathered into one,
And split up too in many parts.

Then Dhanañjay, amazement filled,
Thrilled through and through, his hair on end,
Before the lord bowed low his head,
And with joined palms him thus addressed.[28]

Assurances from such a powerful being can certainly be counted on. This passage contains one of the verses made famous in the United States by J. Robert Oppenheimer, who also studied Sanskrit as a hobby, in describing the explosion of the first atomic bomb ("The splendor of a thousand suns ... ").[29]

---

[28] ibid., 11.9-14

[29] "If the radiance of a thousand suns were to burst at once into the sky that would be like the splendor of the Mighty One ... I am become Death, the Shatterer of Worlds." J. Robert Oppenheimer, quoting *The Bhagavad Gita*, Alamogordo, New Mexico, 1945. He was a US administrator and astrophysicist (1904-1967). The other verse he cites is 11.32:

I am the world effacer, mighty Time,
Made manifest to overthrow these worlds.
Without thy aid none shall indeed survive
Of all the warriors now for battle met.

Bhakti in the Middle

Students of the *Gītā* often make much of the distinction between action, *bhakti*, and knowledge, seeing them as mutually exclusive, distinct paths to liberation. Thus, according to this view, action means ritual action or action dictated by duty (*dharma*) from the results of which one should remain aloof and unattached. Knowledge is the assiduous cultivation of knowledge of the self by carefully listening to the revealed texts (the *śruti* or the Upaniṣads), thinking about what one has heard and logically probing it, and then meditating on it to arrive at a direct realization or experience of its meaning.[30] And *bhakti* means developing an emotional attachment or love for someone, in this case for Kṛṣṇa. In actuality, however, the distinction is not as clear cut as one might claim. Madhusūdana Sarasvatī (1540-1630 CE) in his opening comments on the *Gītā* suggests that the reason *bhakti* is placed in the middle six chapters of the text, between action and knowledge, is that it shares aspects of each.[31] Some, too, have compared the structure of the *Gītā*, though for different reasons, with a barley corn in which the most valuable kernel is in the middle protected on each side by halves of the hull.[32] Thus, *bhakti*, it may be claimed, is the real kernel of the text. And, indeed, *bhakti* as it has come to be understood and practiced over the intervening centuries does indeed incorporate both action and knowledge and, one might argue, does tend to unite and invigorate them. The preeminent text on *bhakti*, the *Bhāgavata Purāṇa* characterizes *bhakti* in this way:

> Listening, praising, and remembering Viṣṇu, serving him, ritually honoring him, extolling him, becoming his servant, his

---

[30]This is the process recommended in the *Bṛhad-āraṇyaka Upaniṣad* itself at 2.4.5: *ātmā vā are draṣṭavyo śrotavyo mantavyo nididhyāsitavyo maitreyi*, "the self, indeed, should be seen, should be heard of, should be thought about, should be meditated on, o Maitreyi!."

[31]Madhusūdana says:

> Ritual action, worship, and knowledge are the three divisions in order. In that way the Gītā with its eighteen chapters also has three divisions. (4) One division with each unit of six chapters is here observed. In the first and the last, preferences for action and knowledge are described. (5) Since there is no combination of those two because they are highly incompatible, the preference for *bhakti* for Bhagavān is proclaimed in the middle six. (6) Since it [*bhakti*] indeed follows both, it eliminates all the obstacles between them. It is of three kinds: *bhakti* mixed with action, pure *bhakti*, and *bhakti* mixed with knowledge. (7)

See his section of the appendix.

[32]See, for instance, D. Dennis Hudson, "The 'Barley-Corn' Pattern of the *Bhagavad-gītā*," in the *Journal of Vaiṣṇava Studies*, 9.2 (2001), 181-194.

> friend, and offering oneself to him; if this kind of ninefold *bhakti* is performed and offered to Viṣṇu by someone, then I think that person the most highly educated.[33]

Bhakti, then, is clearly active and involves actions, even ritual actions, of various sorts. The difference perhaps between *bhakti* and detached action is that instead of remaining unattached to the results of one's action, as in *niṣkāma-karma*, one offers those results to Kṛṣṇa. In both cases, one renounces one's own claim to the results of action, but in the second case, through the influence of *bhakti*, one hopes to please Kṛṣṇa with those results. The results become an offering of love to Kṛṣṇa.

Bhakti is also recognized as a kind of knowledge. Perhaps one of the first to suggest that *bhakti* is a form of knowledge was the great Śaṅkara (7th cent. CE) in his commentary on the *Gītā*. Paraphrasing verse 12.20 of the *Gītā* Śaṅkara says: "My *bhaktas* who are sheltered by the highest *bhakti*, defined as knowledge of the highest truth, are extremely dear to me."[34] Śrī Rāmānuja (11th century CE) also considers *bhakti* a kind of knowledge. He says: "*Bhakti* is a special kind of knowledge that is extremely pleasing, that has no other purpose and that creates disinterest in everything other than itself."[35] Śrī Rūpa Gosvāmin (16th century CE) writes in his *Ocean of the Nectar of the Rapture of Bhakti* (*Bhakti-rasāmṛta-sindhu*) that *bhakti* is of three types: practice (*sādhana*), attraction (*bhāva*), and love (*preman*).[36] The first is the active side of *bhakti*, *bhakti* as a set of actions or practices meant to cultivate or create favorable conditions for the appearance of the latter two forms of *bhakti*. These are forms of cognition or awareness and thus forms of knowledge. In the next verse, which is his definition of *bhakti* as practice, Śrī Rūpa says:

> If it is accomplished by action and has attraction as its goal, it is called *bhakti* as practice. Its goal is the appearance in the

[33]Bhāg., 7,5,23-4:

श्रवणं कीर्तनं विष्णोः पादसेवनम्।
अर्चनं वन्दनं दास्यं सख्यमात्मनिवेदनम्॥
इति पुंसार्पिता विष्णौ भक्तिश्चेन्नवलक्षणा।
क्रियेत भगवत्यद्धा तन्मन्येऽधीतमुत्तमम्॥

[34]Śaṅkara, comm. on 12.20: *madbhaktāśca uttamāṃ paramārthajñānalakṣaṇāṃ bhaktimāśritāste'tīva me priyāḥ.*

[35]Rāmānuja, *Vedārthasaṅgraha*, para. 128: *bhaktirapi niratiśayapriyānanyaprayojanasvetaravaitṛṣṇyāvahajñānaviśeṣa eva.*

[36]Brs., 1.2.1: *sā bhaktiḥ sādhanaṃ bhāvaḥ premā ceti tridhoditā*|.

heart of an eternally existing attraction.[37]

Bhakti as practice is aimed at creating the conditions under which *bhakti* as attraction and *bhakti* as love may appear. The latter two, however, are not thought of as created or caused by the practices of *bhakti*. They are regarded as pre-existing or eternally existing. They merely appear in the hearts of the *bhaktas* but are not born there. Where then do the last two forms of *bhakti* come from? According to the Caitanyite theologians, they are part of the internal or essential power (*svarūpa-śakti*) of Bhagavān himself and they descend into the world in much the same way as Bhagavān himself descends into it for various salvific purposes. Being infused with this power, the *bhakta*, experiencing it as deep attraction and later as love, becomes a source of great pleasure for Kṛṣṇa, too. As Śrī Jīva puts it: "The operation called the pleasure-giving power (*hlādinī-śakti*) is the essential core of the internal power (*svarūpa-śakti*) which is itself the most essential of all of Lord's powers. In turn, the essential core of that pleasure power is the special operation *bhakti* and is also known as attraction (*rati*)."[38] He says next: "That *bhakti* always exists, having placed itself on both sides, Bhagavān and *bhakta*."[39] The presence of this pleasure-giving power on both sides of the relationship insures that each derives great pleasure from the other.

The cognitive or knowledge dimension of *bhakti* is brought out more clearly by a later theologian of the Caitanya tradition, Baladeva Vidyābhūṣaṇa (18th century CE.). Writing in the introduction to his commentary on the *Brahma-sūtras* called the *Jewel of Conclusion* (*Siddhānta-ratna*) he says: "*Bhakti*, too, is a special kind of knowledge."[40] He then says: "Knowledge, also known as scientific knowledge (*vidyā*) and intuitive knowledge (*vedana*), is twofold. One is the perception of the categories of *tat* and *tvam* by a kind of aggressive directness as if staring without blinking; and the second, charming and wonderful as if acquired by gazing furtively through side-long glances, has the form of *bhakti*."[41] The *tat* and *tvam* refer to the

---

[37]Brs., 1.2.2:

कृतिसाध्या भवेत् साध्यभावा सा साधनाभिधा।
नित्यसिद्धस्य भावस्य प्राकट्यं हृदि साध्यता॥

[38]Śrī Jīva, *Paramātma-sandarbha*, para 92: *kiṃca paramasārabhūtāyā api svarūpaśakteḥ sārabhūtā hlādinī nāma yā vṛttistasyā eva sārabhūto vṛttiviśeṣo bhaktiḥ sā ca ratyaparaparyāyā*|

[39]ibid.: *bhaktirbhagavati bhakte ca nikṣiptanijobhayakoṭiḥ sarvadā tiṣṭhati*|

[40]Baladeva Vidyābhūṣaṇa, *Siddhānta-ratna*, para 32: *bhaktirapi jñānaviśeṣo bhavati*

[41]ibid, para 33: *vidyāvedanaparyāyaṃ jñānaṃ dvividham*| *ekaṃ nirnimeṣavīkṣaṇavat tattvam-padārthānubhavarūpaṃ; dvitīyaṃ tvapāṅgavīkṣaṇavadvicitraṃ bhaktirūpamiti*|

famous Upaniṣadic great declaration (*mahāvākya*) *tat tvam asi*, "You are that," which is meant to establish the identity of the self with Brahman or the absolute. The result of the first kind of knowing, the scientific sort, is one of two types of liberation, depending on whether the "you" is more clearly known or the "that" is more clearly known. The former leads to the kind of liberation called isolation (*kaivalya*) which is the goal of many non-dualist traditions. The latter leads to the liberation of the five types beginning with achieving the same transcendent world as the Lord, and so forth.[42]

The result of knowing the second way, however, the *bhakti* way, is achieving the highest goal of humankind, the joy of serving the Lord directly as the recipient of the grace of being able to bring the Lord under one's control as though one were a young woman endowed with attractive qualities like affection, beauty, and so forth. Thus, according to Baladeva knowing in the way of *bhakti* is a much more intimate way of knowing and leads to the highest result. He formalizes his understanding of *bhakti* as a way of knowing by altering Śrī Jīva's definition of *bhakti* as the core of the pleasure-giving power. For Baladeva, *bhakti* is the "essential core of the pleasure-giving and the knowledge-giving powers inseparably united" and that essential core is the "special desire that is favorable to the Lord found in his eternal companions."[43]

Thus, *bhakti*, starting out in the *Gītā* as one of three options, ends in the great flowering of the *bhakti* movements of the 15th and 16th centuries in India by absorbing and transforming the other two paths, the paths of action and knowledge.[44]

---

[42]The five types of liberation are: achieving the same eternal world as the Lord, the same or equal opulence as the Lord, the same beautiful form as the Lord, closeness to the Lord and the opportunity to merge into the Lord. See Bhāg. 3.29.11.

[43]ibid., para 40: *tathā ca hlādasaṃvidoḥ samavetayoḥ sāro bhaktiriti sidhyati| tatsāratvaṃ ca tannityaparikarāśrayakatadānukulyābhilāṣaviśeṣaḥ*

[44]To reinforce the suggestion made in a previous footnote that the *Gītā* is a response to Buddhism, one might point to the similarity between the three paths, action, knowledge and *bhakti* and the Eightfold Noble Path of the Buddhists. The eightfold path is similarly divided into three compoments: wisdom (*prajñā*), character (*śīla*), and concentration (*samādhi*). Wisdom is: right understanding and right intention. Character is: right speech, right action, right livelihood. Concentration is: right effort, right mindfulness, and right meditation. Those three correspond to knowledge, action, and *bhakti*. One might wonder what *bhakti* has to do with meditation, but *bhakti* seems to be closely associated with meditation. Rāmānuja defines it as constant recollection, or *dhruvānusmṛti*. The emotional dimension of *bhakti*, which we have been calling attraction (*bhāva* or *rati*), works to drive or empower the meditation, making it easy to fix one's mind on the object of one's attraction. Thus, in the three paths offered by the Gītā we have a replacement for the Eightfold Noble Path of Buddhism. Moreover, as the great Buddhist scholar Tscherbatsky noted long ago, all Indian philosophical

The Translation

This translation of the *Gītā* was first published a century ago (1911), and does not seem to have been reprinted since then. Needless to say it is a great joy and privilege to be involved in its reproduction. The readers sympathetic to the theme of the poem will acknowledge certain remarkable virtues in Caleb's translation.

There have indeed been other metric renditions such as Sir Edwin Arnold's *Song Celestial*, which is regarded as true to the original text and is worthy as a great poetical work in its own right. For the major portion of the text Arnold chose to use blank verse's unrhymed five-footed lines. Although blank verse may be regarded as suited to the didactic theme of the poem in English, it strays, however, from the feel and flow of the original verses of the *Gītā*. Caleb on the other hand has dropped the measure to rhymed tetrameter couplets, which more closely resemble the *anuṣṭubh* couplets of the original. Deciding on the meter in coordination with the argument is a vital aspect or device of prosody, as Ovid points out:

> For mighty wars I thought to tune my lute,
> And make my measures to my subject suit,
> But Cupid, laughing, when he saw my mind,
> From every second verse a foot purloined ... [45]

There is some variation in meter of the original Sanskrit and Caleb has followed by using blank verse to correspond to the longer *triṣṭubh* meter.

As well as adherence to meter in that way, Caleb has taken great care not to interpret, which is the modern translator's vice, but to be as literal as would be intelligible, avoiding idiomatic usage. Of course there are

---

traditions profess the Four Noble Truths: "All Indian philosophical systems professed to be doctrines of Salvation. They therefore start from the conception of a whole (*sarvam*) which is then split into two halves, Phenomenal life and the Absolute (*saṃsāra* and *nirvāṇa*). The phenomenal part is further divided into an analysis of its actual condition (*duḥkh* [suffering]), its driving forces (*duḥkha-samudaya* [the arising of suffering]) and their gradual extinction (*mārga* [the path]). When extinction (*nirodha*) is reached, life merges into the Absolute about whose essence a variety of constructions exist. These four topics,—the four 'noble truths,' as the term has been very inadequately translated and represented as a fundamental principle of Buddhism,—contain, in reality, no doctrine at all. It is only a scheme for philosophical constructions and is accepted by all Indian systems without exception. They cover, indeed, the Indian conception of philosophy. Uddyotakara says, 'these are the four topics which are investigated by every philosopher in every system of metaphysics.'" (*The Conception of Buddhist Nirvāṇa*, 54-55.)

[45]Ovid, *Amours I*, 1, opening lines. Dryden's 1776 translation. Internet archives. Online publisher Bathurst.

faults in Caleb's translation, such as skipping or stumbling meter and the occasional awkward turn of phrase. Perhaps his fidelity to Sanskrit word order and his mildly archaic vocabulary will prove to be obstacles for some readers today. But we leave sympathetic readers to judge for themselves.

Editorial Notes and Practices

We have tried to make as few editorial changes as possible in the text of the translation. In a couple of cases, verses were inadvertantly left out of the original edition. Mr. Brand supplied the versifications for those missing verses and on a few rare occasions changed the original to a more felicitous expression that nevertheless met the demands of the meter. Beyond that, a few other changes in word order and vocabulary were made by Elizabeth Delmonico; the resulting expressions continued to fit the meter but were less likely to create confusion. On the whole, there were a handful of these kinds of changes per chapter. In each case we endeavored to insure that the resulting translation was as faithful to the original Sanskrit meanings of the verses as the original.

The original work did not include the Sanskrit text. This we have added in two forms, in the original Devanāgarī script and just under that, in the standard diacritic form commonly used for Sanskrit texts. Thus, the layout of the work has the original Sanskrit text in these two forms on the left-hand pages and the translation with footnotes, drawn primarily from the original, on the right-hand pages. This way an interested reader or student of the Sanskrit language can look back and forth from the English verse translation to the Sanskrit text and see how the translator has tried to capture the original in English.

The text followed in the edition is referred to as the "vulgate" version; that is, it is the version accepted by the earliest commentator, Śrī Śaṅkara (7th cent. CE). The text was downloaded from the Gauḍīya Grantha Mandira, a fine collection of Sanskrit and Bengali texts related to the Caitanya tradition. It then was edited and corrected by the Sanskrit editor for this edition, Neal Delmonico. Another version of the text, perhaps an even earlier one, is found in the version accepted by a later commentator named Bhāskara (9th cent. CE).[46] Bhāskara's commentary has survived only in fragments up to the ninth chapter, but some of the readings, especially those in the first chapter make better sense than those in the vulgate.[47]

[46]Not to be confused with the two Indian mathematicians of that name: Bhāskara I (7th cent. CE) and Bhāskara II (12th cent. CE).

[47]See 1.10, for instance.

It was the intention of the Sanskrit editor to include the variant readings wherever they were available, but in this edition only the first chapter has been done in this way. To do the rest would have postponed the publication of this edition. In a later edition the rest of the variants will be added. The version of Bhāskara seems to have been the basis of the development of yet a third version or recension of the *Gītā* referred to as the Kashmiri recension. It contains fourteen whole and four half verses not contained in the vulgate and lacks two verses which the vulgate contains. Perhaps in the next edition of this work, those, too, will be noted.[48]

The bibliography at the end of the book contains the works used for and referred to in this introduction as well as translations and editions of the *Bhagavad-gītā* that were used in the production of this edition or that the editors consider specially significant and worthy of note.

Appendix: Various Interpretations of the Gītā

The *Gītā* has been interpreted in various distinct ways by the different philosophical schools and religious communities of Hinduism. It became, from the time of Śaṅkara (650-700 CE.). part of the structure of authenticity by which each school or community might justify and distinguish itself from the others. Referred to as the three "points of departure" (*prasthāna-traya*), the *Gītā* along with the *Vedānta-sūtras* and the Upaniṣads formed the basis upon which each school could demonstrate, through the composition of commentaries, the authenticity of its teachings. Although our reading of the Sanskrit fully accords with that embodied in Caleb's translation, we have included in the appendix of this work a sampling of six summaries of the teachings of the *Gītā* produced by leading thinkers of some of the major schools and communities.

We start off with the overview Śaṅkara gives of the purpose and central teaching of the *Gītā* in the introductory passage of his commentary on the text. That is followed by the short text called the *Collected Teachings of the Gītā* by Yamunā Muni. Śaṅkara represented the Non-dualist (Advaita) school of Vedānta and Yamunā the Qualified Non-dualist (Viśiṣṭādvaita) school of Vedānta. For Śaṅkara liberation is achieved by knowledge alone. Action, because it is not incompatible with ignorance, is incapable of destroying ignorance and thus it can only be regarded as an indirect means to liberation, indirect in the sense that it brings about a purification of

[48]See the discussion and references in Robert Minor's *Bhagavad-gītā: an exegetical commentary*, pp. li-lii. (Columbia, Missouri: South Asia Books, 1982.)

mind necessary for true knowledge to arise. Śaṅkara says this clearly in his *A Thousand Teachings* (*Upadeśasāhasrī*):

> Since ignorance is its [transmigration's] root, its destruction is desired. Therefore, knowledge of Brahman is started and from that comes liberation. Knowledge alone is for the destruction of ignorance, not action because action is not incompatible [with ignorance]. Without the destruction of ignorance, desire and aversion are not destroyed. If desire and aversion are not destroyed action which is the source of faults is permanent. Therefore, for the accomplishment of liberation, knowledge alone is to be appealed to.[49]

Where does *bhakti* fit in, then? Anyone commenting on the *Gītā* must take into account this central feature of the text. As we have seen, Śaṅkara resolves the problem by recognizing *bhakti*, or rather the highest (*uttamā*) *bhakti*, as the same as knowledge of the highest truth.[50]

---

[49]Śaṅkara, *Upadeśasāhasrī*, Metrical Section, 1.5-7:

अज्ञानं तस्य मूलं स्यादिति तद्धानमिष्यते।
ब्रह्मविद्यात आरब्धा ततो निःश्रेयसं भवेत्॥
विद्यैवाज्ञानहानाय न कर्माप्रतिकूलतः।
नाज्ञानस्याप्रहाणे हि रागद्वेषक्षयो भवेत्॥
रागद्वेषक्षयाभावे कर्म दोषोद्भवं ध्रुवम्।
तस्मान्निःश्रेयसार्थाय विद्यैवात्र विधीयते॥

It would be a much harder and more confusing task to pin Śaṅkara down to a particular set of views were it not for the groundbreaking research of Paul Hacker, Hajime Nakamura, Sengaku Mayeda and others who have determined ways to distinguish Śaṅkara's genuine writings from the numerous works attributed to him. As it turns out most of the three hundred or so works in his name are not by him nor do they reflect his views. When one looks only to the works that are most likely his, the results are often surprizing. Views that have been traditionally assigned to him turn out to be either later developments or to have originated with someone else. As Hacker says: "According to my researches, I regard as authentic, besides the *Brahmasūtrabhāṣya*, the following: the commentaries on thie Upaniṣads, except those on the *Śvetāśvatara* and *Nṛsiṃhapūrvatāpanīya* Upaniṣads, but inclusive of the commentary on *Māṇḍūkyakārikā*, also on the *Bhagavadgītā* and perhaps that on the *Adhyātmapaṭala* of the *Āpastambadharmasūtra*, and finally, *Upadeśasāhasrī*. The last is a collection (perhaps compiled by Śaṅkara's pupil Sureśvara) of all his independent writings. All other commentaries ascribed to him, as also the whole mass of tracts passing under the name of Śaṅkara (mostly Śaṅkarācārya), are not by Śaṅkara the author of the *Brahmasūtrabhāṣya*." (30) As a result, Śaṅkara's views are in serious need of careful reexamination in the light of this new insight into what he really wrote. For more, see the essays by Paul Hacker on the subject in the collection and translation of his essays by Wilhelm Halbfass called *Philology and Confrontation*.

[50]In his comment on 12.20 cited before.

For Yamunā Muni liberation is achieved by *bhakti* which is produced and nourished by a combination of knowledge and action:

> Knowledge and Action, regarded as yogas [disciplines] and well-refined are urged for the achievement of direct perception of the self in the first sextet. In the middle sextet, *bhakti-yoga*, which is produced by knowledge and action, is praised for the success in the actual attainment of the truth of Bhagavān. Distinguishing between *pradhāna*, *puruṣa*, the manifest, and the controller of all, as well as intelligence in action, *bhakti*, and so forth, whatever was left over from before, are described in the final [sextet].[51]

And, the highest goal is achieving Viṣṇu's transcendent abode:

> But the knower who is the most single-minded, whose self and life rest on him, whose only happiness and misery are connection with or separation from him, whose only thought is him, who has gained the self by meditation on, applying himself for, speaking of, praising, eulogizing, and spreading the fame of Bhagavān, whose breath, mind, intellect, senses, and acts are given over to him, who performs everything beginning from his own work up to and including *bhakti* impelled by love alone, should give up the sense of expedience and fearlessly place that on the Lord. With single-minded, unending servitude as one's only love, one reaches his abode. This scripture has this as its primary teaching.[52])

After Yamunā Muni's summary follows the summary of another important member of his school, Rāmānuja, as expressed in the introduction of his commentary on the *Gītā*. His views are much the same as Yamunā Muni's except that he is on record as teaching that *bhakti* is a special kind of knowledge (*jñāna-viśeṣa*) or is a permanent or constant remembering (*dhruvānusmṛti*) of Viṣṇu.

> With the ostensible intention of imparting to the son of Pāṇḍu the martial spirit, he brought about the descent of the *yoga* of *bhakti* directed to himself, promoted with the aid of *jñāna* and *karma*—the *yoga* which has been promulgated by the Vedānta as the pathway to the supreme goal of release.[53]

---

[51] Verses 2-4 of Yamunā's summary.

[52] Verses 29-32.

[53] See the appendix for the whole passage.

Next, comes the summary of Madhusūdana Sarasvatī, a late (1540-1630 CE.) member of Śaṅkara's non-dualist tradition, who coming after the great *bhakti* movement of Śrī Caitanya in Bengal, believed that though knowledge of the truth leads to liberation, without *bhakti* that cannot be fully accomplished.

> "One who has the highest *bhakti* for God and just as for God for the guru, for such a great soul all these described blessings occur."[54] On the basis of the evidence of this scripture and others, in all conditions *bhakti* for Bhagavān, with body, mind, word, is to applied.[55]

He recognized the great power of *bhakti* to fix the mind on the absolute.[56]

For all the writers mentioned so far, *bhakti* understood as a form of knowledge is considered a means to liberation. Liberation or *mukti*, though differently conceived, is the uncontested goal. *Mukti* for Śaṅkara is the blissful attainment of Brahman along with the permanent cessation of suffering and arises with the destruction of ignorance. For Yamunā Muni and Rāmānuja liberation is achieved through *bhakti* produced by knowledge and action and is understood as achieving the privilege of performing direct service to Viṣṇu in his transcendent realm.

For the final two writers, however, *bhakti* itself became the goal. *Mukti* fell into disregard. Perhaps this was because in the view of their tradition *bhakti* became identified with the core of the pleasure-giving power of the Lord, as we saw in the teachings of Śrī Jīva and Baladeva. The pleasure experienced by the presence of this power in one's heart leaves nothing more to be desired. Even the prospect of returning to the world again and again and facing repeatedly birth, disease, old age and death is not displeasing if one is accompanied by this *bhakti* power. The last two summaries are by Viśvanātha Cakravartin (1625-1705 CE.) and Baladeva Vidyābhūṣaṇa (1720-1790 CE.) (of the Caitanya school of Inconceivable Difference and Non-difference (*acintya-bhedābheda*). Their verses, summarizing the teaching of each chapter of the *Gītā*, naturally downplay the importance of liberation and highlight *bhakti*'s place of centrality in the *Gītā*. For them the real goal is preparing for the descent or infusion of *bhakti* into the heart following which it quickly matures into love for Kṛṣṇa. Lib-

---

[54] Śvetāśvatara Upaniṣad, 6.33.

[55] Verses 30 and 31.

[56] In his *Bhakti-rasāyana*, 2.1, he writes: *drute citte hi praviṣṭā yā govindākāratā sthirā| sā bhaktirityabhihitā*, "That which enters into the melted mind and gives it the lasting shape of Govinda is called *bhakti*."

eration, though unsought and even unwanted, then comes automatically as a side effect.[57]

There are many groups and communities whose views have not been mentioned here. This is only because we have not found any summaries of the *Gītā* composed by members of those traditions. It has no bearing on the quality or worthiness of their interpretations of the *Gītā*. Thus, the views of Madhva (1238–1317 CE.), of Nimbārka (13th century), of Vallabha (1479–1531 CE.), and many others have not been discussed. Perhaps summaries of the *Gītā* do exist in those communities. If so, we will try, in later editions of this work, to include them.

The Editors

[57]One is tempted to surmise that the reason the Caitanyite theologians connected *bhakti* so strongly with a pleasure-giving power of Kṛṣṇa had to do with the extraordinary ecstasies Śrī Caitanya, the founder of their tradition, was famous for. No doubt, the connection of *bhakti* with pleasure was anticipated by Rāmānuja and others (*niratiśayapriya*) before. But it seems like much of Caitanyite theology was aimed at making sense of the idiosyncrasies of Caitanya's experiences. Perhaps this is always the case with strong founding figures, however.

Original Preface (1911)

There are so many excellent translations of the *Bhagavad-gītā* (popularly known as the *Gītā*) that the addition of one more translation to those already in existence appears neither necessary nor desirable. The *Gītā*, however, is a poem, forming an integral part of the *Mahābhārata*, the most voluminous epic in literature. Its translations, on the contrary, are for the most part in prose, and as such they fail to attract the student accustomed to the rhythmical movement of the original, or to appeal to the general reader in consequence of their presenting difficult and often highly technical subjects in an unattractive garb. In the present work I have endeavored to overcome these objections by producing for the average reader interested in the sacred literature of India and in the comparative study of religions, a version of the *Gītā* which is pleasant to the ear, and is, at the same time, a literal, accurate and trustworthy representation of the original. The version lays no claim to being the result of critical study or original investigation; it is, so far as my share in the production is concerned, merely a versification based upon existing prose translations, and intended to further the popularization, in the East as well as in the West, of a book which has had an incalculable influence upon the minds and characters of a large section of the people of India, and which has been the means of helping many a weary soul in its endeavor to find, in the midst of the cares and turmoils of life, that perfect peace which results from union with the Divine.

In spite of the fact that the material at my disposal for a metrical rendering has been ample, the *Song Divine*, in consequence of my almost total ignorance of Sanskrit, would never have seen the light of day but for the generous assistance of a friend (whose modesty forbids me to disclose his name), well known to those who have the privilege of his friendship as a profound student of one of the leading systems of Indian philosophy. His translation of every verse of the *Gītā* from the original, founded upon the commentaries of Śrīdhara, Śaṅkarācārya, and Śaṅkarānanda, made solely for my benefit, has provided me with an independent text which has been invaluable in enabling me to come to a correct judgment in regard to textual differences met with in the standard translations I have used as a basis. The *Song Divine* is thus something more than a mere versification; as a joint work, it may be justly considered as a metrical translation.

It will be noticed that I have employed two forms of metre in the *Song Divine*. I have done so in accordance with the metrical differentiation found in the original, in which the major portion of the verses occur in the form of the *anuṣṭubh*, a metre in which each foot or quarter-verse contains eight syllables, and the remainder, in the form of the *triṣṭubh*, which contains eleven syllables in each foot. The *anuṣṭubh* verses appear in my version in the iambic tetrametre, whilst the *triṣṭubh* verses take the form of the iambic pentametre. By way of variation, eleven of the *anuṣṭubh* verses at the commencement of the Tenth Discourse have been rendered in iambic heptametre. For metrical reasons I have in nearly all cases dropped the final *a* of the Sanskrit nouns which appear in the text: in the footnotes, however, the *a* has been retained.

The footnotes I have appended have been compiled from various sources, and are intended to help the reader in understanding technical terms and allusions, and to make the text itself, wherever necessary, more intelligible.[58] Even with the help of these notes, copious as they are, I fear the reader will find it extremely difficult, if not impossible, to grasp the theology, cosmology, psychology, and eschatology of the *Gītā* without some knowledge of the essential teachings of three at least of the six systems of Hindu philosophy---Sāṅkhya, the Yoga of Patañjali, and the Vedānta. The *Gītā* represents the efforts of a master-mind to harmonize the hostile teachings of the schools, and to weld into them a single, connected and consistent system of philosophic idealism and faith, and for this reason its teachings cannot be fully understood without a preliminary acquaintance with the philosophic systems upon which it is based. To the reader wishing to study the *Gītā* profitably, I would strongly recommend Professor Paul Deussen's *The Philosophy of the Upanishads*, as a work presenting in the clearest possible light the many topics of doctrinal interest lightly touched upon, or greatly condensed in the 700 verses which make up the ``dialogue, most wonderful'' of Śrī Kṛṣṇa with Prince Arjuna.

In conclusion, I desire to tender my grateful acknowledgments to the

[58] Most of the footnotes included in the original edition of this translation have not been included in this edition. Only those notes deemed most illuminating and important have been retained. See the introduction of the Sanskrit editor. Eds.

friend to whom I have already referred; to Professor A. Venis, of the Government College, Benares, and to Professor A. C. Woolner, of the Oriental College, Lahore, for their careful revision of the ms; to Pandit Hiranand Śāstrī, of the Archaeological Department, for looking over and correcting the footnotes; and to Pandit Dr. Bal Kishen Kaul, R.S., my former pupil and present colleague, for many useful suggestions and for active help in placing at my disposal literary matter invaluable to the student of the *Gītā*.

Ashfield, Lahore.
August, 1911.

Chapter One: Viewing the Armies (सैन्यदर्शनम्)

धृतराष्ट्र उवाच
धर्मक्षेत्रे कुरुक्षेत्रे समवेता युयुत्सवः।[1]
मामकाः पाण्डवाश्चैव किमकुर्वत सञ्जय॥ १॥

dhṛtarāṣṭra uvāca

dharmakṣetre kurukṣetre samavetā yuyutsavaḥ|
māmakāḥ pāṇḍavāścaiva kimakurvata saṃjaya|| 1||

सञ्जय उवाच
दृष्ट्वा तु पाण्डवानीकं व्यूढं दुर्योधनस्तदा।
आचार्यमुपसंगम्य राजा वचनमब्रवीत्॥ २॥

sañjaya uvāca

dṛṣṭvā tu pāṇḍavānīkaṃ vyūḍhaṃ duryodhanastadā |
ācāryamupasaṃgamya rājā vacanamabravīt || 2 ||

पश्यैतां पाण्डुपुत्राणामाचार्य महतीं चमूम्।
व्यूढां द्रुपदपुत्रेण तव शिष्येण धीमता॥ ३॥

paśyaitāṃ pāṇḍuputrāṇāmācārya mahatīṃ camūm|
vyūḍhāṃ drupadaputreṇa tava śiṣyeṇa dhīmatā|| 3||

अत्र शूरा महेष्वासा भीमार्जुनसमा युधि।
युयुधानो विराटश्च द्रुपदश्च महारथः॥ ४॥

atra śūrā maheṣvāsā bhīmārjunasamā yudhi|
yuyudhāno virāṭaśca drupadaśca mahārathaḥ|| 4||

धृष्टकेतुश्चेकितानः काशिराजश्च वीर्यवान्।
पुरुजित् कुन्तिभोजश्च शैब्यश्च नरपुंगवः॥ ५॥

dhṛṣṭaketuścekitānaḥ kāśirājaśca vīryavān|
purujit kuntibhojaśca śaibyaśca narapuṃgavaḥ|| 5||

---

[1] Alternate reading: सर्वक्षत्रसमागमे

Dhṛtarāṣṭra[2] said:

On Kuru's field,[3] the field of right,
When face to face on war intent,
What were the deeds, O Sañjay,[4] say,
My people[5] and the Pāṇḍu's[6] wraught? 1

Sañjay said:

The king Duryodhan[7] when he saw
The marshalled hosts of Pāṇḍu's sons,
Approached his old preceptor Droṇa,[8]
And unto him these words addressed; 2

Yon mighty army pray observe
Of Pāṇḍu's sons, O teacher mine,
In battle order there arrayed
By thine apt pupil, Drupad's son. 3

What heroes, mighty bowmen these,
Of Bhīm and Arjun,[9] peers in war!
Chiefs like Virat and Yuyudhan,
And Drupad of the mighty car![10] 4

Dhṛṣṭaketu, Chekitan,
And sacred Kāshī's gallant king;
Shaibya, the man most eminent,
And Purujit and Kuntibhoj. 5

---

[2]The congenitally blind father of the Kurus, brother to Pāṇḍu.

[3]Commonly known as Kurukṣetra, a tract of land to the east of the Jamna, near Delhi.

[4]Dhṛtarāṣṭra's attendant.

[5]The Kurus

[6]The sons of Pāṇḍu, the Pāṇḍavas.

[7]The eldest son of Dhṛtarāṣṭra.

[8]The common preceptor or *guru* of the Kurus and the Pāṇḍavas.

[9]Bhīma, Arjuna and Yudhiṣṭhira were the three sons of Pāṇḍu by his first wife Pṛthā, also called Kuntī.

[10]In the original, a *mahāratha*, i.e., a warrior who could fight ten thousand archers single-handed.

युधामन्युश्च विक्रान्त उत्तमौजाश्च वीर्यवान्।
सौभद्रो द्रौपदेयाश्च सर्व एव महारथाः॥ ६॥

yudhāmanyuśca vikrānta uttamaujāśca vīryavān|
saubhadro draupadeyāśca sarva eva mahārathāḥ|| 6||

अस्माकं तु विशिष्टा ये तान्निबोध द्विजोत्तम।
नायका मम सैन्यस्य संज्ञार्थं तान्ब्रवीमि ते॥ ७॥

asmākaṃ tu viśiṣṭā ye tānnibodha dvijottama|
nāyakā mama sainyasya saṃjñārthaṃ tānbravīmi te|| 7||

भवान्भीष्मश्च कर्णश्च कृपश्च समितिंजयः।
अश्वत्थामा विकर्णश्च सौमदत्तिर्जयद्रथः॥ ८॥[11]

bhavānbhīṣmaśca karṇaśca kṛpaśca samitiṃjayaḥ|
aśvatthāmā vikarṇaśca saumadattirjayadrathaḥ|| 8||

अन्ये च बहवः शूरा मदर्थे त्यक्तजीविताः।
नानाशस्त्रप्रहरणाः सर्वे युद्धविशारदाः॥ ९॥

anye ca bahavaḥ śūrā madarthe tyaktajīvitāḥ|
nānāśastrapraharaṇāḥ sarve yuddhaviśāradāḥ|| 9||

अपर्याप्तं तदस्माकं बलं भीष्माभिरक्षितम्।
पर्याप्तं त्विदमेतेषां बलं भीमाभिरक्षितम्॥ १०॥[12]

aparyāptaṃ tadasmākaṃ balaṃ bhīṣmābhirakṣitam|
paryāptaṃ tvidameteṣāṃ balaṃ bhīmābhirakṣitam|| 10||

---

[11] Alternate reading:
भवान्भीष्मश्च कर्णश्च कृपः शल्यो जयद्रथः।
अश्वत्थामा विकर्णश्च सौमदत्तिस्तथैव च॥

[12] Alternate reading:
अपर्याप्तं तदस्माकं बलं भीमाभिरक्षितम्।
पर्याप्तं त्विदमेतेषां बलं भीष्माभिरक्षितम्॥

Yudhāmanyu of prowess rare,
The valiant Uttamaujas too,
Subhadrā's[13] boy, Draupadī's[14] sons,
Each master of a mighty car. 6

And now, O best of twice-born men,
Pray note the chieftains on our side
My army leaders whom I name
That thou mayest recognize them all. 7

Thyself, good sir, and Bhīsma[15] and Karṇa,[16]
And Kṛpa, oft victorious lord,
Vikarṇa and Aśvathāman too,
And Somdatta's son named Jayadrath. 8

And scores of other valiant men
Who for my sake are courting death,
All fully armed with weapons keen,
Past masters of the art of war. 9

Quite adequate our forces are,
And marshaled for the fray by Bhīsma,
Whilst theirs in Bhīm's[17] supreme command,
Compared with ours are small indeed.[18] 10

---

[13]Kṛṣṇa's sister married to Arjuna; her son was named Abhimanyu.

[14]The common wife of the five Pāṇḍavas.

[15]The half-brother of Vicitravīrya, the common grandfather of the Kurus and the Pāṇḍavas.

[16]The son of Kuntī before her marriage to Pāṇḍu. The rivalry between Arjuna and Karṇa, the two greatest leaders on the Pāṇḍava and Kuru sides respectively forms the chief theme of the *Mahābhārata*, as the rivalry between Achilles and Hector forms the leading topic of the *Illiad*. It was not until Karṇa had been slain by Arjuna that Kuntī disclosed the truth regarding the former's birth.

[17]The generalissimo of the Pāṇḍava hosts.

[18]Duryodhana's forces comprised four more divisions than those of Yudhiṣṭhira.

अयनेषु च सर्वेषु यथाभागमवस्थिताः।
भीष्ममेवाभिरक्षन्तु भवन्तः सर्व एव हि॥ ११॥

ayaneṣu ca sarveṣu yathābhāgamavasthitāḥ|
bhīṣmamevābhirakṣantu bhavantaḥ sarva eva hi|| 11||

तस्य संजनयन्हर्षं कुरुवृद्धः पितामहः।
सिंहनादं विनद्योच्चैः शङ्खं दध्मौ प्रतापवान्॥ १२॥

tasya saṃjanayanharṣaṃ kuruvṛddhaḥ pitāmahaḥ|
siṃhanādaṃ vinadyoccaiḥ śaṅkhaṃ dadhmau pratāpavān|| 12||

ततः शङ्खाश्च भेर्यश्च पणवानकगोमुखाः।
सहसैवाभ्यहन्यन्त स शब्दस्तुमुलो ऽभवत्॥ १३॥

tataḥ śaṅkhāśca bheryaśca paṇavānakagomukhāḥ|
sahasaivābhyahanyanta sa śabdastumulo 'bhavat|| 13||

ततः श्वेतैर्हयैर्युक्ते महति स्यन्दने स्थितौ।
माधवः पाण्डवश्चैव दिव्यौ शङ्खौ प्रदध्मतुः॥ १४॥

tataḥ śvetairhayairyukte mahati syandane sthitau|
mādhavaḥ pāṇḍavaścaiva divyau śaṅkhau pradadhmatuḥ|| 14||

पाञ्चजन्यं हृषीकेशो देवदत्तं धनंजयः।
पौण्ड्रं दध्मौ महाशङ्खं भीमकर्मा वृकोदरः॥ १५॥

pāñcajanyaṃ hṛṣīkeśo devadattaṃ dhanaṃjayaḥ|
pauṇḍraṃ dadhmau mahāśaṅkhaṃ bhīmakarmā vṛkodaraḥ|| 15||

अनन्तविजयं राजा कुन्तीपुत्रो युधिष्ठिरः।
नकुलः सहदेवश्च सुघोषमणिपुष्पकौ॥ १६॥

anantavijayaṃ rājā kuntīputro yudhiṣṭhiraḥ|
nakulaḥ sahadevaśca sughoṣamaṇipuṣpakau|| 16||

Ho warriors! then let each remain
At his appointed station firm;
With loyal care protect ye Bhīsma,
Obedient to my royal call. 11

Lo, then the valiant grandsire Bhīsma,
The eldest of the Kuru race,
A loud lion's roar, his conch,
To cheer Duryodhan blew on high. 12

Whereon at once burst forth the clang
Of conches and of kettle drums,
O trumpets and of gongs and horns,
A very din tumultuous! 13

And Mādhav[19] then and Pāṇḍu's son,[20]
Both seated in a mighty car,
Yoked to a team of milk-white steeds,
Blew on their shells divine a blast. 14

And Bhīma too, of gruesome deeds,
Blew on the Paundra, his mighty conch;
On Pāñchajanya Hṛṣīkeś,[21]
And Dhanañjay[22] on God-bestowed. 15

Yudhiṣṭhir, Kuntī's royal son,
Blew on the Endless Victory,
And Nakul on the Dulcet-tone,
And Sahadev[23] on the Gem-bedecked. 16

---

[19]A name of Kṛṣṇa.
[20]Arjuna.
[21]A name of Kṛṣṇa, signifying "Lord of the senses."
[22]A name of Arjuna, signifying "lord of wealth."
[23]Nakula and Sahadeva were half-brothers to Bhīma, Arjuna, and Yudhiṣṭhira, Pāṇḍu's son's by his second wife.

काश्यश्च परमेष्वासः शिखण्डी च महारथः।
धृष्टद्युम्नो विराटश्च सात्यकिश्चापराजितः॥ १७॥

kāśyaśca parameṣvāsaḥ śikhaṇḍī ca mahārathaḥ|
dhṛṣṭadyumno virāṭaśca sātyakiścāparājitaḥ|| 17||

द्रुपदो द्रौपदेयाश्च सर्वशः पृथिवीपते।[24]
सौभद्रश्च महाबाहुः शङ्खान्दध्मुः पृथक्पृथक्॥ १८॥

drupado draupadeyāśca sarvaśaḥ pṛthivīpate|
saubhadraśca mahābāhuḥ śaṅkhān dadhmuḥ pṛthak pṛthak|| 18||

स घोषो धार्तराष्ट्राणां हृदयानि व्यदारयत्।
नभश्च पृथिवीं चैव तुमुलो व्यनुनादयन्[25]॥ १९॥

sa ghoṣo dhārtarāṣṭrāṇāṃ hṛdayāni vyadārayat|
nabhaśca pṛthivīṃ caiva tumulo vyanunādayan|| 19||

अथ व्यवस्थितान्दृष्ट्वा धार्तराष्ट्रान्कपिध्वजः।
प्रवृत्ते शस्त्रसंपाते धनुरुद्यम्य पाण्डवः॥ २०॥

atha vyavasthitān dṛṣṭvā dhārtarāṣṭrān kapidhvajaḥ|
pravṛtte śastrasampāte dhanurudyamya pāṇḍavaḥ|| 20||

हृषीकेशं तदा वाक्यमिदमाह महीपते।
सेनयोरुभयोर्मध्ये रथं स्थापय मे ऽच्युत॥ २१॥

hṛṣīkeśaṃ tadā vākyamidamāha mahīpate|
senayorubhayormadhye rathaṃ sthāpaya me 'cyuta|| 21||

---

[24] Alternate reading for this line:
पाञ्चालश्च महेष्वासो द्रौपदेयाश्च पञ्च ये।
[25] Alternate: व्यनुनादयत्

The famous archer Kāshī's king,
The mighty car-lord Śikhaṇḍin,[26]
Virāṭ and Dṛṣṭadyumna too,
And Sātyaki the unsubdued; 17

And Drupad and Draupadī's sons,
Subhadrā's son of mighty arms,
From all sides each, O lord of earth,
With his own conch the tumult swelled. 18

The hearts of Dhṛtarāṣṭra's men
By that most awful blast were rent,
For suddenly it roused to life
The echos both of earth and sky. 19

Now when ape-bannered Pāṇḍu's son
Dhṛtarāṣṭra's marshaled host beheld,
And showers of missiles falling fast,
He forthwith raised his bow aloft, 20

And in this wise , O lord of earth,
Addressed himself to Hṛṣīkesh;
Half way between those armies twain
Halt thou my car, Immortal One.[27] 21

---

[26]A son of Drupada and brother of Dhṛṣṭadyumna. He is said to have been miraculously changed from a woman into a man. When Arjuna had failed to overcome him, Bhīṣma, the old veteran, refusing to return the blows of one who had once been a woman, was ultimately slain by the young Śikhaṇḍin.

[27]In the original *Acyuta*, meaning undeteriorating or unchanging.

यावदेतान् निरीक्षे ऽहं योद्धुकामानवस्थितान्।
कैर्मया सह योद्धव्यमस्मिन् रणसमुद्यमे॥ २२॥

yāvadetān nirīkṣe 'haṃ yoddhukāmānavasthitān|
kairmayā saha yoddhavyamasmin raṇasamudyame|| 22||

योत्स्यमानानवेक्षे ऽहं य एते ऽत्र समागताः।
धार्तराष्ट्रस्य दुर्बुद्धेर्युद्धे प्रियचिकीर्षवः॥ २३॥

yotsyamānānavekṣe 'haṃ ya ete 'tra samāgatāḥ|
dhārtarāṣṭrasya durbuddheryuddhe priyacikīrṣavaḥ|| 23||

सञ्जय उवाच
एवमुक्तो हृषीकेशो गुडाकेशेन भारत।
सेनयोरुभयोर्मध्ये स्थापयित्वा रथोत्तमम्॥ २४॥

sañjaya uvāca

evamukto hṛṣīkeśo guḍākeśena bhārata|
senayorubhayormadhye sthāpayitvā rathottamam|| 24||

भीष्मद्रोणप्रमुखतः सर्वेषां च महीक्षिताम्।
उवाच पार्थ पश्यैतान् समवेतान् कुरून् इति॥ २५॥

bhīṣmadroṇapramukhataḥ sarveṣāṃ ca mahīkṣitām|
uvāca pārtha paśyaitān samavetān kurūn iti|| 25||

तत्रापश्यत् स्थितान् पार्थः पितृनथ पितामहान्।
आचार्यान् मातुलान् भ्रातृन् पुत्रान् पौत्रान् सखींस्तथा।
श्वशुरान् सुहृदश्चैव सेनयोरुभयोरपि॥ २६॥

tatrāpaśyat sthitān pārthaḥ pitṛnatha pitāmahān|
ācāryān mātulān bhrātṛn putrān pautrān sakhīṃstathā|
śvaśurān suhṛdaścaiva senayorubhayorapi|| 26||

That I may scrutinize the foes
Who with us now desire to fight;
With whom indeed I must contend
In this fierce war that now begins. 22

That I may see those gathered here,
All eager for the coming fray;
Who anxious are to serve in war,
Dhṛtarāṣṭra's evil minded son. 23

Sañjay said:

Then Hṛṣīkesh, O Bharat's son,[28]
Requested thus by Guḍākesh,[29]
At once did halt that mighty car
Half way between those armies twain. 24

Directly facing Bhīṣma, Droṇa,
And all those rulers of the earth,
And said, "Behold, O Pṛthā's son
The host of Kurus gathered here." 25

There Pṛthā's son in both those hosts
His forebears, sons and cousins saw,
Relations, comrades, friends as well,
And fathers-in-law, holy teachers,
Maternal uncles, grandsons too,[30]
On fratricidal deeds intent. 26

---

[28]The expression "Bharat's son," wherever it occurs in the text, stands for "descendant of Bharata" and should be so understood. Bharata was the son of Duṣyanta and Śakuntalā, and was the ancestor of both the Pāṇḍavas and Kurus. India is often called "Bhāratavarṣa" after him.

[29]A name of Arjuna, signifying "lord of sleep," i.e., sleepless or not indolent. The word is also translated as "thick or curly-haired."

[30]This verse was left out of Caleb's translation. It has been supplied by the editor.

तान्समीक्ष्य स कौन्तेयः सर्वान्बन्धूनवस्थितान्।
कृपया परयाविष्टो विषीदन्निदमब्रवीत्॥ २७॥[31]
tān samīkṣya sa kaunteyaḥ sarvān bandhūnavasthitān|
kṛpayā parayāviṣṭo viṣīdann idam abravīt|| 27||

अर्जुन उवाच

दृष्ट्वेमं स्वजनं कृष्ण युयुत्सुं समुपस्थितम्।
सीदन्ति मम गात्राणि मुखं च परिशुष्यति॥ २८॥
arjuna uvāca

dṛṣṭvemaṃ svajanaṃ kṛṣṇa yuyutsuṃ samupasthitam|
sīdanti mama gātrāṇi mukhaṃ ca pariśuṣyati|| 28||

वेपथुश्च शरीरे मे रोमहर्षश्च जायते।
गाण्डीवं स्रंसते[32] हस्तात्त्वक् चैव परिदह्यते॥ २९॥
vepathuśca śarīre me romaharṣaśca jāyate|
sraṃsate gāṇḍīvaṃ hastāt tvak caiva paridahyate|| 29||

न च शक्नोम्यवस्थातुं भ्रमतीव च मे मनः।
निमित्तानि च पश्यामि विपरीतानि केशव॥ ३०॥
na ca śaknomyavasthātuṃ bhramatīva ca me manaḥ|
nimittāni ca paśyāmi viparītāni keśava|| 30||

न च श्रेयो ऽनुपश्यामि हत्वा स्वजनमाहवे॥ ३१॥
na ca śreyo 'nupaśyāmi hatvā svajanamāhave|| 31||

न काङ्क्षे विजयं कृष्ण न च राज्यं सुखानि च।
किं नो राज्येन गोविन्द किं भोगैर्जीवितेन वा॥ ३२॥
na kāṅkṣe vijayaṃ kṛṣṇa na ca rājyaṃ sukhāni ca|
kiṃ no rājyena govinda kiṃ bhogairjīvitena vā|| 32||

---

[31]Alternate: सीदमानो ऽब्रवीदिदम्।
[32]Alternate: स्रंसते गाण्डीवं

When Kuntī's son beheld the host
Of all his friends for battle met,[33]
With deep compassion overcome,
And sad at heart, he spake these words: 27

Arjuna said:

O Krishna, seeing these my kin
All standing eager for the fight,
My members fail, bereft of strength,
And all my mouth is parched and dry. 28

There thrills a shudder through my frame,
My hair with horror stands on end.
And from my hand the Gaṇḍīva slips,
And all my skin with fever burns. 29

I scarce can dare to stand upright,
My mind distracted madly whirls.
And I, O Keśava,[34] also see
Dread signs portending ill and woe. 30

I fail to see what good can come
By slaying these my kith and kin! 31

For vict'ry have I no desire,
For kingdom, Krishna, or delights;
To us, O Govinda,[35] kingship's naught,
Not even life with all its joys, 32

[33]This verse was left out of Caleb's translation. It has been supplied by the editor.
[34]A name of Kṛṣṇa.
[35]A name of Kṛṣṇa.

येषामर्थे काङ्क्षितं नो राज्यं भोगाः सुखानि च।
त इमे ऽवस्थिता युद्धे[36] प्राणांस्त्यक्त्वा धनानि च[37] ॥ ३३॥

yeṣāmarthe kāṅkṣitaṃ no rājyaṃ bhogāḥ sukhāni ca|
ta ime 'vasthitā yuddhe prāṇāṃstyaktvā dhanāni ca|| 33||

आचार्याः पितरः पुत्रास्तथैव च पितामहाः।
मातुलाः श्वशुराः पौत्राः श्यालाः संबन्धिनस्तथा॥ ३४॥

ācāryāḥ pitaraḥ putrāstathaiva ca pitāmahāḥ|
mātulāḥ śvaśurāḥ pautrāḥ śyālāḥ saṃbandhinastathā|| 34||

एतान्न हन्तुमिच्छामि घ्नतो ऽपि मधुसूदन।
अपि त्रैलोक्यराज्यस्य हेतोः किं नु महीकृते॥ ३५॥

etān na hantumicchāmi ghnato 'pi madhusūdana|
api trailokyarājyasya hetoḥ kiṃ nu mahīkṛte|| 35||

निहत्य धार्तराष्ट्रान्नः का प्रीतिः स्याज्जनार्दन।
पापमेवाश्रयेदस्मान् हत्वैतानाततायिनः॥ ३६॥

nihatya dhārtarāṣṭrān naḥ kā prītiḥ syājjanārdana|
pāpamevāśrayedasmān hatvaitān ātatāyinaḥ|| 36||

तस्मान्नार्हा वयं हन्तुं धार्तराष्ट्रान् स्वबान्धवान्।
स्वजनं हि कथं हत्वा सुखिनः स्याम माधव॥ ३७॥

tasmān nārhā vayaṃ hantuṃ dhārtarāṣṭrān svabāndhavān|
svajanaṃ hi kathaṃ hatvā sukhinaḥ syāma mādhava|| 37||

---

[36] Alternate: त एव नः स्थिता योद्धुं
[37] Alternate: सुदुस्त्यजान्

When they for whom we wish to gain
Dominion, pleasures and delights,
Stand here engaged in mutual strife,
Prepared to give up wealth and life. 33

Reverend teachers, fathers, sons,
And with them the great grandsires,
Fathers and brothers in-law, grandsons,
And all our dearest kinsmen here. 34[38]

I'd fain not slaughter kith and kin,[39]
Though slain by them, not e'en to win
The kingship of the triple world,[40]
Far less to gain an earthly crown. 35

What joy, Janārdan,[41] will ours be
When we have slain Dhṛtarāṣṭra's sons?
Nay, only sin shall cling to us
If we destroy these wicked ones! 36

It thus behooves us ill to slay
Our kinsmen—Dhṛtarāṣṭra's sons;
Our kinsmen slain, O Mādhav, how
Can we be happy e'er again? 37

---

[38]This stanza was left out of Caleb's translation. It has been supplied by the editor.

[39]The vocative "o Madhusūdana" has been omitted.

[40]The earth, intermediate regions, and heaven, or the terrene, aerial, and celestial regions.

[41]"Destroyer of the people." This is one of Kṛṣṇa's names, He being the warrior conquering all forms of evil.

यद्यप्येते न पश्यन्ति लोभोपहतचेतसः।
कुलक्षयकृतं दोषं मित्रद्रोहे च पातकम्॥ ३८॥

yadyapyete na paśyanti lobhopahatacetasaḥ|
kulakṣayakṛtaṃ doṣaṃ mitradrohe ca pātakam|| 38||

कथं न ज्ञेयमस्माभिः पापादस्मान् निवर्तितुम्।
कुलक्षयकृतं दोषं प्रपश्यद्भिर्जनार्दन॥ ३९॥

kathaṃ na jñeyamasmābhiḥ pāpādasmān nivartitum|
kulakṣayakṛtaṃ doṣaṃ prapaśyadbhirjanārdana|| 39||

कुलक्षये प्रणश्यन्ति कुलधर्माः सनातनाः।
धर्मे नष्टे कुलं कृत्स्नमधर्मो ऽभिभवत्युत॥ ४०॥

kulakṣaye praṇaśyanti kuladharmāḥ sanātanāḥ|
dharme naṣṭe kulaṃ kṛtsnamadharmo 'bhibhavatyuta|| 40||

अधर्माभिभवात्कृष्ण प्रदुष्यन्ति कुलस्त्रियः।
स्त्रीषु दुष्टासु वार्ष्णेय जायते वर्णसंकरः॥ ४१॥

adharmābhibhavātkṛṣṇa praduṣyanti kulastriyaḥ|
strīṣu duṣṭāsu vārṣṇeya jāyate varṇasaṃkaraḥ|| 41||

संकरो नरकायैव कुलघ्नानां कुलस्य च।
पतन्ति पितरो ह्येषां लुप्तपिण्डोदकक्रियाः॥ ४२॥

saṃkaro narakāyaiva kulaghnānāṃ kulasya ca|
patanti pitaro hyeṣāṃ luptapiṇḍodakakriyāḥ|| 42||

दोषैरेतैः कुलघ्नानां वर्णसंकरकारकैः।
उत्साद्यन्ते जातिधर्माः कुलधर्माश्च शाश्वताः॥ ४३॥

doṣairetaiḥ kulaghnānāṃ varṇasaṃkarakārakaiḥ|
utsādyante jātidharmāḥ kuladharmāśca śāśvatāḥ|| 43||

For if indeed they cannot see,
Their reason overpowered by greed,
The sin of wiping out a race,
The crime of enmity to friends, 38

Should we therefore, who plainly see,
O Janārdan, the sinfulness
Of wholesale slaughter of a race,
This evil deed not learn to shun? 39

The time-honored ancestral rites[42]
By such extinction are destroyed;
When this occurs the clan becomes
The prey of sheer iniquity.[43] 40

Where, Krishna, iniquity prevails,
Corrupt become the women-folk;
From such corruption, Vṛshṇi's son,
Caste mingling follows in its train. 41

With mingling up of castes ensues
A hellward march of sinning folk,
And their ancestors fall from heaven,
Deprived of ritual offerings.[44] 42

By these misdeeds which mingle castes,
Of those who extirpate a clan,
The time-honored ancestral rites,
And those of caste, are lost for aye. 43

---

[42] *Dharma*, which generally means the essential nature of a thing, hence the laws that govern its being; hence its duties. It also signifies religious rites as enjoined in the *śāstras* (scriptures), righteousness, piety, virtue.

[43] *Adharma*, the opposite of *dharma*.

[44] I.e., rice-balls and libations. This refers to the *śraddhā* ceremony, the periodical offering of rice-cakes, water, etc., to dead ancestors. Such offerings reach the dead if made by legitimate offspring; in the absence of such offerings the ancestors are necessarily deprived of food, and in consequence suffer.

उत्सन्नकुलधर्माणां मनुष्याणां जनार्दन।
नरके नियतं वासो भवतीत्यनुशुश्रुम॥ ४४॥

utsannakuladharmāṇāṃ manuṣyāṇāṃ janārdana|
narake niyataṃ vāso bhavatītyanuśuśruma|| 44||

अहो बत महत् पापं कर्तुं व्यवसिता वयम्।
यद्राज्यसुखलोभेन हन्तुं स्वजनमुद्यताः॥ ४५॥

aho bata mahat pāpaṃ kartuṃ vyavasitā vayam|
yadrājyasukhalobhena hantuṃ svajanamudyatāḥ|| 45||

यदि मामप्रतीकारमशस्त्रं शस्त्रपाणयः।
धार्तराष्ट्रा रणे हन्युस्तन् मे क्षेमतरं भवेत्॥ ४६॥

yadi māmapratīkāramaśastraṃ śastrapāṇayaḥ|
dhārtarāṣṭrā raṇe hanyustan me kṣemataraṃ bhavet|| 46||

सञ्जय उवाच

एवमुक्त्वार्जुनः संख्ये रथोपस्थ उपाविशत्।
विसृज्य सशरं चापं शोकसंविग्नमानसः॥ ४७॥

sañjaya uvāca

evamuktvārjunaḥ saṃkhye rathopastha upāviśat|
visṛjya saśaraṃ cāpaṃ śokasaṃvignamānasaḥ|| 47||

And, O Janārdan, we have heard
The dwelling place of all such men
Whose ancestral rites have ceased to be
Is everlastingly in hell. 44

Alas! Alas how grievous is
The sin we now have ventured on,
Since for the greed of kingship's joys
We wish to slaughter kith and kin! 45

'Twere better far that I be slain,
Resisting not and weaponless,
By Dhṛtarāṣṭra's armed sons,
Than answer them with blow for blow. 46

Sañjay said:

So speaking on the battle field,
Arjun, his mind distraught by grief,
His bow and arrows flung away,
And sank upon the chariot seat. 47

Chapter Two: The Yoga of the Reason-Method (साङ्ख्ययोगः)

संजय उवाच

तं तथा कृपयाविष्टमश्रुपूर्णाकुलेक्षणम्।
विषीदन्तमिदं[45] वाक्यमुवाच मधुसूदनः॥ १॥

saṃjaya uvāca

taṃ tathā kṛpayāviṣṭamaśrupūrṇākulekṣaṇam|
viṣīdantamidaṃ vākyamuvāca madhusūdanaḥ|| 1||

श्रीभगवानुवाच

कुतस्त्वा कश्मलमिदं विषमे समुपस्थितम्।
अनार्यजुष्टमस्वर्ग्यमकीर्तिकरमर्जुन॥ २॥

śrībhagavān uvāca

kutastvā kaśmalamidaṃ viṣame samupasthitam|
anāryajuṣṭamasvargyamakīrtikaramarjuna|| 2||

क्लैब्यं मा स्म गमः पार्थ[46] नैतत्त्वय्युपपद्यते।
क्षुद्रं हृदयदौर्बल्यं त्यक्त्वोत्तिष्ठ परंतप॥ ३॥

klaibyaṃ mā sma gamaḥ pārtha naitat tvayyupapadyate|
kṣudraṃ hṛdayadaurbalyaṃ tyaktvottiṣṭha paraṃtapa|| 3||

अर्जुन उवाच

कथं भीष्ममहं संख्ये द्रोणं च मधुसूदन।
इषुभिः प्रतियोत्स्यामि पूजार्हावरिसूदन॥ ४॥

arjuna uvāca

kathaṃ bhīṣmamahaṃ saṃkhye droṇaṃ ca madhusūdana|
iṣubhiḥ pratiyotsyāmi pūjārhāvarisūdana|| 4||

---

[45]Alternate: सीदमानमिदं

[46]Alternate: मा क्लैब्यं गच्छ कौन्तेय

Sañjay said:

To him with pity thus o'ercome,
With smarting eyes bedimmed with tears,
Depressed in spirit, grief opressed,
Lord Madhusūdan spake these words. 1

The Blessed Lord said:

Whence this dejection, Arjun, say,
Which grips thee in this danger's hour?
Inglorious, shutting out from heaven,
And always by the brave abhored. 2

O Pārtha, yield not to impotence,
For surely it becomes thee not;
Shake off this faintness of the heart,
And rouse thyself, O Parantap![47] 3

Arjun said:

O Madhusūdan, how can I
Assail with arrows Bhīṣma, Droṇa?
O foe destroyer, both these chiefs
Deserve my worship reverent. 4

[47] A name of Arjuna, signifying "foe-tormentor."

गुरूनहत्वा हि महानुभावाञ्
श्रेयो भोक्तुं[48] भैक्ष्यमपीह लोके।
हत्वार्थकामांस्तु गुरूनिहैव
भुञ्जीय भोगान्रुधिरप्रदिग्धान्॥ ५॥

gurūn ahatvā hi mahānubhāvāñ
śreyo bhoktuṃ bhaikṣyam apīha loke|
hatvārthakāmāṃstu gurūn ihaiva
bhuñjīya bhogān rudhirapradigdhān|| 5||

न चैतद्विद्मः कतरन् नो गरीयो
यद्वा जयेम यदि वा नो जयेयुः।
यानेव हत्वा न जिजीविषामस्
ते ऽवस्थिताः[49] प्रमुखे धार्तराष्ट्राः॥ ६॥

na caitadvidmaḥ kataran no garīyo
yadvā jayema yadi vā no jayeyuḥ|
yān eva hatvā na jijīviṣāmas
te 'vasthitāḥ pramukhe dhārtarāṣṭrāḥ|| 6||

कार्पण्यदोषोपहतस्वभावः
पृच्छामि त्वां धर्मसंमूढचेताः।
यच्छ्रेयः स्यान्निश्चितं ब्रूहि तन्मे
शिष्यस्ते ऽहं शाधि मां त्वां प्रपन्नम्॥ ७॥

kārpaṇyadoṣopahatasvabhāvaḥ
pṛcchāmi tvāṃ dharmasaṃmūḍhacetāḥ|
yacchreyaḥ syān niścitaṃ brūhi tan me
śiṣyaste 'haṃ śādhi māṃ tvāṃ prapannam|| 7||

---

[48] Alternate: श्रेयश्चर्तुं
[49] Alternate: ते नः स्थिताः

Rather than slay these teachers noble souled
Let my repast be beggars' daily bread;
By killing them, greed tainted though they be,
Blood stained delights alone should I enjoy. 5

Nor do I know for us which better is,
To vanquish them or by them vanquished be;
Our foes indeed are Dhṛtarāṣṭra's sons,
Whom having slain, we could not care to live. 6

By helplessness oppressed, by doubts assailed,
I do not see the path of duty plain,
Be thou my guide and tell me what is best,
My teacher thou, in mercy lead me now. 7

न हि प्रपश्यामि ममापनुद्याद्
यच्छोकमुच्छोषणमिन्द्रियाणाम्।
अवाप्य भूमावसपत्नमृद्धं
राज्यं सुराणामपि चाधिपत्यम्॥ ८॥

na hi prapaśyāmi mamāpanudyād
yacchokam ucchoṣaṇam indriyāṇām|
avāpya bhūmāvasapatnam ṛddhaṃ
rājyaṃ surāṇām api cādhipatyam|| 8||

संजय उवाच
एवमुक्त्वा हृषीकेशं गुडाकेशः परंतपः।
न योत्स्य इति गोविन्दमुक्त्वा तूष्णीं बभूव ह॥ ९॥

saṃjaya uvāca

evam uktvā hṛṣīkeśaṃ guḍākeśaḥ paraṃtapaḥ|
na yotsya iti govindam uktvā tūṣṇīṃ babhūva ha|| 9||

तमुवाच हृषीकेशः प्रहसन्निव भारत।
सेनयोरुभयोर्मध्ये विषीदन्तमिदं वचः॥ १०॥

tam uvāca hṛṣīkeśaḥ prahasann iva bhārata|
senayorubhayormadhye viṣīdantam idaṃ vacaḥ|| 10||

श्रीभगवानुवाच
अशोच्यानन्वशोचस्त्वं प्रज्ञावादांश्च भाषसे।
गतासूनगतासूंश्च नानुशोचन्ति पण्डिताः॥ ११॥

śrībhagavān uvāca

aśocyān anvaśocastvaṃ prajñāvādāṃśca bhāṣase|
gatāsūn agatāsūṃśca nānuśocanti paṇḍitāḥ|| 11||

I do not see what will dispell the grief,
Which never more will leave my spirit free,
When I a matchless kingdom have obtained,
Nay more, become the sovereign of the gods! 8

Sañjay said:

Thus having answered Hṛṣīkeś,
To Govind, Guḍākeś then said;
In battle I will not engage,
And having spoken, silence held. 9

To him, dejected and depressed,
Whilst stationed 'midst those armies twain,
O son of Bharat, Hṛṣīkeś then
Softly smiling, spake these words; 10

The Blessed Lord said:

Thou grievest where no grief should be,
Yet speakest words of wisdom thou!
They who are wise grieve not for those
Who live or who have passed away. 11

न त्वेवाहं जातु नासं न त्वं नेमे जनाधिपाः।
न चैव न भविष्यामः सर्वे वयमतः परम्॥ १२॥

na tvevāhaṃ jātu nāsaṃ na tvaṃ neme janādhipāḥ|
na caiva na bhaviṣyāmaḥ sarve vayam ataḥ param|| 12||

देहिनो ऽस्मिन् यथा देहे कौमारं यौवनं जरा।
तथा देहान्तरप्राप्तिर्धीरस्तत्र न मुह्यति॥ १३॥

dehino 'smin yathā dehe kaumāraṃ yauvanaṃ jarā|
tathā dehāntaraprāptirdhīrastatra na muhyati|| 13||

मात्रास्पर्शास्तु कौन्तेय शीतोष्णसुखदुःखदाः।
आगमापायिनो ऽनित्यास्तांस्तितिक्षस्व भारत॥ १४॥

mātrāsparśāstu kaunteya śītoṣṇasukhaduḥkhadāḥ|
āgamāpāyino 'nityāstāṃstitikṣasva bhārata|| 14||

यं हि न व्यथयन्त्येते पुरुषं पुरुषर्षभ।
समदुःखसुखं धीरं सो ऽमृतत्वाय कल्पते॥ १५॥

yaṃ hi na vyathayantyete puruṣaṃ puruṣarṣabha|
samaduḥkhasukhaṃ dhīraṃ so 'mṛtatvāya kalpate|| 15||

नासतो विद्यते भावो नाभावो विद्यते सतः।
उभयोरपि दृष्टो ऽन्तस्त्वनयोस्तत्त्वदर्शिभिः॥ १६॥

nāsato vidyate bhāvo nābhāvo vidyate sataḥ|
ubhayorapi dṛṣṭo 'ntastvanayostattvadarśibhiḥ|| 16||

अविनाशि तु तद्विद्धि येन सर्वमिदं ततम्।
विनाशमव्ययस्यास्य न कश्चित्कर्तुमर्हति॥ १७॥

avināśi tu tadviddhi yena sarvam idaṃ tatam|
vināśam avyayasyāsya na kaścit kartum arhati|| 17||

For verily I ne'er was not,
Nor thou, nor any of these lords,
And none of us who live this day
Hereafter ever cease to be. 12

Just as the dweller[50] in these frames
Puts on his childhood, youth and age,
So doth he clothe himself afresh;
At this the wise are not perplexed. 13

Sensations, O thou Kuntī's son,
Of heat and cold, of joy and pain,
Are fleeting, unabiding things,
With courage do thou bear them then. 14

That wise man who, O chief of men,
Is not perturbed by these at all,
To whom alike are joy and pain,
The life immortal he deserves. 15

What is can never cease to be,
What never was cannot exist,
This dual truth is plain to them
Who essence part from accident. 16

Know him as indestructible
By whom pervaded is the world,
And none can bring about the death
Of him, the undecaying self. 17

[50] i.e., the embodied Self.

अन्तवन्त इमे देहा नित्यस्योक्ताः शरीरिणः।
अनाशिनो ऽप्रमेयस्य तस्माद्युध्यस्व भारत॥ १८॥

antavanta ime dehā nityasyoktāḥ śarīriṇaḥ|
anāśino 'prameyasya tasmādyudhyasva bhārata|| 18||

य एनं वेत्ति हन्तारं यश्चैनं मन्यते हतम्।
उभौ तौ न विजानीतो नायं हन्ति न हन्यते॥ १९॥

ya enaṃ vetti hantāraṃ yaścainaṃ manyate hatam|
ubhau tau na vijānīto nāyaṃ hanti na hanyate|| 19||

न जायते म्रियते वा कदाचिन्
नायं भूत्वा भविता वा न भूयः।
अजो नित्यः शाश्वतो ऽयं पुराणो
न हन्यते हन्यमाने शरीरे॥ २०॥

na jāyate mriyate vā kadācin
nāyaṃ bhūtvā bhavitā vā na bhūyaḥ|
ajo nityaḥ śāśvato 'yaṃ purāṇo
na hanyate hanyamāne śarīre|| 20||

वेदाविनाशिनं नित्यं य एनमजमव्ययम्।
कथं स पुरुषः पार्थ कं घातयति हन्ति कम्॥ २१॥

vedāvināśinaṃ nityaṃ ya enam ajam avyayam|
kathaṃ sa puruṣaḥ pārtha kaṃ ghātayati hanti kam|| 21||

These bodies in which he abides,
The deathless, eternal, infinite,
They only perish, Bharat's son,
Arise therefore and fight thy foes. 18

Who think of him as one who slays,
Or who believe that he is slain,
They both are steeped in ignorance,
He slayeth not nor is he slain. 19

He never enters birth nor doth he die,
And having been, he cannot cease to be;
Eternal, primal, changeless and unborn,
He is not killed though killed the body be. 20

O Pṛthā's son, how can that man
Who knoweth him to be unborn,
Eternal and immutable,
Kill anyone or have him killed? 21

वासांसि जीर्णानि यथा विहाय
नवानि गृह्णाति नरो ऽपराणि।
तथा शरीराणि विहाय जीर्णानि
अन्यानि संयाति नवानि देही॥ २२॥

vāsāṃsi jīrṇāni yathā vihāya
navāni gṛhṇāti naro 'parāṇi|
tathā śarīrāṇi vihāya jīrṇāni
anyāni saṃyāti navāni dehī|| 22||

नैनं छिन्दन्ति शस्त्राणि नैनं दहति पावकः।
न चैनं क्लेदयन्त्यापो न शोषयति मारुतः॥ २३॥

nainaṃ chindanti śastrāṇi nainaṃ dahati pāvakaḥ|
na cainaṃ kledayantyāpo na śoṣayati mārutaḥ|| 23||

अच्छेद्यो ऽयमदाह्यो ऽयमक्लेद्यो ऽशोष्य एव च।
नित्यः सर्वगतः स्थाणुरचलो ऽयं सनातनः॥ २४॥

acchedyo 'yam adāhyo 'yam akledyo 'śoṣya eva ca|
nityaḥ sarvagataḥ sthāṇuracalo 'yaṃ sanātanaḥ|| 24||

अव्यक्तो ऽयमचिन्त्यो ऽयमविकार्यो ऽयमुच्यते।
तस्मादेवं विदित्वैनं नानुशोचितुमर्हसि॥ २५॥

avyakto 'yam acintyo 'yam avikāryo 'yam ucyate|
tasmādevaṃ viditvainaṃ nānuśocitum arhasi|| 25||

अथ चैनं नित्यजातं नित्यं वा मन्यसे मृतम्।
तथापि त्वं महाबाहो नैवं शोचितुम् अर्हसि॥ २६॥

atha cainaṃ nityajātaṃ nityaṃ vā manyase mṛtam|
tathāpi tvaṃ mahābāho naivaṃ śocitum arhasi|| 26||

Like to the man who casts off garments old,
And clothes himself in other raiment new,
So too doth he, the dweller in these frames,
Discard the old to live in bodies fresh. 22

He never is by weapons cleft,
Nor burnt by raging flames of fire,
He cannot be by waters drenched,
Nor ever withered by the wind. 23

And he divided cannot be,
Nor burnt nor drenched nor dried;
He's immovable, ancient, firm,
Eternal and pervading all. 24

Unmanifest, unthinkable,
Unchangable, he's said to be.
Hence, knowing him to be as such
It is not meet that thou shouldst mourn. 25

But if indeed thou think that he
Is ever born and ever dies,[51]
It is not meet that even then,
O mighty armed, thou thus shouldst grieve. 26

[51]This means that assuming that the Self, according to popular belief (which confounds the Self with the body in which He dwells), is born again and again, and dies again and again whenever the body comes into existence or ceases to be, even then it is futile to grieve, for, as pointed out in the succeeding verse, it is a universal law that what is born must die, and what is dead must live again.

जातस्य हि ध्रुवो मृत्युर्ध्रुवं जन्म मृतस्य च।
तस्मादपरिहार्ये ऽर्थे न त्वं शोचितुमर्हसि॥ २७॥

jātasya hi dhruvo mṛtyurdhruvaṃ janma mṛtasya ca|
tasmād aparihārye 'rthe na tvaṃ śocitum arhasi|| 27||

अव्यक्तादीनि भूतानि व्यक्तमध्यानि भारत।
अव्यक्तनिधनान्येव तत्र का परिदेवना॥ २८॥

avyaktādīni bhūtāni vyaktamadhyāni bhārata|
avyaktanidhanānyeva tatra kā paridevanā|| 28||

आश्चर्यवत्पश्यति कश्चिदेनम्
आश्चर्यवद्वदति तथैव चान्यः।
आश्चर्यवच्चैनमन्यः शृणोति
श्रुत्वाप्येनं वेद न चैव कश्चित्॥ २९॥

āścaryavat paśyati kaścidenam
āścaryavadvadati tathaiva cānyaḥ|
āścaryavaccainam anyaḥ śṛṇoti
śrutvāpyenaṃ veda na caiva kaścit|| 29||

देही नित्यमवध्यो ऽयं देहे सर्वस्य भारत।
तस्मात्सर्वाणि भूतानि न त्वं शोचितुमर्हसि॥ ३०॥

dehī nityam avadhyo 'yaṃ dehe sarvasya bhārata|
tasmātsarvāṇi bhūtāni na tvaṃ śocitum arhasi|| 30||

स्वधर्ममपि चावेक्ष्य न विकम्पितुमर्हसि।
धर्म्याद्धि युद्धाच्छ्रेयो ऽन्यत्क्षत्रियस्य न विद्यते॥ ३१।

svadharmam api cāvekṣya na vikampitum arhasi|
dharmyāddhi yuddhācchreyo 'nyatkṣatriyasya na vidyate|| 31|

For who is born must surely die,
And who is dead must surely live,
Therefore, for that which must befall
Thou shouldst not vainly grieve. 27

Before their birth and after death
All beings are unmanifest,
We only see them whilst they live,
Why therefore should we mourn for them?[52] 28

As wonderful he's adjudged by one,
As wonderful a second speaks of him,
As wonderful he's heard of by another,
And yet his mystery none ever knows. 29

Th' embodied self, O Bharat's son,
Is past all wounding, past all hurt,
Therefore, for any creature thou
Hast not the slightest cause to grieve. 30

Think too of what is due from thee,[53]
And in thy duty do not fail.
Since, for a warrior nothing is
More wholesome than a righteous war. 31

---

[52] This means that all beings, though ever-existent, have a non-manifest ante-natal condition, a manifest middle condition—the phase intervening between birth and death—and again an unmanifest post-mortem condition. Therefore, about these illusions or vicissitudes, first unseen, then seen, and again unseen, there should be no grief, since these constitute a natural law of being.

[53] Arjuna being a *kṣatriya*, it was part of his duties to engage in lawful war.

यदृच्छया चोपपन्नं स्वर्गद्वारमपावृतम्।
सुखिनः क्षत्रियाः पार्थ लभन्ते युद्धमीदृशम्॥ ३२॥

yadṛcchayā copapannaṃ svargadvāram apāvṛtam|
sukhinaḥ kṣatriyāḥ pārtha labhante yuddham īdṛśam|| 32||

अथ चेत्त्वम् इमं धर्म्यं संग्रामं न करिष्यसि।
ततः स्वधर्मं कीर्तिं च हित्वा पापमवाप्स्यसि॥ ३३॥

atha cet tvam imaṃ dharmyaṃ saṃgrāmaṃ na kariṣyasi|
tataḥ svadharmaṃ kīrtiṃ ca hitvā pāpam avāpsyasi|| 33||

अकीर्तिं चापि भूतानि कथयिष्यन्ति ते ऽव्ययाम्।
संभावितस्य चाकीर्तिर् मरणाद् अतिरिच्यते॥ ३४॥

akīrtiṃ cāpi bhūtāni kathayiṣyanti te 'vyayām|
saṃbhāvitasya cākīrtirmaraṇādatiricyate|| 34||

भयाद्रणादुपरतं मंस्यन्ते त्वां महारथाः।
येषां च त्वं बहुमतो भूत्वा यास्यसि लाघवम्॥ ३५॥

bhayād raṇād uparataṃ maṃsyante tvāṃ mahārathāḥ|
yeṣāṃ ca tvaṃ bahumato bhūtvā yāsyasi lāghavam|| 35||

अवाच्यवादांश्च बहून्वदिष्यन्ति तवाहिताः।
निन्दन्तस्तव सामर्थ्यं ततो दुःखतरं नु किम्॥ ३६॥

avācyavādāṃśca bahūn vadiṣyanti tavāhitāḥ|
nindantastava sāmarthyaṃ tato duḥkhataraṃ nu kim|| 36||

हतो वा प्राप्स्यसि स्वर्गं जित्वा वा भोक्ष्यसे महीम्।
तस्मादुत्तिष्ठ कौन्तेय युद्धाय कृतनिश्चयः॥ ३७॥

hato vā prāpsyasi svargaṃ jitvā vā bhokṣyase mahīm|
tasmāduttiṣṭha kaunteya yuddhāya kṛtaniścayaḥ|| 37||

Happy the warriors, Pṛthā's son,
To whom a battle such as this,
Comes of itself, unsought, unasked,
An open door which leads to heaven. 32

But if thou wilt refuse to fight
This righteous battle, fair and just,
Thy fame and duty thrown away,
Thou shalt most surely sin incur. 33

The tale of thy undying shame
Shall be renewed from age to age.
Who in the past have honoured been
Must count such fate as worse than death. 34

The chiefs who own great battle cars
Will think thou didst not fight through fear,
And th' esteem which now is thine
Will be transformed to cold contempt. 35

Unutterable and evil things
Thy enemies will speak of thee,
And mock thy mighty prowess, Prince,
What can be sadder fate than this! 36

If slain thou wilt to heaven go,
If victor thou wilt gain the earth;
Arise therefore, O Kuntī's son,
With full resolve to fight thy foes! 37

सुखदुःखे समे कृत्वा लाभालाभौ जयाजयौ।
ततो युद्धाय युज्यस्व नैवं पापमवाप्स्यसि॥ ३८॥

sukhaduḥkhe same kṛtvā lābhālābhau jayājayau|
tato yuddhāya yujyasva naivaṃ pāpam avāpsyasi|| 38||

एषा ते ऽभिहिता सांख्ये बुद्धिर्योगे त्विमां शृणु।
बुद्ध्या युक्तो यया पार्थ कर्मबन्धं प्रहास्यसि॥ ३९॥

eṣā te 'bhihitā sāṃkhye buddhiryoge tvimāṃ śṛṇu|
buddhyā yukto yayā pārtha karmabandhaṃ prahāsyasi|| 39||

नेहाभिक्रमनाशो ऽस्ति प्रत्यवायो न विद्यते।
स्वल्पमप्यस्य धर्मस्य त्रायते महतो भयात्॥ ४०॥

nehābhikramanāśo 'sti pratyavāyo na vidyate|
svalpam apyasya dharmasya trāyate mahato bhayāt|| 40||

व्यवसायात्मिका बुद्धिरेकेह कुरुनन्दन।
बहुशाखा ह्यनन्ताश्च बुद्धयो ऽव्यवसायिनाम्॥ ४१॥

vyavasāyātmikā buddhirekeha kurunandana|
bahuśākhā hyanantāśca buddhayo 'vyavasāyinām|| 41||

यामिमां पुष्पितां वाचं प्रवदन्त्यविपश्चितः।
वेदवादरताः पार्थ नान्यदस्तीति वादिनः॥ ४२॥

yām imāṃ puṣpitāṃ vācaṃ pravadantyavipaścitaḥ|
vedavādaratāḥ pārtha nānyadastīti vādinaḥ|| 42||

कामात्मानः स्वर्गपरा जन्मकर्मफलप्रदाम्।
क्रियाविशेषबहुलां भोगैश्वर्यगतिं प्रति॥ ४३॥

kāmātmānaḥ svargaparā janmakarmaphalapradām|
kriyāviśeṣabahulāṃ bhogaiśvaryagatiṃ prati|| 43||

Let pain and pleasure, gain and loss,
And triumph also, and defeat,
Have equal value in thy sight,
For thus no sin shall cling to thee. 38

This is the knowledge thou hast heard
Of Saṅkhyā;[54] now also hear of Yoga.[55]
This knowledge gained, thou shalt indeed
All action-fetters cast away. 39

No effort here is ever lost,
Nor any difficulties known;[56]
A little even of this lore
Delivers man from mortal fear.[57] 40

O joy of Kuru's, on this path
There is but one determined thought,
But manifold and endless are
The thoughts of weak and wavering men. 41

O Pṛthā's son, the speech of those
Is florid froth and foolishness,
Who love the letter of the Veda,
And say, naught better is than this. 42

Hearts full of hope, with heaven for goal,
They offer birth as actions's fruit,
And earthly pow'r and joys to win,
On ceremonial rites insist. 43

---

[54]*Sāṅkhya* (lit. a numeral, and therefore, counting—the counting forth, or separation, of spirit from matter) here, refers to the doctrine or science of the soul—soul-knowledge, God-knowledge, wisdon, or knowledge.

[55]i.e., *karma-yoga*, briefly named *yoga* here, is the way of salvation by works without seeking reward or the "fruits" of work. The term *yoga*, from the root *yuj* (to join) means union, or that which unites man to God—"the harmonizing of all the constituents in man till they vibrate in perfect unison with the One, the Supreme Self." The *yuktah* is the man who is thus united with God, or as rendered in the text, the man who is attuned with God. Telang translates *yoga* and *yuktah* by the words "devotioin" and "devoted" respectively.

[56]No effort, however, small or discontinuous, becomes abortive in *yoga*, in contrast, for example, to the ritualistic methods for self-purification described in the Vedas; in the latter case, a single omission or mistake renders the whole nugatory.

[57]i.e., the fear of *saṃsāra* (lit. that which runs) or the course or cycle of births and deaths alternating—briefly mundane existence.

भोगैश्वर्यप्रसक्तानां तयापहृतचेतसाम्।
व्यवसायात्मिका बुद्धिः समाधौ न विधीयते॥ ४४॥

bhogaiśvaryaprasaktānāṃ tayāpahṛtacetasām|
vyavasāyātmikā buddhiḥ samādhau na vidhīyate|| 44||

त्रैगुण्यविषया वेदा निस्त्रैगुण्यो भवार्जुन।
निर्द्वन्द्वो नित्यसत्त्वस्थो निर्योगक्षेम आत्मवान्॥ ४५॥

traiguṇyaviṣayā vedā nistraiguṇyo bhavārjuna|
nirdvandvo nityasattvastho niryogakṣema ātmavān|| 45||

यावानर्थ उदपाने सर्वतः संप्लुतोदके।
तावान्सर्वेषु वेदेषु ब्राह्मणस्य विजानतः॥ ४६॥

yāvānartha udapāne sarvataḥ saṃplutodake|
tāvān sarveṣu vedeṣu brāhmaṇasya vijānataḥ|| 46||

कर्मण्येवाधिकारस्ते मा फलेषु कदाचन।
मा कर्मफलहेतुर्भूर्मा ते सङ्गो ऽस्त्वकर्मणि॥ ४७॥

karmaṇyevādhikāraste mā phaleṣu kadācana|
mā karmaphalaheturbhūrmā te saṅgo 'stvakarmaṇi|| 47||

योगस्थः कुरु कर्माणि सङ्गं त्यक्त्वा धनंजय।
सिद्ध्यसिद्ध्योः समो भूत्वा समत्वं योग उच्यते॥ ४८॥

yogasthaḥ kuru karmāṇi saṅgaṃ tyaktvā dhanaṃjaya|
siddhyasiddhyoḥ samo bhūtvā samatvaṃ yoga ucyate|| 48||

Misled by doctrine such as this,
Enslaved by earthly wealth and power,
The single thought can ne'er be theirs
On steady contemplation[58] bent. 44

Above the three-fold *guṇas* then,[59]
The Veda's theme, O Arjun, rise,
And casting off the "pairs,"[60] be thou
Unanxious, self-controlled and pure.[61] 45

As in a place with waters whelmed,
A tank can serve no useful end,
So to the brahman, knowing all,
Of little use can be the Veda.[62] 46

Thy business is with deeds alone,
Not with the fruits the deeds may yield;
Act not for what the act may bring,
Nor to inaction be attatched. 47

Steadfast in Yoga do all thy works,
But unattatched, O Dhanañjay,
Success and failure see as one,
For Yoga is equanimity. 48

---

[58] *Samādhi.*

[59] The *guṇas* (translated as "qualities" or "attributes") are *sattva*, purity, *rajas*, activity or passion, and *tamas*, inertness or darkness. These *guṇas* are the characteristics or affections of matter, or Nature (*Prakṛti*), and their existence is to be inferred from the effects which they are instrumental in producing, such as brightness, dullness, etc.

[60] Often called the "pairs" of opposites," such as pleasure and pain, heat and cold, etc.

[61] i.e., *sattva*-filled.

[62] This is one possible version of this verse. The idea appears to be that to the man who has realized that salvation can be had by Wisdom (*Sāṅkhya* and *Yoga*), the ritualistic ordinances of the Vedas are of little worth, since these lead to results such as residence in Heaven, which compared to salvation are of no moment whatever. The verse may also be rendered thus:

To the enlightened Brāhmaṇ, know
The usefulness of all the Vedas
Is just as much as of a pool
Where ample floods o'erspread the land.

That is, the utility of the Vedas as a means of securing pleasure is comprehended in the infinite bliss which comes to him who possesses self-knowledge.

दूरेण ह्यवरं कर्म बुद्धियोगाद्धनंजय।
बुद्धौ शरणमन्विच्छ कृपणाः फलहेतवः॥ ४९॥

dūreṇa hyavaraṃ karma buddhiyogāddhanaṃjaya|
buddhau śaraṇamanviccha kṛpaṇāḥ phalahetavaḥ|| 49||

बुद्धियुक्तो जहातीह उभे सुकृतदुष्कृते।
तस्माद्योगाय युज्यस्व योगः कर्मसु कौशलम्॥ ५०॥

buddhiyukto jahātīha ubhe sukṛtaduṣkṛte|
tasmādyogāya yujyasva yogaḥ karmasu kauśalam|| 50||

कर्मजं बुद्धियुक्ता हि फलं त्यक्त्वा मनीषिणः।
जन्मबन्धविनिर्मुक्ताः पदं गच्छन्त्यनामयम्॥ ५१॥

karmajaṃ buddhiyuktā hi phalaṃ tyaktvā manīṣiṇaḥ|
janmabandhavinirmuktāḥ padaṃ gacchantyanāmayam|| 51||

यदा ते मोहकलिलं बुद्धिर्व्यतितरिष्यति।
तदा गन्तासि निर्वेदं श्रोतव्यस्य श्रुतस्य च॥ ५२॥

yadā te mohakalilaṃ buddhirvyatitariṣyati|
tadā gantāsi nirvedaṃ śrotavyasya śrutasya ca|| 52||

श्रुतिविप्रतिपन्ना ते यदा स्थास्यति निश्चला।
समाधावचला बुद्धिस्तदा योगमवाप्स्यसि॥ ५३॥

śrutivipratipannā te yadā sthāsyati niścalā|
samādhāvacalā buddhistadā yogamavāpsyasi|| 53||

अर्जुन उवाच

स्थितप्रज्ञस्य का भाषा समाधिस्थस्य केशव।
स्थितधीः किं प्रभाषेत किमासीत व्रजेत किम्॥ ५४॥

arjuna uvāca

sthitaprajñasya kā bhāṣā samādhisthasya keśava|
sthitadhīḥ kiṃ prabhāṣeta kim āsīta vrajeta kim|| 54||

For wisdom[63] is, O Dhanañjay,
Far better, far, than any deed.
Do thou in wisdom shelter take;
They wretched are who work for gain. 49

Whoso with wisdom is endued,
E'en here[64] casts off deeds good and ill;
Wherefore, apply thyself to Yoga,
For Yoga is naught but skill in deeds. 50

The sages who have wisdom gained
Renounce the fruit which action brings,
And from the bonds of re-birth freed,
Achieve the state which knows no pain. 51

Thy reason when it has gone past,
Beyond delussion's tangled maze,
Then shalt thou cease to be concerned
With things both heard and yet unheard.[65] 52

Nay, thy reason now sore perplexed
By doctrinal perplexities,[66]
When 'tis in contemplation based[67]
Then unto Yoga thou shalt attain. 53

Arjun said:

How is the steady-minded known[68]
Who is in contemplation wrapt?
How doth, O Keśav, such a man
Deport himself, sit, talk and walk? 54

---

[63]Wisdom here and in the succeeding verses stands for *buddhi-yoga. Buddhi* is the discriminative faculty of the mind. The word throughout this work has been translated reason.

[64]in this world.

[65]i.e., the doctrinal teachings other than those referring to the Self.

[66]In the original: the *śruti* or revealed scriptures

[67]*Samādhi*, contemplation of the Self.

[68]*Sthita-prajña*, translated here as "the steady-minded" or as the man with a steady or balanced mind, is the man who by sustained intellectual effort arrives at the conviction that he is the Supreme Brahman. This is the conviction or knowledge which in the Third Discourse is spoken of as *jñāna*, devotion to which is regarded by some commentators as the chief, if not the only means, by which *mokṣa*, or salvation—the Brahmic Bliss—can be obtained.

श्रीभगवानुवाच
प्रजहाति यदा कामान् सर्वान् पार्थ मनोगतान्।
आत्मन्येवात्मना तुष्टः स्थितप्रज्ञस्तदोच्यते॥ ५५॥

śrībhagavān uvāca
prajahāti yadā kāmān sarvān pārtha manogatān|
ātmany evātmanā tuṣṭaḥ sthitaprajñas tadocyate|| 55||

दुःखेष्वनुद्विग्नमनाः सुखेषु विगतस्पृहः।
वीतरागभयक्रोधः स्थितधीर्मुनिरुच्यते॥ ५६॥

duḥkheṣv anudvignamanāḥ sukheṣu vigataspṛhaḥ|
vītarāgabhayakrodhaḥ sthitadhīr munir ucyate|| 56||

यः सर्वत्रानभिस्नेहस्तत्तत् प्राप्य शुभाशुभम्।
नाभिनन्दति न द्वेष्टि तस्य प्रज्ञा प्रतिष्ठिता॥ ५७॥

yaḥ sarvatrānabhisnehas tat tat prāpya śubhāśubham|
nābhinandati na dveṣṭi tasya prajñā pratiṣṭhitā|| 57||

यदा संहरते चायं कूर्मो ऽङ्गानीव सर्वशः।
इन्द्रियाणीन्द्रियार्थेभ्यस्तस्य प्रज्ञा प्रतिष्ठिता॥ ५८॥

yadā saṃharate cāyaṃ kūrmo 'ṅgānīva sarvaśaḥ|
indriyāṇīndriyārthebhyastasya prajñā pratiṣṭhitā|| 58||

विषया विनिवर्तन्ते निराहारस्य देहिनः।
रसवर्जं रसो ऽप्यस्य परं दृष्ट्वा निवर्तते॥ ५९॥

viṣayā vinivartante nirāhārasya dehinaḥ|
rasavarjaṃ raso 'pyasya paraṃ dṛṣṭvā nivartate|| 59||

The Blessed Lord said:

Whene'er a man, O Pṛthā's son,
Abandons all his heart's desires,
With self alone by self's content,[69]
Then steady minded is he called. 55

Whose mind 'midst pain is not distressed,
Who has for pleasures no desire,
Who's freed from passion, fear and wrath,
Is called a sage of steady mind. 56

The man whose heart is unattatched,
Who, come what may of good or ill,
Is not elated or depressed,
The mind of such is balanced well. 57

And when a man draws in all round
Just as the turtle doth its limbs,
His senses from the things of sense,
Then is his mind in perfect poise. 58

Sense-objects leave alone the man
Who is in all things abstinent,
But not the taste for them; e'en this
Departs when the supreme is seen. 59

[69] i.e., who is satisfied, as a result of his own meditation, with the Self alone, with nothing that falls short of the supreme reality.

यततो ह्यपि कौन्तेय पुरुषस्य विपश्चितः।
इन्द्रियाणि प्रमाथीनि हरन्ति प्रसभं मनः॥ ६०॥

yatato hyapi kaunteya puruṣasya vipaścitaḥ|
indriyāṇi pramāthīni haranti prasabhaṃ manaḥ|| 60||

तानि सर्वाणि संयम्य युक्त आसीत मत्परः।
वशे हि यस्येन्द्रियाणि तस्य प्रज्ञा प्रतिष्ठिता॥ ६१॥

tāni sarvāṇi saṃyamya yukta āsīta matparaḥ|
vaśe hi yasyendriyāṇi tasya prajñā pratiṣṭhitā|| 61||

ध्यायतो विषयान् पुंसः सङ्गस्तेषूपजायते।
सङ्गात्संजायते कामः कामात्क्रोधो ऽभिजायते॥ ६२॥

dhyāyato viṣayān puṃsaḥ saṅgasteṣūpajāyate|
saṅgātsaṃjāyate kāmaḥ kāmātkrodho 'bhijāyate|| 62||

क्रोधाद्भवति संमोहः संमोहात्स्मृतिविभ्रमः।
स्मृतिभ्रंशाद्बुद्धिनाशो बुद्धिनाशात्प्रणश्यति॥ ६३॥

krodhād bhavati saṃmohaḥ saṃmohāt smṛtivibhramaḥ|
smṛtibhraṃśād buddhināśo buddhināśāt praṇaśyati|| 63||

रागद्वेषवियुक्तैस्तु विषयानिन्द्रियैश्चरन्।
आत्मवश्यैर्विधेयात्मा प्रसादमधिगच्छति॥ ६४॥

rāgadveṣaviyuktais tu viṣayān indriyaiścaran|
ātmavaśyair vidheyātmā prasādam adhigacchati|| 64||

प्रसादे सर्वदुःखानां हानिरस्योपजायते।
प्रसन्नचेतसो ह्याशु बुद्धिः पर्यवतिष्ठते॥ ६५॥

prasāde sarvaduḥkhānāṃ hānirasyopajāyate|
prasannacetaso hyāśu buddhiḥ paryavatiṣṭhate|| 65||

The boisterous senses, Kuntī's son,
Wrench forcibly away the mind
In sooth, of even him who's wise,
Though struggling hard to stem them back. 60

Restraining them, a man should live
Attuned with me, intent on me;
Of such whose senses are controlled
The mind indeed is balanced well. 61

The man who dotes on things of sense,
For them he soon attachment forms;
From this attachment springs desire,
And anger from desire is born. 62

From anger comes delusion next,
And loss of memory in its turn;
From memory's loss the reason's lost,
And then is lost the man himself. 63

But who with self restraint doth move
In 'midst of things, with senses free
From love and hate, and well controlled,
Attaineth peacefulness of mind. 64

And having peace of mind attained,
All his afflictions cease to be;
For of the tranquil minded man
The reason steady soon becomes. 65

नास्ति बुद्धिरयुक्तस्य न चायुक्तस्य भावना।
न चाभावयतः शान्तिरशान्तस्य कुतः सुखम्॥ ६६॥

nāsti buddhirayuktasya na cāyuktasya bhāvanā|
na cābhāvayataḥ śāntiraśāntasya kutaḥ sukham|| 66||

इन्द्रियाणां हि चरतां यन्मनो ऽनुविधीयते।
तदस्य हरति प्रज्ञां वायुर्नावमिवाम्भसि॥ ६७॥

indriyāṇāṃ hi caratāṃ yanmano 'nuvidhīyate|
tadasya harati prajñāṃ vāyurnāvamivāmbhasi|| 67||

तस्माद्यस्य महाबाहो निगृहीतानि सर्वशः।
इन्द्रियाणीन्द्रियार्थेभ्यस्तस्य प्रज्ञा प्रतिष्ठिता॥ ६८॥

tasmādyasya mahābāho nigṛhītāni sarvaśaḥ|
indriyāṇīndriyārthebhyastasya prajñā pratiṣṭhitā|| 68||

या निशा सर्वभूतानां तस्यां जागर्ति संयमी।
यस्यां जाग्रति भूतानि सा निशा पश्यतो मुनेः॥ ६९॥

yā niśā sarvabhūtānāṃ tasyāṃ jāgarti saṃyamī|
yasyāṃ jāgrati bhūtāni sā niśā paśyato muneḥ|| 69||

आपूर्यमाणमचलप्रतिष्ठं
समुद्रमापः प्रविशन्ति यद्वत्।
तद्वत्कामा यं प्रविशन्ति सर्वे
स शान्तिमाप्नोति न कामकामी॥ ७०॥

āpūryamāṇamacalapratiṣṭhaṃ
samudramāpaḥ praviśanti yadvat|
tadvatkāmā yaṃ praviśanti sarve
sa śāntimāpnoti na kāmakāmī|| 70||

Wisdom and concentration both
Are to the unattuned denied,
To the unconcentrated, peace,
And to the peaceless, happiness. 66

For by the roving senses led,
The mind his judgment leads astray,
Just as a storm-tossed ship at sea
Is driven far from out her course. 67

Therefore, O thou of mighty arms,
The judgment balanced is of those
Whose senses fully are restrained
From roving to the things of sense. 68

The self-controlled man's awake,
When for all other men 'tis night;
The sage who seeth finds it night
When other beings are awake.[70] 69

Just as the sea its level changeth not,
Though fed it be by rivers constantly,
So he in whom thus enter all desires,
Finds peace; not he who craves for things. 70

---

[70]The sage is awake to spiritual matters which are hidden from the ordinary man, and *vice versa*, worldly pursuits which are realities to the masses are a mere illusion to the sage—to the man who knows the supreme reality.

विहाय कामान् यः सर्वान्पुमांश्चरति निःस्पृहः।
निर्ममो निरहंकारः स शान्तिमधिगच्छति॥ ७१॥

vihāya kāmān yaḥ sarvānpumāṃścarati niḥspṛhaḥ|
nirmamo nirahaṃkāraḥ sa śāntimadhigacchati|| 71||

एषा ब्राह्मी स्थितिः पार्थ नैनां प्राप्य विमुह्यति।
स्थित्वास्यामन्तकाले ऽपि ब्रह्मनिर्वाणमृच्छति॥ ७२॥

eṣā brāhmī sthitiḥ pārtha naināṃ prāpya vimuhyati|
sthitvāsyāmantakāle 'pi brahmanirvāṇamṛcchati|| 72||

The man who casting off desire,
Without attachment goes through life,
Who is not vain,[71] who selfless is,[72]
At last attains to perfect peace.[73] 71

O Pārtha this is the Brahman state,[74]
None is deluded having this;
If e'en at death he's found therein,
A man attains the Brahman bliss.[75] 72

---

[71]Lit. free from egoism.
[72]Lit. free from the sense of I-ness and My-ness.
[73]i.e., *nirvāṇa*—the end of *saṃsāra*; in short, he becomes Brahma.
[74]i.e., the divine state—the state of Brahma.
[75]*Brahma-nirvāṇa*

Chapter Three: The Yoga of Action (कर्मयोगः)

अर्जुन उवाच

ज्यायसी चेत्कर्मणस्ते मता बुद्धिर्जनार्दन।
तत्किं कर्मणि घोरे मां नियोजयसि केशव॥ १॥

arjuna uvāca

jyāyasī cet karmaṇaste matā buddhirjanārdana|
tat kiṃ karmaṇi ghore māṃ niyojayasi keśava|| 1||

व्यामिश्रेणैव वाक्येन बुद्धिं मोहयसीव मे।
तदेकं वद निश्चित्य येन श्रेयो ऽहमाप्नुयाम्॥ २॥

vyāmiśreṇaiva vākyena buddhiṃ mohayasīva me|
tadekaṃ vada niścitya yena śreyo 'ham āpnuyām|| 2||

श्रीभगवानुवाच

लोके ऽस्मिन्द्विविधा निष्ठा पुरा प्रोक्ता मयानघ।
ज्ञानयोगेन सांख्यानां कर्मयोगेन योगिनाम्॥ ३॥

śrībhagavān uvāca

loke 'smin dvividhā niṣṭhā purā proktā mayānagha|
jñānayogena sāṃkhyānāṃ karmayogena yogināṃ|| 3||

न कर्मणामनारम्भान्नैष्कर्म्यं पुरुषो ऽश्नुते।
न च संन्यसनादेव सिद्धिं समधिगच्छति॥ ४॥

na karmaṇām anārambhān naiṣkarmyaṃ puruṣo 'śnute|
na ca saṃnyasanād eva siddhiṃ samadhigacchati|| 4||

Arjun said:

If thou thinkest, O Janārdan,
That knowledge better is than work,
Wherefore dost thou, O Keśav, then
This dreadful act on me enjoin? 1

Thou seemest only to confuse
My mind by thy ambiguous words;
Tell me one thing decisively
By which I may to bliss attain. 2

The Blessed Lord said:

O sinless one, I've said before
This world a two-fold path contains;[76]
Of knowledge, by the *Sāṅkhyas* trod,
And works in which the *Yogins* walk.3

A man cannot by shunning work
From action total freedom gain,
Nor to perfection can he rise
By mere renouncement of all work. 4

---

[76]These two paths referred to in the Second Discourse, verse 39, as the Sāṅkhya and the Yoga, are known in the *Gītā* as *jñāna-yoga* (*yoga* by knowledge) and and *karma-yoga* (*yoga* by works). The latter is the dedication of physical energies to God's services.

न हि कश्चित्क्षणमपि जातु तिष्ठत्यकर्मकृत्।
कार्यते ह्यवशः कर्म सर्वः प्रकृतिजैर्गुणैः॥ ५॥

na hi kaścit kṣaṇam api jātu tiṣṭhaty akarmakṛt|
kāryate hy avaśaḥ karma sarvaḥ prakṛtijair guṇaiḥ|| 5||

कर्मेन्द्रियाणि संयम्य य आस्ते मनसा स्मरन्।
इन्द्रियार्थान् विमूढात्मा मिथ्याचारः स उच्यते॥ ६॥

karmendriyāṇi saṃyamya ya āste manasā smaran|
indriyārthān vimūḍhātmā mithyācāraḥ sa ucyate|| 6||

यस्त्विन्द्रियाणि मनसा नियम्यारभते ऽर्जुन।
कर्मेन्द्रियैः कर्मयोगमसक्तः स विशिष्यते॥ ७॥

yas tv indriyāṇi manasā niyamyārabhate 'rjuna|
karmendriyaiḥ karmayogam asaktaḥ sa viśiṣyate|| 7||

नियतं कुरु कर्म त्वं कर्म ज्यायो ह्यकर्मणः।
शरीरयात्रापि च ते न प्रसिध्येदकर्मणः॥ ८॥

niyataṃ kuru karma tvaṃ karma jyāyo hy akarmaṇaḥ|
śarīrayātrāpi ca te na prasidhyed akarmaṇaḥ|| 8||

यज्ञार्थात्कर्मणो ऽन्यत्र लोको ऽयं कर्मबन्धनः।
तदर्थं कर्म कौन्तेय मुक्तसङ्गः समाचर॥ ९॥

yajñārthāt karmaṇo 'nyatra loko 'yaṃ karmabandhanaḥ|
tadarthaṃ karma kaunteya muktasaṅgaḥ samācara|| 9||

सहयज्ञाः प्रजाः सृष्ट्वा पुरोवाच प्रजापतिः।
अनेन प्रसविष्यध्वमेष वो ऽस्त्विष्टकामधुक्॥ १०॥

sahayajñāḥ prajāḥ sṛṣṭvā purovāca prajāpatiḥ|
anena prasaviṣyadhvam eṣa vo 'stv iṣṭakāmadhuk|| 10||

For verily no man can be
E'en for an instant actionless,
As by the *guṇas*, nature-born,
He's driven to work against his will. 5

The self-deluded man who lives,
His active powers[77] held well in hand,
Yet doting on the things of sense,
That man is called a hypocrite. 6

But who his senses, mind controlled,
Without attachment doth employ
His active powers for Karma-yoga,
That man indeed is worthier far. 7

Do thine alloted task, for work
Is better far than idleness;
Thy body even cannot thrive
Without its daily round of work. 8

By action fettered is the world,
Except by acts of sacrifice,
Therefore, detached, O Kuntī's son,
In works of sacrifice engage. 9

Creating men and sacrifice
In days of yore the Maker[78]said;
By sacrifice increase your kind,
May this your wishes gratify.[79] 10

---

[77]Lit. the organs of action. These are, according to Hindu philosophy, eleven in number, five organs of action, five of perception, and the mind.

[78]*Prajāpati*, the demi-urge or creative element of God personified. The term is generally applied to the four-faced Brahmā, the Lord commissioned to create his single system in the cosmos, viz, the *brahmāṇḍa*. It is also used to designate the Prajāpatis, the sons of Brahmā. Here it applies to God himself.

[79]Lit. may this be to you the *kāmadhuk*, Indra's cow of plenty, from which each could milk what he wanted.

देवान् भावयतानेन ते देवा भावयन्तु वः।
परस्परं भावयन्तः श्रेयः परमवाप्स्यथ॥ ११॥

devān bhāvayatānena te devā bhāvayantu vaḥ|
parasparaṃ bhāvayantaḥ śreyaḥ param avāpsyatha|| 11||

इष्टान्भोगान्हि वो देवा दास्यन्ते यज्ञभाविताः।
तैर्दत्तानप्रदायैभ्यो यो भुङ्क्ते स्तेन एव सः॥ १२॥

iṣṭān bhogān hi vo devā dāsyante yajñabhāvitāḥ|
tairdattān apradāyaibhyo yo bhuṅkte stena eva saḥ|| 12||

यज्ञशिष्टाशिनः सन्तो मुच्यन्ते सर्वकिल्बिषैः।
भुञ्जते ते त्वघं पापा ये पचन्त्यात्मकारणात्॥ १३॥

yajñaśiṣṭāśinaḥ santo mucyante sarvakilbiṣaiḥ|
bhuñjate te tvaghaṃ pāpā ye pacantyātmakāraṇāt|| 13||

अन्नाद्भवन्ति भूतानि पर्जन्यादन्नसंभवः।
यज्ञाद्भवति पर्जन्यो यज्ञः कर्मसमुद्भवः॥ १४॥

annādbhavanti bhūtāni parjanyādannasaṃbhavaḥ|
yajñādbhavati parjanyo yajñaḥ karmasamudbhavaḥ|| 14||

कर्म ब्रह्मोद्भवं विद्धि ब्रह्माक्षरसमुद्भवम्।
तस्मात्सर्वगतं ब्रह्म नित्यं यज्ञे प्रतिष्ठितम्॥ १५॥

karma brahmodbhavaṃ viddhi brahmākṣarasam udbhavam|
tasmāt sarvagataṃ brahma nityaṃ yajñe pratiṣṭhitam|| 15||

एवं प्रवर्तितं चक्रं नानुवर्तयतीह यः।
अघायुरिन्द्रियारामो मोघं पार्थ स जीवति॥ १६॥

evaṃ pravartitaṃ cakraṃ nānuvartayatīha yaḥ|
aghāyur indriyārāmo moghaṃ pārtha sa jīvati|| 16||

With this sustain the shining ones,[80]
And may you be by them sustained,
By mutual sustinence as this,
Thou shalt attain the highest good.[81] 11

They shall, by sacrifice sustained,
On you bestow your heart's desires.
A thief indeed is he who takes
Their gifts without returning aught. 12

The good who eat whate'er is left
Of sacrifice are freed from sin;
The bad who cook for self alone,
Their food is sin assuredly.[82] 13

In food all creatures have their birth,
From rain in turn is food produced,
From sacrifice proceedeth rain,
And sacrifice from action springs. 14

Learn thou all action springs from Brahm,[83]
Brahm comes from Him Who ever lives,[84]
Therefore, the all-pervading Brahm
Is ever found in sacrifice. 15

Who here on earth doth follow not
The world-wheel thus in motion set,
Who lives a sensuous, sinful life,
That man, O Pārtha, lives in vain. 16

---

[80]The *devas* (translated in other passages as "gods") or the immortals who live in *svarga*—the heaven of Hindu mythology.

[81]This may mean either *mokṣa*, or *svarga*.

[82]The righteous who eat of sacrificial remains (known as *amṛta*, or ambrosia) are freed from the sin of cruelty, etc., involved in the slaughter of animals for sacrificial purposes, but the sinful who think that God's gifts are intended for themselves alone, and prepare and eat food with this notion, eat sin itself.

[83]Brahman, here, stands for the Vedas; the all-pervading Brahman being found in sacrifice means that the all-comprehending Vedas treat of everything relating to sacrificial rites.

[84]Lit. the imperishable—the supreme being.

यस्त्वात्मरतिरेव स्यादात्मतृप्तश्च मानवः।
आत्मन्येव च संतुष्टस्तस्य कार्यं न विद्यते॥ १७॥

yas tv ātmaratir eva syād ātmatṛptaśca mānavaḥ|
ātmany eva ca saṃtuṣṭas tasya kāryaṃ na vidyate|| 17||

नैव तस्य कृतेनार्थो नाकृतेनेह कश्चन।
न चास्य सर्वभूतेषु कश्चिदर्थव्यपाश्रयः॥ १८॥

naiva tasya kṛtenārtho nākṛteneha kaścana|
na cāsya sarvabhūteṣu kaścidarthavyapāśrayaḥ|| 18||

तस्मादसक्तः सततं कार्यं कर्म समाचर।
असक्तो ह्याचरन् कर्म परमाप्नोति पूरुषः॥ १९॥

tasmād asaktaḥ satataṃ kāryaṃ karma samācara|
asakto hy ācaran karma param āpnoti pūruṣaḥ|| 19||

कर्मणैव हि संसिद्धिमास्थिता जनकादयः।
लोकसंग्रहमेवापि संपश्यन् कर्तुमर्हसि॥ २०॥

karmaṇaiva hi saṃsiddhim āsthitā janakādayaḥ|
lokasaṃgraham evāpi saṃpaśyan kartum arhasi|| 20||

यद्यदाचरति श्रेष्ठस्तत्तदेवेतरो जनः।
स यत्प्रमाणं कुरुते लोकस्तदनुवर्तते॥ २१॥

yadyadācarati śreṣṭhastattadevetaro janaḥ|
sa yatpramāṇaṃ kurute lokastadanuvartate|| 21||

न मे पार्थास्ति कर्तव्यं त्रिषु लोकेषु किं चन।
नानवाप्तमवाप्तव्यं वर्त एव च कर्मणि॥ २२॥

na me pārthāsti kartavyaṃ triṣu lokeṣu kiṃ cana|
nānavāptamavāptavyaṃ varta eva ca karmaṇi|| 22||

But who rejoiceth in the self,
And with the self is satisfied,
Who's in the self alone content,
Has nought whatever here to do. 17

He is not in the least concerned
In aught that's done or left undone,
And no concern of his depends
On any being whatsoe'er. 18

Therefore, without attachment, thou
E'er do that work which should be done;
Work done without attachment is
Man's passport sure to the supreme. 19

Of old did Janak[85] and the rest,
By work alone perfection gain;
Thou also shouldst engage in work,
The world's welfare thy only aim. 20

Whate'er the thing a great man does,
That copied is by other men;
Whatever standard he sets up,
By that the common people go. 21

There nothing is, O Pṛthā's son,
In all the worlds for me to do,
Naught unattained that I might gain,
Yet even I engage in work. 22

[85] One of the royal sages—kings who lived the life of ascetics.

यदि ह्यहं न वर्तेयं जातु कर्मण्यतन्द्रितः।
मम वर्त्मानुवर्तन्ते मनुष्याः पार्थ सर्वशः॥ २३॥

yadi hyahaṃ na varteyaṃ jātu karmaṇyatandritaḥ|
mama vartmānuvartante manuṣyāḥ pārtha sarvaśaḥ|| 23||

उत्सीदेयुरिमे लोका न कुर्यां कर्म चेदहम्।
संकरस्य च कर्ता स्यामुपहन्यामिमाः प्रजाः॥ २४॥

utsīdeyurime lokā na kuryāṃ karma cedaham|
saṃkarasya ca kartā syām upahanyāmimāḥ prajāḥ|| 24||

सक्ताः कर्मण्यविद्वांसो यथा कुर्वन्ति भारत।
कुर्याद्विद्वांस्तथासक्तश्चिकीर्षुर्लोकसंग्रहम्॥ २५॥

saktāḥ karmaṇyavidvāṃso yathā kurvanti bhārata|
kuryādvidvāṃstathāsaktaścikīrṣurlokasaṃgraham|| 25||

न बुद्धिभेदं जनयेदज्ञानां कर्मसङ्गिनाम्।
योजयेत्[86]सर्वकर्माणि विद्वान् युक्तः समाचरन्॥ २६॥

na buddhibhedaṃ janayedajñānāṃ karmasaṅginām|
yojayetsarvakarmāṇi vidvān yuktaḥ samācaran|| 26||

प्रकृतेः क्रियमाणानि गुणैः कर्माणि सर्वशः।
अहंकारविमूढात्मा कर्ताहमिति मन्यते॥ २७॥

prakṛteḥ kriyamāṇāni guṇaiḥ karmāṇi sarvaśaḥ|
ahaṃkāravimūḍhātmā kartāhamiti manyate|| 27||

तत्त्ववित्तु महाबाहो गुणकर्मविभागयोः।
गुणा गुणेषु वर्तन्त इति मत्वा न सज्जते॥ २८॥

tattvavit tu mahābāho guṇakarmavibhāgayoḥ|
guṇā guṇeṣu vartanta iti matvā na sajjate|| 28||

---

[86]जोषयेदिति पाथः वा

And if unwearied I worked not,
O son of Pṛthā, every man
Would imitate the lead I gave,
And idle be and actionless. 23

These worlds would into ruin fall
If I withdrew myself from work;
Caste mingling would through me ensue,
And all these people wrecked through me. 24

As fools, O son of Bharat, act,
Because they are to action bound,
So too the wise, unbound, should act,
The world's welfare their only aim. 25

Let no wise man upset the minds
Of foolish ones to action bound,
But working with them heartily,
Let him to work the people draw. 26

The gunas, born of nature, are
The sole mainspring of every act;
Whose mind is warped by egoism,
Imagines, 'I perform those acts'. 27

But who the *guṇas* understands,[87]
Their functions and divisions too,
Is unattached, for well he knows,
The *guṇas* on the *guṇas* act.[88] 28

---

[87]The vocative "O stalwart-armed" in this line is omitted.
[88]The *guṇas* as sense-organs move amongst the *guṇas* as sense-objects.

प्रकृतेर्गुणसंमूढाः सज्जन्ते गुणकर्मसु।
तानकृत्स्नविदो मन्दान् कृत्स्नविन्न विचालयेत्॥ २९॥

prakṛterguṇasaṃmūḍhāḥ sajjante guṇakarmasu|
tānakṛtsnavido mandān kṛtsnavin na vicālayet|| 29||

मयि सर्वाणि कर्माणि संन्यस्याध्यात्मचेतसा।
निराशीर्निर्ममो भूत्वा युध्यस्व विगतज्वरः॥ ३०॥

mayi sarvāṇi karmāṇi saṃnyasyādhyātmacetasā|
nirāśīrnirmamo bhūtvā yudhyasva vigatajvaraḥ|| 30||

ये मे मतमिदं नित्यमनुतिष्ठन्ति मानवाः।
श्रद्धावन्तो ऽनसूयन्तो मुच्यन्ते ते ऽपि कर्मभिः॥ ३१॥

ye me matam idaṃ nityamanutiṣṭhanti mānavāḥ|
śraddhāvanto 'nasūyanto mucyante te 'pi karmabhiḥ|| 31||

ये त्वेतदभ्यसूयन्तो नानुतिष्ठन्ति मे मतम्।
सर्वज्ञानविमूढांस्तान्विद्धि नष्टानचेतसः॥ ३२॥

ye tvetadabhyasūyanto nānutiṣṭhanti me matam|
sarvajñānavimūḍhāṃstān viddhi naṣṭān acetasaḥ|| 32||

सदृशं चेष्टते स्वस्याः प्रकृतेर्ज्ञानवानपि।
प्रकृतिं यान्ति भूतानि निग्रहः किं करिष्यति॥ ३३॥

sadṛśaṃ ceṣṭate svasyāḥ prakṛterjñānavānapi|
prakṛtiṃ yānti bhūtāni nigrahaḥ kiṃ kariṣyati|| 33||

इन्द्रियस्येन्द्रियस्यार्थे रागद्वेषौ व्यवस्थितौ।
तयोर्न वशमागच्छेत्तौ ह्यस्य परिपन्थिनौ॥ ३४॥

indriyasyendriyasyārthe rāgadveṣau vyavasthitau|
tayorna vaśamāgacchettau hyasya paripanthinau|| 34||

Those by the *guṇas* led astray,
Are to their functions e'er attached;
Who are with perfect knowledge blest,
Should not perplex the ignorant.[89] 29

Surrend'ring all thy acts to me,
And resting in the self thy thoughts,
Rid of desire and selfishness,[90]
Thy fever cured, wage thou this war! 30

Those men who practise constantly
This teaching that from me proceeds,
Not captiously, but trustingly,
They too from action's bonds are freed. 31

But who my teaching disregard,
And carp at it and criticize,
Deluded in all knowledge, know
These senseless ones are doomed to death. 32

Yea, e'en the man of knowledge acts
As by his nature he is bid;
All creatures own their nature's sway,
What can therefore restraint avail? 33

Both love and hate for things of sense
Inherent in the senses are;
Let none become a slave to them,[91]
For they his foes are verily. 34

---

[89]Lit. men of imperfect knowledge.
[90]The notion of "I"-ness and "my"-ness.
[91]I.e., to love and hate (desire and aversion) for sense-objects.

श्रेयान् स्वधर्मो विगुणः परधर्मात्स्वनुष्ठितात्।
स्वधर्मे निधनं श्रेयः परधर्मो भयावहः॥ ३५॥

śreyān svadharmo viguṇaḥ paradharmātsvanuṣṭhitāt|
svadharme nidhanaṃ śreyaḥ paradharmo bhayāvahaḥ|| 35||

अर्जुन उवाच

अथ केन प्रयुक्तो ऽयं पापं चरति पूरुषः।
अनिच्छन्नपि वार्ष्णेय बलादिव नियोजितः॥ ३६॥

arjuna uvāca

atha kena prayukto 'yaṃ pāpaṃ carati pūruṣaḥ|
anicchannapi vārṣṇeya balādiva niyojitaḥ|| 36||

श्रीभगवानुवाच

काम एष क्रोध एष रजोगुणसमुद्भवः।
महाशनो महापाप्मा विद्धेनमिह वैरिणम्॥ ३७॥

śrībhagavān uvāca

kāma eṣa krodha eṣa rajoguṇasamudbhavaḥ|
mahāśano mahāpāpmā viddhy enam iha vairiṇam|| 37||

धूमेनाव्रियते वह्निर्यथादर्शो मलेन च।
यथोल्बेनावृतो गर्भस्तथा तेनेदमावृतम्॥ ३८॥

dhūmenāvriyate vahniryathādarśo malena ca|
yatholbenāvṛto garbhas tathā tenedamāvṛtam|| 38||

आवृतं ज्ञानमेतेन ज्ञानिनो नित्यवैरिणा।
कामरूपेण कौन्तेय दुष्पूरेणानलेन च॥ ३९॥

āvṛtaṃ jñānametena jñānino nityavairiṇā|
kāmarūpeṇa kaunteya duṣpūreṇānalena ca|| 39||

Though meritless, ones own work is
Better than alien work well done;
Better is death at duty's post,
In other's work doth danger lurk. 35

Arjun said:

Then what is it, O Vṛṣṇi's son,
That prompts a man to sinful deeds,
As if he were against his will
By some resistless pow'r impelled? 36

The Blessed Lord said:

It is desire, yea, it is wrath,
Which always is of *rajas* born,
Consuming all, polluting all,
Know this to be man's foe on earth. 37

Surrounded as is fire by smoke,
As mirror clouded is by dust,
And as the child within the womb,
So by desire is *this*[92] concealed. 38

By this, the ever present foe
Of those who're wise is wisdom hid;
Yea, by desire, O Kuntī's son,
Unsated like a flame of fire. 39

---

[92]The universe according to some commentators; but *this* obviously refers to wisdom mentioned in the following verse.

इन्द्रियाणि मनो बुद्धिरस्याधिष्ठानमुच्यते।
एतैर्विमोहयत्येष ज्ञानमावृत्य देहिनम्॥ ४०॥

indriyāṇi mano buddhirasyādhiṣṭhānamucyate|
etairvimohayatyeṣa jñānamāvṛtya dehinam|| 40||

तस्मात्त्वमिन्द्रियाण्यादौ नियम्य भरतर्षभ।
पाप्मानं प्रजहि ह्येनं ज्ञानविज्ञाननाशनम्॥ ४१॥

tasmāt tvam indriyāṇy ādau niyamya bharatarṣabha|
pāpmānaṃ prajahi hyenaṃ jñānavijñānanāśanam|| 41||

इन्द्रियाणि पराण्याहुरिन्द्रियेभ्यः परं मनः।
मनसस्तु परा बुद्धिर्यो बुद्धेः परतस्तु सः॥ ४२॥

indriyāṇi parāṇy āhur indriyebhyaḥ paraṃ manaḥ|
manasas tu parā buddhiryo buddheḥ paratastu saḥ|| 42||

एवं बुद्धेः परं बुद्ध्वा संस्तभ्यात्मानमात्मना।
जहि शत्रुं महाबाहो कामरूपं दुरासदम्॥ ४३॥

evaṃ buddheḥ paraṃ buddhvā saṃstabhyātmānamātmanā|
jahi śatrum mahābāho kāmarūpaṃ durāsadam|| 43||

The reason, senses and the mind,
Are said to be its seat; through these,
By veiling wisdom it deludes
The self who in the body dwells. 40

Therefore, O thou the Bharat's lord,
Thy senses conquering first of all,
Do thou cast off this sinful thing,
Knowledge and wisdom both which kills. 41

The wise have called the senses great,
And held the mind yet greater still,
And reason greater than the mind,
But self than reason's greater far. 42

Thus knowing him who's reason's lord,
And self subduing by the self,
Slay thou desire, O mighty armed,
The foe which is so hard to kill! 43

Chapter Four: The Yoga of the Divisions of Knowledge (ज्ञानविभागयोगः)

श्रीभगवानुवाच

इमं विवस्वते योगं प्रोक्तवानहमव्ययम्।
विवस्वान् मनवे प्राह मनुरिक्ष्वाकवे ऽब्रवीत्॥ १॥

śrībhagavān uvāca

imaṃ vivasvate yogaṃ proktavān aham avyayam|
vivasvān manave prāha manurikṣvākave 'bravīt|| 1||

एवं परम्पराप्राप्तमिमं राजर्षयो विदुः।
स कालेनेह महता योगो नष्टः परंतप॥ २॥

evaṃ paramparāprāptam imaṃ rājarṣayo viduḥ|
sa kāleneha mahatā yogo naṣṭaḥ paraṃtapa|| 2||

स एवायं मया ते ऽद्य योगः प्रोक्तः पुरातनः।
भक्तो ऽसि मे सखा चेति रहस्यं ह्येतदुत्तमम्॥ ३॥

sa evāyaṃ mayā te 'dya yogaḥ proktaḥ purātanaḥ|
bhakto 'si me sakhā ceti rahasyaṃ hyetaduttamam|| 3||

अर्जुन उवाच

अपरं भवतो जन्म परं जन्म विवस्वतः।
कथमेतद्विजानीयां त्वमादौ प्रोक्तवानिति॥ ४॥

arjuna uvāca

aparaṃ bhavato janma paraṃ janma vivasvataḥ|
katham etadvijānīyāṃ tvam ādau proktavān iti|| 4||

The Blessed Lord said:

This everlasting *yoga* I taught
To Vivasvān,[93] who in his turn
To Manu[94] fully made it known,
And Manu to Ikṣvāku[95] next. 1

Thus in succession handed down,
By royal sages it was learnt;
By flight of ages, Parantap,
This Yoga has vanished from the world. 2

This self-same and primeval Yoga,
The greatest of all mysteries,
To thee, my friend and devotee,
Has been declared by me this day. 3

Arjun said:

But later, teacher, is thy birth,
Compared with that of Vivasvān;
How then am I to understand,
'Twas thou who first declared this *yoga*? 4

---

[93]The sun-god, said to be the progenitor of the solar dynasty, the history of which is related in the *Rāmāyaṇa*.

[94]The son of the sun-god.

[95]Manu's son.

श्रीभगवानुवाच

बहूनि मे व्यतीतानि जन्मानि तव चार्जुन।
तान्यहं वेद सर्वाणि न त्वं वेत्थ परंतप॥ ५॥

śrībhagavān uvāca

bahūni me vyatītāni janmāni tava cārjuna|
tāny ahaṃ veda sarvāṇi na tvaṃ vettha paraṃtapa|| 5||

अजो ऽपि सन्नव्ययात्मा भूतानामीश्वरो ऽपि सन्।
प्रकृतिं स्वामधिष्ठाय संभवाम्यात्ममायया॥ ६॥
ajo 'pi sann avyayātmā bhūtānām īśvaro 'pi san|
prakṛtiṃ svām adhiṣṭhāya saṃbhavāmy ātmamāyayā|| 6||

यदा यदा हि धर्मस्य ग्लानिर्भवति भारत।
अभ्युत्थानमधर्मस्य तदात्मानं सृजाम्यहम्॥ ७॥

yadā yadā hi dharmasya glānir bhavati bhārata|
abhyutthānam adharmasya tadātmānaṃ sṛjāmy aham|| 7||

परित्राणाय साधूनां विनाशाय च दुष्कृताम्।
धर्मसंस्थापनार्थाय संभवामि युगे युगे॥ ८॥

paritrāṇāya sādhūnāṃ vināśāya ca duṣkṛtām|
dharmasaṃsthāpanārthāya saṃbhavāmi yuge yuge|| 8||

जन्म कर्म च मे दिव्यमेवं यो वेत्ति तत्त्वतः।
त्यक्त्वा देहं पुनर्जन्म नैति मामेति सो ऽर्जुन॥ ९॥

janma karma ca me divyam evaṃ yo vetti tattvataḥ|
tyaktvā dehaṃ punarjanma naiti mām eti so 'rjuna|| 9||

The Blessed Lord said:

O Arjun, know both thou and I
Have left unnumbered births behind;
I know them all, O Parantap,
But they have faded from thy mind. 5

Though I'm unborn—the changeless[96] self,
Although all creatures lord I am—
Yet passing into matter[97] I
By my own *māyā* enter birth.[98] 6

Whenever righteousness[99] declines,
And sinfulness[100] the victory gains,
On such occasions, Bharat's son,
I always incarnate myself. 7

The virtuous people to protect,
And to destroy the wicked ones,
To set up firmly righteousness,
From age to age I enter birth. 8

Whoever thus in very truth
My births divine and action knows,
He, Arjun, on departing hence
Is not reborn, but comes to me. 9

---

[96]Lit. imperishable.

[97]Lit. my *prakṛti*, i.e., the nature or matter-stuff of which I myself am the creator. Entering, or establishing myself in this nature, which goes to the formation of the material body in which I appear, I manifest myself from time to time according to the moral needs of the world.

[98]*Māyā*, i.e., illusion; I appear to be born, though I am not really born. [Śaṅkara in his commentary says that the *prakṛti* and *māyā* mentioned in this verse are the same thing. That *māyā* consists of the three *guṇa* and the whole universe exists under its control. Moreover, it confuses the whole world so that it does not know Vāsudeva (Kṛṣṇa). Kṛṣṇa exerts his control over that *māyā* and appears as if he has a body, as if he were born. Since it is his own *māyā* his birth is not ultimately real like that of an ordinary person. Sans. Ed.]

[99]*Dharma*.

[100]*Adharma*.

वीतरागभयक्रोधा मन्मया मामुपाश्रिताः।
बहवो ज्ञानतपसा पूता मद्भावमागताः॥ १०॥

vītarāgabhayakrodhā manmayā mām upāśritāḥ|
bahavo jñānatapasā pūtā madbhāvam āgatāḥ|| 10||

ये यथा मां प्रपद्यन्ते तांस्तथैव भजाम्यहम्।
मम वर्त्मानुवर्तन्ते मनुष्याः पार्थ सर्वशः॥ ११॥

ye yathā māṃ prapadyante tāṃstathaiva bhajāmyaham|
mama vartmānuvartante manuṣyāḥ pārtha sarvaśaḥ|| 11||

काङ्क्षन्तः कर्मणां सिद्धिं यजन्त इह देवताः।
क्षिप्रं हि मानुषे लोके सिद्धिर्भवति कर्मजा॥ १२॥

kāṅkṣantaḥ karmaṇāṃ siddhiṃ yajanta iha devatāḥ|
kṣipraṃ hi mānuṣe loke siddhir bhavati karmajā|| 12||

चातुर्वर्ण्यं मया सृष्टं गुणकर्मविभागशः।
तस्य कर्तारमपि मां विद्ध्यकर्तारमव्ययम्॥ १३॥

cāturvarṇyaṃ mayā sṛṣṭaṃ guṇakarmavibhāgaśaḥ|
tasya kartāram api māṃ viddhy akartāram avyayam|| 13||

न मां कर्माणि लिम्पन्ति न मे कर्मफले स्पृहा।
इति मां यो ऽभिजानाति कर्मभिर्न स बध्यते॥ १४॥

na māṃ karmāṇi limpanti na me karmaphale spṛhā|
iti māṃ yo 'bhijānāti karmabhir na sa badhyate|| 14||

From passion, fear and anger freed,
Absorbed in me, engrossed in me,
And purified in wisdom's fire,
Full many a soul hath come to me. 10

However men may come to me,
Thus even do I welcome them;
By whatsoever path they come,
That path is mine, O Pṛthā's son.[101] 11

Those here who seek success in work
Make offerings to the shining ones,
For swiftly in this world of men
Success from action is achieved. 12

According to the *guṇas* three,[102]
And acts, I made the four-fold caste,[103]
But though its author yet I am
Immutable and actionless.[104] 13

No action e'er polluteth me,
Nor do I wish for action's fruit,
Whoso thus knoweth me in truth,
Is fettered not by action's chains. 14

---

[101] This is a remarkable verse showing the catholicity of the religion inculcated in the *Gītā*. Its purport is that to the true seeker God is always accessible, the particular way in which He is sought being of no account.

[102] Lit. "according to the apportionment of the *guṇas* and duties" (Telang).

[103] The *brāhmaṇas*, *kṣatriyas*, *vaiśyas*, and the *śūdras*.

[104] I.e., though I am their author yet I am not the author or agent.

एवं ज्ञात्वा कृतं कर्म पूर्वैरपि मुमुक्षुभिः।
कुरु कर्मैव तस्मात्त्वं पूर्वैः पूर्वतरं कृतम्॥ १५॥

evaṃ jñātvā kṛtaṃ karma pūrvair api mumukṣubhiḥ|
kuru karmaiva tasmāt tvaṃ pūrvaiḥ pūrvataraṃ kṛtam|| 15||

किं कर्म किमकर्मेति कवयो ऽप्यत्र मोहिताः।
तत्ते कर्म प्रवक्ष्यामि यज्ज्ञात्वा मोक्ष्यसे ऽशुभात्॥ १६॥

kiṃ karma kim akarmeti kavayo 'py atra mohitāḥ|
tat te karma pravakṣyāmi yaj jñātvā mokṣyase 'śubhāt|| 16||

कर्मणो ह्यपि बोद्धव्यं बोद्धव्यं च विकर्मणः।
अकर्मणश्च बोद्धव्यं गहना कर्मणो गतिः॥ १७॥

karmaṇo hy api boddhavyaṃ boddhavyaṃ ca vikarmaṇaḥ|
akarmaṇaśca boddhavyaṃ gahanā karmaṇo gatiḥ|| 17||

कर्मण्यकर्म यः पश्येदकर्मणि च कर्म यः।
स बुद्धिमान्मनुष्येषु स युक्तः कृत्स्नकर्मकृत्॥ १८॥

karmaṇy akarma yaḥ paśyed akarmaṇi ca karma yaḥ|
sa buddhimān manuṣyeṣu sa yuktaḥ kṛtsnakarmakṛt|| 18||

यस्य सर्वे समारम्भाः कामसंकल्पवर्जिताः।
ज्ञानाग्निदग्धकर्माणं तमाहुः पण्डितं बुधाः॥ १९॥

yasya sarve samārambhāḥ kāmasaṃkalpavarjitāḥ|
jñānāgnidagdhakarmāṇaṃ tam āhuḥ paṇḍitaṃ budhāḥ|| 19||

Thus knowing me, the men of old
Did act in order to be freed;
Thou too should act as they did act,
The ancients in the olden time. 15

What action and inaction are
The sages even do not know;
Of action hence I'll speak to thee,
Which knowing thou shalt freedom[105] gain. 16

'Tis needful one should understand
What action and inaction are,
And what unlawful action means,
For action's nature is abstruse. 17

Who in inaction action sees,
And action in inaction finds,
Attuned is he and wise 'mongst men,
E'en though he doeth every act. 18

The man whose every act is free
From fancies[106] and from all desire,
Whose acts are burnt in wisdom's fire,
Is by the learned called a sage. 19

---

[105] i.e., freedom from the evil of *saṃsāra*.
[106] *Saṅkalpa*, delusion, fancy or imaginings.

त्यक्त्वा कर्मफलासङ्गं नित्यतृप्तो निराश्रयः।
कर्मण्यभिप्रवृत्तो ऽपि नैव किं चित्करोति सः॥ २०॥

tyaktvā karmaphalāsaṅgaṃ nityatṛpto nirāśrayaḥ|
karmaṇy abhipravṛtto 'pi naiva kiṃ cit karoti saḥ|| 20||

निराशीर्यतचित्तात्मा त्यक्तसर्वपरिग्रहः।
शारीरं केवलं कर्म कुर्वन्नाप्नोति किल्बिषम्॥ २१॥

nirāśīryatacittātmā tyaktasarvaparigrahaḥ|
śārīraṃ kevalaṃ karma kurvannāpnoti kilbiṣam|| 21||

यदृच्छालाभसंतुष्टो द्वन्द्वातीतो विमत्सरः।
समः सिद्धावसिद्धौ च कृत्वापि न निबध्यते॥ २२॥

yadṛcchālābhasaṃtuṣṭo dvandvātīto vimatsaraḥ|
samaḥ siddhāv asiddhau ca kṛtvāpi na nibadhyate|| 22||

गतसङ्गस्य मुक्तस्य ज्ञानावस्थितचेतसः।
यज्ञायाचरतः कर्म समग्रं प्रविलीयते॥ २३॥

gatasaṅgasya muktasya jñānāvasthitacetasaḥ|
yajñāyācarataḥ karma samagraṃ pravilīyate|| 23||

ब्रह्मार्पणं ब्रह्म हविर्ब्रह्माग्नौ ब्रह्मणा हुतम्।
ब्रह्मैव तेन गन्तव्यं ब्रह्मकर्मसमाधिना॥ २४॥

brahmārpaṇaṃ brahma havir brahmāgnau brahmaṇā hutam|
brahmaiva tena gantavyaṃ brahmakarmasamādhinā|| 24||

All greed for action's fruit cast off,
On none relying, e'er content,
Although in work he is engaged,
Yet such an one doth naught at all. 20

Hope-free,[107] his mind and self controlled,
And all his earthly goods renounced,
Corporeal merely all his acts,
And hence no sin doth cling to him. 21

Content with what he gets unsought,
Above the `pairs', from malice free,
The same in failure and success,
Though acting he is never bound. 22

The man in whom attachment's dead,
Who's freed,[108] with mind in wisdom wrapt,
Whose acts are done for sacrifice,[109]
From him all actions melt away.[110] 23

To him the sacrifice,[111] the ghee,
The priest, the fire are only Brahm,
He verily to Brahm shall go,
Who in his acts sees Brahm alone.[112] 24

---

[107]Free from expectations.
[108]Freed from attachment to worldly concerns.
[109]Sacrifice here means all works done for the supreme being.
[110]I.e., are reduced to nothing.
[111]I.e., the act of sacrifice.
[112]This verse is translated as follows by Mahādev Śāstrī: Brahman is the offering, Brahman the oblation; by Brahman is the oblation poured into the fire of Brahman; Brahman verily shall be reached by him who sees Brahman in action.

दैवमेवापरे यज्ञं योगिनः पर्युपासते।
ब्रह्माग्नावपरे यज्ञं यज्ञेनैवोपजुह्वति॥ २५॥

daivamevāpare yajñaṃ yoginaḥ paryupāsate|
brahmāgnāvapare yajñaṃ yajñenaivopajuhvati|| 25||

श्रोत्रादीनीन्द्रियाण्यन्ये संयमाग्निषु जुह्वति।
शब्दादीन् विषयानन्य इन्द्रियाग्निषु जुह्वति॥ २६॥

śrotrādīnīndriyāṇyanye saṃyamāgniṣu juhvati|
śabdādīn viṣayānanya indriyāgniṣu juhvati|| 26||

सर्वाणीन्द्रियकर्माणि प्राणकर्माणि चापरे।
आत्मसंयमयोगाग्नौ जुह्वति ज्ञानदीपिते॥ २७॥

sarvāṇīndriyakarmāṇi prāṇakarmāṇi cāpare|
ātmasaṃyamayogāgnau juhvati jñānadīpite|| 27||

द्रव्ययज्ञास्तपोयज्ञा योगयज्ञास्तथापरे।
स्वाध्यायज्ञानयज्ञाश्च यतयः संशितव्रताः॥ २८॥

dravyayajñāstapoyajñā yogayajñāstathāpare|
svādhyāyajñānayajñāśca yatayaḥ saṃśitavratāḥ|| 28||

अपाने जुह्वति प्राणं प्राणे ऽपानं तथापरे।
प्राणापानगती रुद्ध्वा प्राणायामपरायणाः॥ २९॥

apāne juhvati prāṇaṃ prāṇe 'pānaṃ tathāpare|
prāṇāpānagatī ruddhvā prāṇāyāmaparāyaṇāḥ|| 29||

Some *yogins* offer sacrifice
In worship of the shining ones,
Whilst others in the fire of Brahm
Make sacrifice through sacrifice.[113] 25

The senses, such as hearing, some
Pour in the fires of self-restraint,[114]
Whilst others yet sense objects pour,
Like sound, into the fires of sense.[115] 26

Some others pour as sacrifice
The vital functions and of sense,
Into the wisdom-kindled fire
Of *yoga* that's wrought by self-restraint. 27

Yet others make a sacrifice
Of wealth, of penance and of *yoga*,[116]
Of knowledge and of Vedic lore;
Ascetics these of rigid vows. 28

Some offer up the life breaths twain,
The one into the other breath,
Controlling too their ebb and tide,
Upon their mastery are bent.[117] 29

---

[113] I.e., they offer up all their actions to Brahman *as* a sacrifice *by means* of an act of sacrifice.
[114] By this is meant the restraint of the senses for practical *yoga*.
[115] I.e., are unattached to the objects of the senses.
[116] I.e., the various kinds of control effected by *yoga*.
[117] Lit. "Some offer up the upward life-breath (*prāṇa*) into the downward life-breath (*apāna*), and the downward life-breath into the upward life-breath, and stopping up the motions of the upward and downward life-breaths devote themselves to the restraint of the life-breaths (*prāṇāyāma*)." This verse refers to the practice of the *Haṭha-yogins*, who believe that salvation can be obtained through various physical exercises. According to them the life-breaths (the "vital airs") flow from one region of the body to another, thus carrying on the vital functions.

अपरे नियताहाराः प्राणान्प्राणेषु जुह्वति।
सर्वे ऽप्येते यज्ञविदो यज्ञक्षपितकल्मषाः॥ ३०॥

apare niyatāhārāḥ prāṇānprāṇeṣu juhvati|
sarve 'pyete yajñavido yajñakṣapitakalmaṣāḥ|| 30||

यज्ञशिष्टामृतभुजो यान्ति ब्रह्म सनातनम्।
नायं लोको ऽस्त्ययज्ञस्य कुतो ऽन्यः कुरुसत्तम॥ ३१॥

yajñaśiṣṭāmṛtabhujo yānti brahma sanātanam|
nāyaṃ loko 'styayajñasya kuto 'nyaḥ kurusattama|| 31||

एवं बहुविधा यज्ञा वितता ब्रह्मणो मुखे।
कर्मजान्विद्धि तान्सर्वानेवं ज्ञात्वा विमोक्ष्यसे॥ ३२॥

evaṃ bahuvidhā yajñā vitatā brahmaṇo mukhe|
karmajānviddhi tānsarvānevaṃ jñātvā vimokṣyase|| 32||

श्रेयान्द्रव्यमयाद्यज्ञाज्ज्ञानयज्ञः परंतप।
सर्वं कर्माखिलं पार्थ ज्ञाने परिसमाप्यते॥ ३३॥

śreyāndravyamayādyajñājjñānayajñaḥ paraṃtapa|
sarvaṃ karmākhilaṃ pārtha jñāne parisamāpyate|| 33||

तद्विद्धि प्रणिपातेन परिप्रश्नेन सेवया।
उपदेक्ष्यन्ति ते ज्ञानं ज्ञानिनस्तत्त्वदर्शिनः॥ ३४॥

tadviddhi praṇipātena paripraśnena sevayā|
upadekṣyanti te jñānaṃ jñāninastattvadarśinaḥ|| 34||

And others too, retrenching food,[118]
The life breaths in the life breaths pour,
These[119] know what sacrifice denotes,
By sacrifice their sins destroyed. 30

O best of Kurus, they who eat
Ambrosial food[120] reach changeless Brahm,
This world is not for those who make
No sacrifice; much less the next.[121] 31

Thus sacrifices manifold
Are laid out at the mouth of Brahm;[122]
Know thou they all from action spring,
So knowing, thou shalt freedom gain. 32

O Parantap. the sacrifice
Of wisdom's better than of things,
Without exception, Pṛthā's son,
In wisdom action culminates. 33

This learn thou by discipleship,
By service and by questionings;
The wise who have perceived the truth,
Will guide thee unto wisdom's ways. 34

---

[118]Refers to those who believe starvation and other forms of restraint to be works of merit.
[119]I.e., all the different kinds of sacrificers mentioned in vv. 25-30.
[120]The life-giving remains of the sacrificial food.
[121]Svarga.
[122]If by Brahman the Vedas are meant, the meaning of these lines would be that all these diverse sacrifices are described in the Vedas.

यज्ज्ञात्वा न पुनर्मोहमेवं यास्यसि पाण्डव।
येन भूतान्यशेषेण द्रक्ष्यस्यात्मन्यथो मयि॥ ३५॥

yaj jñātvā na punar moham evaṃ yāsyasi pāṇḍava|
yena bhūtāny aśeṣeṇa drakṣyasy ātmany atho mayi|| 35||

अपि चेदसि पापेभ्यः सर्वेभ्यः पापकृत्तमः।
सर्वं ज्ञानप्लवेनैव वृजिनं संतरिष्यसि॥ ३६॥

api cedasi pāpebhyaḥ sarvebhyaḥ pāpakṛttamaḥ|
sarvaṃ jñānaplavenaiva vṛjinaṃ saṃtariṣyasi|| 36||

यथैधांसि समिद्धो ऽग्निर्भस्मसात्कुरुते ऽर्जुन।
ज्ञानाग्निः सर्वकर्माणि भस्मसात्कुरुते तथा॥ ३७॥

yathaidhāṃsi samiddho 'gnirbhasmasāt kurute 'rjuna|
jñānāgniḥ sarvakarmāṇi bhasmasāt kurute tathā|| 37||

न हि ज्ञानेन सदृशं पवित्रमिह विद्यते।
तत्स्वयं योगसंसिद्धः कालेनात्मनि विन्दति॥ ३८॥

na hi jñānena sadṛśaṃ pavitram iha vidyate|
tat svayaṃ yogasaṃsiddhaḥ kālenātmani vindati|| 38||

श्रद्धावाँल्लभते ज्ञानं तत्परः संयतेन्द्रियः।
ज्ञानं लब्ध्वा परां शान्तिमचिरेणाधिगच्छति॥ ३९॥

śraddhāvā̃l labhate jñānaṃ tatparaḥ saṃyatendriyaḥ|
jñānaṃ labdhvā parāṃ śāntim acireṇādhigacchati|| 39||

Thou shalt, O Pāṇḍav, knowing this,
Again not into error fall,
By means of this thou shalt behold
All beings in thy self and me.[123] 35

Yea, even though 'mongst sinful men,
The chief of sinners thou shouldst be,
Thou shalt indeed cross safely o'er
The sea of sin in wisdom's bark. 36

As kindled fire on fuel feeds
And all to ashes doth reduce,
Likewise, O Arjun, wisdom's fire
Reduceth every act to ash. 37

For verily no cleanser can
On earth with wisdom be compared,
He who perfected is in *yoga*,
In time finds wisdom in the self. 38

The full of faith, the devotee,[124]
He who his senses has controlled,
Finds wisdom, and possessing it,
Ere long attains to peace supreme. 39

[123]Implying the essential unity of the supreme and the individual soul and the universe. [Śaṅkara interprets the words *ātmani*, "in the self," and *mayi*, "in me," to be referring to the same being, namely Kṛṣṇa. So "All beings in the self, in me." Sans. Ed.]

[124]I.e., devoted to or intent on faith.

अज्ञश्चाश्रद्दधानश्च संशयात्मा विनश्यति।
नायं लोको ऽस्ति न परो न सुखं संशयात्मनः॥ ४०॥

ajñaścāśraddadhānaśca saṃśayātmā vinaśyati|
nāyaṃ loko 'sti na paro na sukhaṃ saṃśayātmanaḥ|| 40||

योगसंन्यस्तकर्माणं ज्ञानसंछिन्नसंशयम्।
आत्मवन्तं न कर्माणि निबध्नन्ति धनंजय॥ ४१॥

yogasaṃnyastakarmāṇaṃ jñānasaṃchinnasaṃśayam|
ātmavantaṃ na karmāṇi nibadhnanti dhanaṃjaya|| 41||

तस्मादज्ञानसंभूतं हृत्स्थं ज्ञानासिनात्मनः।
छित्त्वैनं संशयं योगमातिष्ठोत्तिष्ठ भारत॥ ४२॥

tasmād ajñānasaṃbhūtaṃ hṛtsthaṃ jñānāsinātmanaḥ|
chittvainaṃ saṃśayaṃ yogam ātiṣṭhottiṣṭha bhārata|| 42||

But ruined is the self which doubts,
Which faithless and unknowing is;
Nor joy, nor this, nor world to come,
Can be the doubter's heritage. 40

O Dhanañjay, who's self-controlled,
Who hath by Yoga renounced all acts,
Whose doubts have been by wisdom cleft,
From action's bonds that man is free. 41

O Bhārat, thus with wisdom's sword,
Cleave thou the doubt which fills thy breast,
And which is born of ignorance;
In Yoga established be. Arise! 42

Chapter Five: The Yoga of Renunciation of Action (कर्मसन्न्यासयोगः)

अर्जुन उवाच
संन्यासं कर्मणां कृष्ण पुनर्योगं च शंससि।
यच्छ्रेय एतयोरेकं तन्मे ब्रूहि सुनिश्चितम्॥ १॥

arjuna uvāca

saṃnyāsaṃ karmaṇāṃ kṛṣṇa punar yogaṃ ca śaṃsasi|
yacchreya etayor ekaṃ tan me brūhi suniścitam|| 1||

श्रीभगवानुवाच
संन्यासः कर्मयोगश्च निःश्रेयसकरावुभौ।
तयोस्तु कर्मसंन्यासात्कर्मयोगो विशिष्यते॥ २॥

śrībhagavān uvāca
saṃnyāsaḥ karmayogaśca niḥśreyasakarāv ubhau|
tayos tu karmasaṃnyāsāt karmayogo viśiṣyate|| 2||

ज्ञेयः स नित्यसंन्यासी यो न द्वेष्टि न काङ्क्षति।
निर्द्वन्द्वो हि महाबाहो सुखं बन्धात्प्रमुच्यते॥ ३॥

jñeyaḥ sa nityasaṃnyāsī yo na dveṣṭi na kāṅkṣati|
nirdvandvo hi mahābāho sukhaṃ bandhāt pramucyate|| 3||

सांख्ययोगौ पृथग्बालाः प्रवदन्ति न पण्डिताः।
एकमप्यास्थितः सम्यगुभयोर्विन्दते फलम्॥ ४॥

sāṃkhyayogau pṛthag bālāḥ pravadanti na paṇḍitāḥ|
ekam apy āsthitaḥ samyag ubhayor vindate phalam|| 4||

Arjun said:

O Krishna, laudest thou at once,
Surcease from work[125] and its pursuit;[126]
Pray tell me now decisively
Which of the twain the better is.[127] 1

The Blessed Lord said:

Surcease from work and its pursuit,
Both lead a man to bliss supreme,
But of the twain pursuit of work
Is better than renouncing deeds. 2

The man who neither hates nor craves,
A true[128] renouncer should be deemed;
Free from the 'pairs', O mighty armed,
He is from bondage freed with ease. 3

'Tis not the wise, but childish minds,
Who speak of Sāṅkhya and of *yoga*
As paths distinct; who follows well
The one, obtains the fruit of both. 4

---

[125] *Sannyāsa.*
[126] *Yoga.*
[127] The question is: "Of the two—renunciation of action (Sāṅkhya = *sannyāsa* = *jñāna-yoga*) and performance of action (*yoga* = *karma-yoga*) which is superior?"
[128] In the original, a perpetual (*nitya*) renouncer.

यत्सांख्यैः प्राप्यते स्थानं तद्योगैरपि गम्यते।
एकं सांख्यं च योगं च यः पश्यति स पश्यति॥ ५॥

yat sāṃkhyaiḥ prāpyate sthānaṃ tadyogair api gamyate|
ekaṃ sāṃkhyaṃ ca yogaṃ ca yaḥ paśyati sa paśyati|| 5||

संन्यासस्तु महाबाहो दुःखमाप्तुमयोगतः।
योगयुक्तो मुनिर्ब्रह्म न चिरेणाधिगच्छति॥ ६॥

saṃnyāsas tu mahābāho duḥkham āptum ayogataḥ|
yogayukto munir brahma na cireṇādhigacchati|| 6||

योगयुक्तो विशुद्धात्मा विजितात्मा जितेन्द्रियः।
सर्वभूतात्मभूतात्मा कुर्वन्नपि न लिप्यते॥ ७॥

yogayukto viśuddhātmā vijitātmā jitendriyaḥ|
sarvabhūtātmabhūtātmā kurvann api na lipyate|| 7||

नैव किंचित् करोमीति युक्तो मन्येत तत्त्ववित्।
पश्यञ् शृण्वन्स्पृशञ्जिघ्रन्नश्नन्गच्छन्स्वपञ् श्वसन्॥ ८॥

naiva kiṃ cit karomīti yukto manyeta tattvavit|
paśyañ śṛṇvan spṛśañ jighrann aśnan gacchan svapañ śvasan|| 8||

प्रलपन्विसृजन्गृह्णन्नुन्मिषन्निमिषन्नपि।
इन्द्रियाणीन्द्रियार्थेषु वर्तन्त इति धारयन्॥ ९॥

pralapan visṛjan gṛhṇann unmiṣan nimiṣann api|
indriyāṇīndriyārtheṣu vartanta iti dhārayan|| 9||

The goal which by the Saṅkhyās' reached,
Is by the *yogins* also gained;
The true seer is the man
Who *yoga* and Sāṅkhya sees as one. 5

'Tis hard to reach, O mighty armed,
Renunciation without *yoga*;
The sage who is with *yoga* equipped,
Doth swiftly wend his way to Brahm. 6

The *yoga*-equipped, the pure in heart,
The self-controlled, the sense-subdued,
Whose self becomes the self of all,[129]
Remains untainted though he acts. 7

'I nothing do', should be the thought
Of the attuned who knows the truth,
And whilst he hears, or sees, or smells,
Or touches, moves, or eats, or sleeps, 8

Or breathes, or speaks, or gives, or grasps,
Or ope's and shuts his eyelids twain,
This is his sure and certain thought;
"The senses 'midst their objects move."[130] 9

---

[129] I.e., who identifies himself with all beings.
[130] Compare with Third Discourse, verse 28.

ब्रह्मण्याधाय कर्माणि सङ्गं त्यक्त्वा करोति यः।
लिप्यते न स पापेन पद्मपत्रमिवाम्भसा॥ १०॥

brahmaṇy ādhāya karmāṇi saṅgaṃ tyaktvā karoti yaḥ|
lipyate na sa pāpena padmapatram ivāmbhasā|| 10||

कायेन मनसा बुद्ध्या केवलैरिन्द्रियैरपि।
योगिनः कर्म कुर्वन्ति सङ्गं त्यक्त्वात्मशुद्धये॥ ११॥

kāyena manasā buddhyā kevalair indriyair api|
yoginaḥ karma kurvanti saṅgaṃ tyaktvātmaśuddhaye|| 11||

युक्तः कर्मफलं त्यक्त्वा शान्तिमाप्नोति नैष्ठिकीम्।
अयुक्तः कामकारेण फले सक्तो निबध्यते॥ १२॥

yuktaḥ karmaphalaṃ tyaktvā śāntim āpnoti naiṣṭhikīm|
ayuktaḥ kāmakāreṇa phale sakto nibadhyate|| 12||

सर्वकर्माणि मनसा संन्यस्यास्ते सुखं वशी।
नवद्वारे पुरे देही नैव कुर्वन्न कारयन्॥ १३॥

sarvakarmāṇi manasā saṃnyasyās te sukhaṃ vaśī|
navadvāre pure dehī naiva kurvan na kārayan|| 13||

न कर्तृत्वं न कर्माणि लोकस्य सृजति प्रभुः।
न कर्मफलसंयोगं स्वभावस्तु प्रवर्तते॥ १४॥

na kartṛtvaṃ na karmāṇi lokasya sṛjati prabhuḥ|
na karmaphalasaṃyogaṃ svabhāvas tu pravartate|| 14||

Who acts, but gives all acts to Brahm,
Who all attachments casts away,
He is by sin not touched at all,
As lotus leaf unwet by rain. 10

With reason, body and the mind,
E'en with the senses they possess,
The yogins, unattached, do deeds,
For thorough cleansing of the self. 11

Renouncing fruits, the man attuned
Attains to everlasting peace;
The unattuned, by lust led on,
Attached to fruits, live firmly bound.12

Self-ruled, all actions mind-controlled,
The embodied self serenely dwells,
Within his own nine-gated town,[131]
Nor doing deeds nor prompting them. 13

The lord doth not, in this our world,
Do deeds nor prompts he men to act,
He links not action with its fruit;
These are indeed by nature wrought.[132] 14

---

[131]The body is often said to be the City of Brahman, with nine gates—seven in the head (the eyes, ears, nostrils, and mouth), and two in the trunk, anal and urinary.

[132]A more literal rendering of this verse would be—

Nor actorship, nor acts doth He,
The Ruler of the world create,
Nor yet the link 'twixt act and "fruit,"
These are indeed by nature wrought.

नादत्ते कस्यचित्पापं न चैव सुकृतं विभुः।
अज्ञानेनावृतं ज्ञानं तेन मुह्यन्ति जन्तवः॥ १५॥

nādatte kasya cit pāpaṃ na caiva sukṛtaṃ vibhuḥ|
ajñānenāvṛtaṃ jñānaṃ tena muhyanti jantavaḥ|| 15||

ज्ञानेन तु तदज्ञानं येषां नाशितमात्मनः।
तेषामादित्यवज्ज्ञानं प्रकाशयति तत्परम्॥ १६॥

jñānena tu tadajñānaṃ yeṣāṃ nāśitam ātmanaḥ|
teṣām ādityavaj jñānaṃ prakāśayati tatparam|| 16||

तद्बुद्धयस्तदात्मानस्तन्निष्ठास्तत्परायणाः।
गच्छन्त्यपुनरावृत्तिं ज्ञाननिर्धूतकल्मषाः॥ १७॥

tadbuddhayas tadātmānas tanniṣṭhās tatparāyaṇāḥ|
gacchanty apunarāvṛttiṃ jñānanirdhūtakalmaṣāḥ|| 17||

विद्याविनयसंपन्ने ब्राह्मणे गवि हस्तिनि।
शुनि चैव श्वपाके च पण्डिताः समदर्शिनः॥ १८॥

vidyāvinayasaṃpanne brāhmaṇe gavi hastini|
śuni caiva śvapāke ca paṇḍitāḥ samadarśinaḥ|| 18||

इहैव तैर्जितः सर्गो येषां साम्ये स्थितं मनः।
निर्दोषं हि समं ब्रह्म तस्माद्ब्रह्मणि ते स्थिताः॥ १९॥

ihaiva tairjitaḥ sargo yeṣāṃ sāmye sthitaṃ manaḥ|
nirdoṣaṃ hi samaṃ brahma tasmād brahmaṇi te sthitāḥ|| 19||

The lord accepteth not the deeds,
Nor good nor ill of any man,
By ignorance is wisdom cloaked,
'Tis this which all men doth delude. 15

But as for those whose ignorance
By wisdom of the self's dispelled,
This wisdom, like the noonday sun,
Revealeth the supreme to them. 16

Thinking of him, yea, merged in him,
Intent on him, with him for goal,
They go from whence they come not back,
Their sins by wisdom all dispelled. 17

The humble minded brahmin wise,
An elephant, a cow, a dog,
Yea, e'en the lowest outcaste, know,
Are to the sages all the same. 18

All things[133] e'en here are overcome,
By those whose minds are balanced well;
Balanced is Brahm and with no stain,
Therefore at rest are they in Brahm. 19

---

[133]Rendered "rebirths" by some.

न प्रहृष्येत्प्रियं प्राप्य नोद्विजेत्प्राप्य चाप्रियम्।
स्थिरबुद्धिरसंमूढो ब्रह्मविद्ब्रह्मणि स्थितः॥ २०॥

na prahṛṣyet priyaṃ prāpya nodvijet prāpya cāpriyam|
sthirabuddhir asaṃmūḍho brahmavid brahmaṇi sthitaḥ|| 20||

बाह्यस्पर्शेष्वसक्तात्मा विन्दत्यात्मनि यत्सुखम्।
स ब्रह्मयोगयुक्तात्मा सुखमक्षयमश्नुते॥ २१॥

bāhyasparśeṣv asaktātmā vindaty ātmani yat sukham|
sa brahmayogayuktātmā sukham akṣayam aśnute|| 21||

ये हि संस्पर्शजा भोगा दुःखयोनय एव ते।
आद्यन्तवन्तः कौन्तेय न तेषु रमते बुधः॥ २२॥

ye hi saṃsparśajā bhogā duḥkhayonaya eva te|
ādyantavantaḥ kaunteya na teṣu ramate budhaḥ|| 22||

शक्नोतीहैव यः सोढुं प्राक् शरीरविमोक्षणात्।
कामक्रोधोद्भवं वेगं स युक्तः स सुखी नरः॥ २३॥

śaknotīhaiva yaḥ soḍhuṃ prāk śarīravimokṣaṇāt|
kāmakrodhodbhavaṃ vegaṃ sa yuktaḥ sa sukhī naraḥ|| 23||

यो ऽन्तःसुखो ऽन्तरारामस्तथान्तर्ज्योतिरेव यः।
स योगी ब्रह्मनिर्वाणं ब्रह्मभूतो ऽधिगच्छति॥ २४॥

yo 'ntaḥsukho 'ntarārāmas tathāntarjyotir eva yaḥ|
sa yogī brahmanirvāṇaṃ brahmabhūto 'dhigacchati|| 24||

Who's undeluded, firm in mind,
Who knoweth Brahm and rests in Brahm,
Is not elated or depressed
When joy or woe befalls[134] him. 20

To outer contacts unattached,[135]
He finds the joy that's in the self;
Whose self by *yoga* is merged in Brahm,
Attains to everlasting joy. 21

For all delights of contact born
Are verily the wombs of pain,
As surely as they're born they die,
Hence wise men find in them no joy. 22

Whoso can here on earth endure,
Ere casting off this mortal coil,
The impulses of lust and wrath,
He is a *yogin* full of joy. 23

The man who finds his joy within,
His pastime and his light within,[136]
This *yogin*, thus transformed to Brahm,
Attains at last to bliss of Brahm. 24

---

[134]Lit. he does not rejoice on obtaining the pleasant, nor grieve on obtaining the unpleasant.
[135]I.e., contact of the sense with their objects.
[136]I.e., in the Self (Śaṅkara).

लभन्ते ब्रह्मनिर्वाणमृषयः क्षीणकल्मषाः।
छिन्नद्वैधा यतात्मानः सर्वभूतहिते रताः॥ २५॥

labhante brahmanirvāṇam ṛṣayaḥ kṣīṇakalmaṣāḥ|
chinnadvaidhā yatātmānaḥ sarvabhūtahite ratāḥ|| 25||

कामक्रोधवियुक्तानां यतीनां यतचेतसाम्।
अभितो ब्रह्मनिर्वाणं वर्तते विदितात्मनाम्॥ २६॥

kāmakrodhaviyuktānāṃ yatīnāṃ yatacetasām|
abhito brahmanirvāṇaṃ vartate viditātmanām|| 26||

स्पर्शान्कृत्वा बहिर्बाह्यांश्चक्षुश्चैवान्तरे भ्रुवोः।
प्राणापानौ समौ कृत्वा नासाभ्यन्तरचारिणौ॥ २७॥

sparśān kṛtvā bahirbāhyāṃścakṣuścaivāntare bhruvoḥ|
prāṇāpānau samau kṛtvā nāsābhyantaracāriṇau|| 27||

यतेन्द्रियमनोबुद्धिर्मुनिर्मोक्षपरायणः।
विगतेच्छाभयक्रोधो यः सदा मुक्त एव सः॥ २८॥

yatendriyamanobuddhir munir mokṣaparāyaṇaḥ|
vigatecchābhayakrodho yaḥ sadā mukta eva saḥ|| 28||

भोक्तारं यज्ञतपसां सर्वलोकमहेश्वरम्।
सुहृदं सर्वभूतानां ज्ञात्वा मां शान्तिमृच्छति॥ २९॥

bhoktāraṃ yajñatapasāṃ sarvalokamaheśvaram|
suhṛdaṃ sarvabhūtānāṃ jñātvā māṃ śāntim ṛcchati|| 29||

The wise whose sins have been destroyed,
Whose doubts are gone and selves restrained,
Whose only aim's the good of all,
Attain at last to bliss of Brahm. 25

For those ascetics, mind-controlled,
Who are from lust and wrath disjoined,
Who have full knowledge of the self,
The Brahman-bliss lies everywhere.[137] 26

All outer contacts left without,[138]
The gaze betwixt the eyebrows fixed,
The dual tide of breath which flows
Between the nostrils equalized. 27

With reason, mind, and senses curbed,
And having freedom for his goal,
With no desire or wrath or fear,
Such sage indeed is freed for aye. 28

And knowing me, the lord who loves
Austerities and sacrifice,
The mighty ruler of the worlds,
The friend of all, he enters peace. 29

---

[137] I.e., on both sides of death.
[138] I.e., excluded from the mind.

Chapter Six: The Yoga of Meditation (ध्यानयोगः)

श्रीभगवानुवाच
अनाश्रितः कर्मफलं कार्यं कर्म करोति यः।
स संन्यासी च योगी च न निरग्निर्न चाक्रियः॥ १॥

śrībhagavān uvāca

anāśritaḥ karmaphalaṃ kāryaṃ karma karoti yaḥ|
sa saṃnyāsī ca yogī ca na niragnirna cākriyaḥ|| 1||

यं संन्यासमिति प्राहुर्योगं तं विद्धि पाण्डव।
न ह्यसंन्यस्तसंकल्पो योगी भवति कश्चन॥ २॥

yaṃ saṃnyāsam iti prāhuryogaṃ taṃ viddhi pāṇḍava|
na hy asaṃnyastasaṃkalpo yogī bhavati kaścana|| 2||

आरुरुक्षोर्मुनेर्योगं कर्म कारणमुच्यते।
योगारूढस्य तस्यैव शमः कारणमुच्यते॥ ३॥

ārurukṣor muner yogaṃ karma kāraṇam ucyate|
yogārūḍhasya tasyaiva śamaḥ kāraṇam ucyate|| 3||

यदा हि नेन्द्रियार्थेषु न कर्मस्वनुषज्जते।
सर्वसंकल्पसंन्यासी योगारूढस्तदोच्यते॥ ४॥

yadā hi nendriyārtheṣu na karmasv anuṣajjate|
sarvasaṃkalpasaṃnyāsī yogārūḍhas tadocyate|| 4||

उद्धरेदात्मनात्मानं नात्मानमवसादयेत्।
आत्मैव ह्यात्मनो बन्धुरात्मैव रिपुरात्मनः॥ ५॥

uddhared ātmanātmānaṃ nātmānam avasādayet|
ātmaiva hy ātmano bandhur ātmaiva ripur ātmanaḥ|| 5||

बन्धुरात्मात्मनस्तस्य येनात्मैवात्मना जितः।
अनात्मनस्तु शत्रुत्वे वर्ततात्मैव शत्रुवत्॥ ६॥

bandhur ātmātmanas tasya yenātmaivātmanā jitaḥ|
anātmanas tu śatrutve vartetātmaiva śatruvat|| 6||

The Blessed Lord said:

Who doeth work which should be done,
Not seeking fruits, a *yogin* is,
And a *sannyāsin* too, not he
Who lights no ritual fires[139] nor works. 1

What people call renouncing works,
O Pāṇḍav, know that that is *yoga*;
No man a *yogin* e'er can be
Who all his thoughts[140] has not renounced. 2

For that wise man who seeketh yoga,
The means[141] is action said to be,
For that same sage, when yoga-enthroned,
'Tis said the means quiescence is. 3

A man when he is not attached
To action nor to things of sense,
When all his thoughts he has forsworn,
He then is called the *yoga*-enthroned. 4

Let each man raise himself by self,
Let him not debase the self,
For self alone is friend of self,
And self too is the foe of self. 5

Self is self's friend of him in whom
The self has vanquished been by self,[142]
But of the self that's unsubdued,
The foe is verily the self. 6

---

[139]Lighting fires for religious rites is a prescribed duty.
[140]Which are the cause of desires which impel one to action (*saṅkalpa*).
[141]To perfect knowledge (Śrīdhara).
[142]By this is meant restraint of the senses by the mind.

जितात्मनः प्रशान्तस्य परमात्मा समाहितः।
शीतोष्णसुखदुःखेषु तथा मानापमानयोः॥ ७॥

jitātmanaḥ praśāntasya paramātmā samāhitaḥ|
śītoṣṇasukhaduḥkheṣu tathā mānāpamānayoḥ|| 7||

ज्ञानविज्ञानतृप्तात्मा कूटस्थो विजितेन्द्रियः।
युक्त इत्युच्यते योगी समलोष्टाश्मकाञ्चनः॥ ८॥

jñānavijñānatṛptātmā kūṭastho vijitendriyaḥ|
yukta ity ucyate yogī samaloṣṭāśmakāñcanaḥ|| 8||

सुहृन्मित्रार्युदासीनमध्यस्थद्वेष्यबन्धुषु।
साधुष्वपि च पापेषु समबुद्धिर्विशिष्यते॥ ९॥

suhṛnmitrāryudāsīnamadhyasthadveṣyabandhuṣu|
sādhuṣv api ca pāpeṣu samabuddhir viśiṣyate|| 9||

योगी युञ्जीत सततमात्मानं रहसि स्थितः।
एकाकी यतचित्तात्मा निराशीरपरिग्रहः॥ १०॥

yogī yuñjīta satatam ātmānaṃ rahasi sthitaḥ|
ekākī yatacittātmā nirāśīr aparigrahaḥ|| 10||

शुचौ देशे प्रतिष्ठाप्य स्थिरमासनमात्मनः।
नात्युच्छ्रितं नातिनीचं चैलाजिनकुशोत्तरम्॥ ११॥

śucau deśe pratiṣṭhāpya sthiram āsanam ātmanaḥ|
nātyucchritaṃ nātinīcaṃ cailājinakuśottaram|| 11||

तत्रैकाग्रं मनः कृत्वा यतचित्तेन्द्रियक्रियः।
उपविश्यासने युञ्ज्याद्योगमात्मविशुद्धये॥ १२॥

tatraikāgraṃ manaḥ kṛtvā yatacittendriyakriyaḥ|
upaviśyāsane yuñjyād yogam ātmaviśuddhaye|| 12||

The Self[143] of him who is serene,
And self-subdued, is equipoised
In heat and cold, in joy and pain,
In honor too and in disgrace.[144] 7

With wisdom and with knowledge filled,[145]
Unwavering and sense-subdued,
The *yogin* who regards alike
Gold, stone or clod, is saint[146] indeed. 8

Who views alike friends, lovers, foes,
And strangers, neutrals, hated ones,
Relations, good and evil men,
He is 'mongst *yogins* most esteemed. 9

Alone and in a secret place,
A yogin should compose his mind[147]
Unceasingly, with mind and self[148]
Restrained, and free from hope and greed. 10

Established on a seat secure,
Too lofty neither nor too low,
And in some clean place, and covered o'er
With pelt and cloth and *kuśa* grass,[149] 11

He should, his mind one-pointed made,
Its workings, and of sense, restrained,
There firmly seated practice *yoga*,
For thorough cleansing of the self. 12

---

[143]I.e., the Supreme Self.

[144]Or, thus—

> In him who hath his mind controlled,
> Who placid is in cold and heat,
> In pain and pleasure, fame and shame,
> The Self Supreme becomes his Self.

[145]Lit. satisfied.

[146]*Yukta*: here, meaning the man who has ceased to be in any way related to the world—who has attained to *samādhi*, or steadfastness of mind.

[147]I.e., in *samādhi* (Śaṅkara and Śrīdhara).

[148]Self here stands for the senses.

[149]*Eragrostis cynosoroides*. The three articles mentioned here should be spread over the seat in the reverse order of their ennumeration.

समं कायशिरोग्रीवं धारयन्नचलं स्थिरः।
संप्रेक्ष्य नासिकाग्रं स्वं दिशश्चानवलोकयन्॥ १३॥

samaṃ kāyaśirogrīvaṃ dhārayann acalaṃ sthiraḥ|
saṃprekṣya nāsikāgraṃ svaṃ diśaś cānavalokayan|| 13||

प्रशान्तात्मा विगतभीर्ब्रह्मचारिव्रते स्थितः।
मनः संयम्य मच्चित्तो युक्त आसीत मत्परः॥ १४॥

praśāntātmā vigatabhīr brahmacārivrate sthitaḥ|
manaḥ saṃyamya maccitto yukta āsīta matparaḥ|| 14||

युञ्जन्नेवं सदात्मानं योगी नियतमानसः।
शान्तिं निर्वाणपरमां मत्संस्थामधिगच्छति॥ १५॥

yuñjann evaṃ sadātmānaṃ yogī niyatamānasaḥ|
śāntiṃ nirvāṇaparamāṃ matsaṃsthām adhigacchati|| 15||

नात्यश्नतस्तु योगो ऽस्ति न चैकान्तमनश्नतः।
न चातिस्वप्नशीलस्य जाग्रतो नैव चार्जुन॥ १६॥

nātyaśnatastu yogo 'sti na caikāntam anaśnataḥ|
na cātisvapnaśīlasya jāgrato naiva cārjuna|| 16||

युक्ताहारविहारस्य युक्तचेष्टस्य कर्मसु।
युक्तस्वप्नावबोधस्य योगो भवति दुःखहा॥ १७॥

yuktāhāravihārasya yuktaceṣṭasya karmasu|
yuktasvapnāvabodhasya yogo bhavati duḥkhahā|| 17||

यदा विनियतं चित्तमात्मन्येवावतिष्ठते।
निःस्पृहः सर्वकामेभ्यो युक्त इत्युच्यते तदा॥ १८॥

yadā viniyataṃ cittam ātmany evāvatiṣṭhate|
niḥspṛhaḥ sarvakāmebhyo yukta ity ucyate tadā|| 18||

With body, head and neck erect,
And steady, sitting motionless,
The gaze upon the nose-tip fixed,
And roaming not to things around. 13

With self serene and free from fear,
And firm in vows of continence,[150]
The mind controlled and on me fixed,
Let him, attuned, sit rapt in me.[151] 14

Thus e'er attuned with the self,
With mind brought under full control,
The *yogin* doth attain that peace,
The bliss supreme[152] which dwells in me. 15

O Arjun, *yoga* is not for him
Who eats too much, who starves himself,
Nor yet for him who slumbers much,
Or who excessive vigils keeps. 16

The man who moderation knows
In play, in work, in daily food,
In sleeping and in wakefulness,
Attains to yoga that wipes out pain. 17

And when his mind, full well restrained,
Established is in self alone,
And craveth not for things of sense,
Then is he called the man attuned. 18

---

[150]*Brahmacārin*: one vowed to study and continence, etc.
[151]I.e., meditating on me as his final goal.
[152]*Mokṣa* or *nirvāṇa*.

यथा दीपो निवातस्थो नेङ्गते सोपमा स्मृता।
योगिनो यतचित्तस्य युञ्जतो योगमात्मनः॥ १९॥

yathā dīpo nivātastho neṅgate sopamā smṛtā|
yogino yatacittasya yuñjato yogam ātmanaḥ|| 19||

यत्रोपरमते चित्तं निरुद्धं योगसेवया।
यत्र चैवात्मनात्मानं पश्यन्नात्मनि तुष्यति॥ २०॥

yatroparamate cittaṃ niruddhaṃ yogasevayā|
yatra caivātmanātmānaṃ paśyann ātmani tuṣyati|| 20||

सुखमात्यन्तिकं यत्तद्बुद्धिग्राह्यमतीन्द्रियम्।
वेत्ति यत्र न चैवायं स्थितश्चलति तत्त्वतः॥ २१॥

sukham ātyantikaṃ yat tadbuddhigrāhyam atīndriyam|
vetti yatra na caivāyaṃ sthitaś calati tattvataḥ|| 21||

यं लब्ध्वा चापरं लाभं मन्यते नाधिकं ततः।
यस्मिन्स्थितो न दुःखेन गुरुणापि विचाल्यते॥ २२॥

yaṃ labdhvā cāparaṃ lābhaṃ manyate nādhikaṃ tataḥ|
yasmin sthito na duḥkhena guruṇāpi vicālyate|| 22||

तं विद्याद्दुःखसंयोगवियोगं योगसंज्ञितम्।
स निश्चयेन योक्तव्यो योगो ऽनिर्विण्णचेतसा॥ २३॥

taṃ vidyād duḥkhasaṃyogaviyogaṃ yogasaṃjñitam|
sa niścayena yoktavyo yogo 'nirviṇṇacetasā|| 23||

संकल्पप्रभवान्कामांस्त्यक्त्वा सर्वानशेषतः।
मनसैवेन्द्रियग्रामं विनियम्य समन्ततः॥ २४॥

saṃkalpaprabhavān kāmāṃs tyaktvā sarvān aśeṣataḥ|
manasaivendriyagrāmaṃ viniyamya samantataḥ|| 24||

The *yogin* who with mind controlled,
Becomes absorbed in *yoga* of self,
Has been to that bright flame compared,
Which, sheltered, flickers not at all. 19

That state in which the mind finds rest,
By *yoga* practices restrained,
In which by self beholding self,
He rests content in self alone; 20

Wherein he finds that joy supreme[153]
Which reason, not the senses, can
Enjoy; in which established well,
The truth[154] he never then forsakes; 21

Which having gained, he is assured
He can obtain no greater thing;
In which, when he is fully based,
By direst pain he is unmoved. 22

This state, the breaking loose from pain,
Let it be known is named as *yoga*;
This *yoga* should e'er be practicéd
With dauntless heart and firm resolve. 23

Without exception, leaving all
Desires which from the fancy spring,
Restraining by the mind alone,
Each of his senses from all sides; 24

---

[153]The infinite joy of seeing the Self by the self.
[154]Lit. the reality.

शनैः शनैरुपरमेद्बुद्ध्या धृतिगृहीतया।
आत्मसंस्थं मनः कृत्वा न किं चिदपि चिन्तयेत्॥ २५॥

śanaiḥ śanair uparamed buddhyā dhṛtigṛhītayā|
ātmasaṃsthaṃ manaḥ kṛtvā na kiṃ cid api cintayet|| 25||

यतो यतो निश्चरति मनश्चञ्चलमस्थिरम्।
ततस्ततो नियम्यैतदात्मन्येव वशं नयेत्॥ २६॥

yato yato niścarati manaś cañcalam asthiram|
tatastato niyamyaitadātmanyeva vaśaṃ nayet|| 26||

प्रशान्तमनसं ह्येनं योगिनं सुखमुत्तमम्।
उपैति शान्तरजसं ब्रह्मभूतमकल्मषम्॥ २७॥

praśāntamanasaṃ hyenaṃ yoginaṃ sukham uttamam|
upaiti śāntarajasaṃ brahmabhūtam akalmaṣam|| 27||

युञ्जन्नेवं सदात्मानं योगी विगतकल्मषः।
सुखेन ब्रह्मसंस्पर्शमत्यन्तं सुखम् अश्नुते॥ २८॥

yuñjann evaṃ sadātmānaṃ yogī vigatakalmaṣaḥ|
sukhena brahmasaṃsparśam atyantaṃ sukhamaśnute|| 28||

सर्वभूतस्थमात्मानं सर्वभूतानि चात्मनि।
ईक्षते योगयुक्तात्मा सर्वत्र समदर्शनः॥ २९॥

sarvabhūtastham ātmānaṃ sarvabhūtāni cātmani|
īkṣate yogayuktātmā sarvatra samadarśanaḥ|| 29||

यो मां पश्यति सर्वत्र सर्वं च मयि पश्यति।
तस्याहं न प्रणश्यामि स च मे न प्रणश्यति॥ ३०॥

yo māṃ paśyati sarvatra sarvaṃ ca mayi paśyati|
tasyāhaṃ na praṇaśyāmi sa ca me na praṇaśyati|| 30||

By reason held in firm control,
He slowly tranquil should become;[155]
With mind established in the self,
On nought his thoughts should ever dwell. 25

And from whatsoever cause, the mind,
Unsteady, wavering, wandering goes,
He should restrain and bring it back
To self's direct and sole control. 26

The *yogin* who has stilled the mind,
And all his passions has subdued,
Who has no sins, and Brahm become,
Finds verily the bliss supreme. 27

Thus keeping steadfast e'er the self,
And from his sins the *yogin* cleansed,
With ease attains the final joy
Of coming into touch with Brahm. 28

Whose self has been attuned by *yoga*,
Who looks alike on everything,
The self in every creature sees,
And every creature in the self.[156] 29

Whoso beholds me everywhere,
And seeth everything in me,
To him I never can be lost,
Nor he be ever lost to me. 30

---

[155] I.e., cease to think of sense-objects.
[156] Who realizes the essential unity of all things.

सर्वभूतस्थितं यो मां भजत्येकत्वमास्थितः।
सर्वथा वर्तमानो ऽपि स योगी मयि वर्तते॥ ३१॥

sarvabhūtasthitaṃ yo māṃ bhajaty ekatvam āsthitaḥ|
sarvathā vartamāno 'pi sa yogī mayi vartate|| 31||

आत्मौपम्येन सर्वत्र समं पश्यति यो ऽर्जुन।
सुखं वा यदि वा दुःखं स योगी परमो मतः॥ ३२॥

ātmaupamyena sarvatra samaṃ paśyati yo 'rjuna|
sukhaṃ vā yadi vā duḥkhaṃ sa yogī paramo mataḥ|| 32||

अर्जुन उवाच

यो ऽयं योगस्त्वया प्रोक्तः साम्येन मधुसूदन।
एतस्याहं न पश्यामि चञ्चलत्वात्स्थितिं स्थिराम्॥ ३३॥

arjuna uvāca

yo 'yaṃ yogas tvayā proktaḥ sāmyena madhusūdana|
etasyāhaṃ na paśyāmi cañcalatvāt sthitiṃ sthirām|| 33||

चञ्चलं हि मनः कृष्ण प्रमाथि बलवद्दृढम्।
तस्याहं निग्रहं मन्ये वायोरिव सुदुष्करम्॥ ३४॥

cañcalaṃ hi manaḥ kṛṣṇa pramāthi balavad dṛḍham|
tasyāhaṃ nigrahaṃ manye vāyor iva suduṣkaram|| 34||

श्रीभगवानुवाच

असंशयं महाबाहो मनो दुर्निग्रहं चलम्।
अभ्यासेन तु कौन्तेय वैराग्येण च गृह्यते॥ ३५॥

śrībhagavān uvāca

asaṃśayaṃ mahābāho mano durṇigrahaṃ calam|
abhyāsena tu kaunteya vairāgyeṇa ca gṛhyate|| 35||

असंयतात्मना योगो दुष्प्राप इति मे मतिः।
वश्यात्मना तु यतता शक्यो ऽवाप्तुमुपायतः॥ ३६॥

asaṃyatātmanā yogo duṣprāpa iti me matiḥ|
vaśyātmanā tu yatatā śakyo 'vāptum upāyataḥ|| 36||

The man who holds that all is one,
And worships me enshrined in all,
This *yogin* lives in me indeed,
Whate'er his mode of life may be. 31

Who knoweth that all other things
Affected are as he himself,
By pleasure, Arjun, or by pain,[157]
He is the best of *yogins* deemed. 32

Arjun said:

O Madhusūdan, for this *yoga*,
By evenness, now taught by thee,
I do not see a basis firm,
Because of mental restlessness. 33

Krishna, how restless is the mind,
Perverse, impetuous, obstinate!
To curb it seems to me as hard
As to control the wayward wind. 34

The Blessed Lord said:

O mighty armed, undoubtedly
The mind is restless, hard to curb,
Yet, Kuntī's son, it can be checked
By effort and indifference.[158] 35

Methinks that *yoga*-attainment is
Not easy for the uncontrolled,
But by the self-controlled who strive
It may by proper means[159] be won. 36

---

[157]Who sees that whatever is pleasant to himself is pleasant to others, and whatever is painful to him is painful to them.
[158]I.e., to worldly objects.
[159]Such as those described in verses 10-17.

अर्जुन उवाच

अयतिः श्रद्धयोपेतो योगाच्चलितमानसः।
अप्राप्य योगसंसिद्धिं कां गतिं कृष्ण गच्छति॥ ३७॥

arjuna uvāca

ayatiḥ śraddhayopeto yogāc calitamānasaḥ|
aprāpya yogasaṃsiddhiṃ kāṃ gatiṃ kṛṣṇa gacchati|| 37||

कच्चिन्नोभयविभ्रष्टश्छिन्नाभ्रमिव नश्यति।
अप्रतिष्ठो महाबाहो विमूढो ब्रह्मणः पथि॥ ३८॥

kaccin nobhayavibhraṣṭaś chinnābhramiva naśyati|
apratiṣṭho mahābāho vimūḍho brahmaṇaḥ pathi|| 38||

एतन्मे संशयं कृष्ण छेत्तुमर्हस्यशेषतः।
त्वदन्यः संशयस्यास्य छेत्ता न ह्युपपद्यते॥ ३९॥

etan me saṃśayaṃ kṛṣṇa chettum arhasy aśeṣataḥ|
tvadanyaḥ saṃśayasyāsya chettā na hy upapadyate|| 39||

श्रीभगवानुवाच

पार्थ नैवेह नामुत्र विनाशस्तस्य विद्यते।
न हि कल्याणकृत्कश्चिद्दुर्गतिं तात गच्छति॥ ४०॥

śrībhagavān uvāca

pārtha naiveha nāmutra vināśas tasya vidyate|
na hi kalyāṇakṛt kaścid durgatiṃ tāta gacchati|| 40||

प्राप्य पुण्यकृतां लोकानुषित्वा शाश्वतीः समाः।
शुचीनां श्रीमतां गेहे योगभ्रष्टो ऽभिजायते॥ ४१॥

prāpya puṇyakṛtāṃ lokān uṣitvā śāśvatīḥ samāḥ|
śucīnāṃ śrīmatāṃ gehe yogabhraṣṭo 'bhijāyate|| 41||

अथ वा योगिनामेव कुले भवति धीमताम्।
एतद्धि दुर्लभतरं लोके जन्म यदीदृशम्॥ ४२॥

atha vā yoginām eva kule bhavati dhīmatām|
etad dhi durlabhataraṃ loke janma yadīdṛśam|| 42||

Arjun said:

He who has faith but will not strive,
Whose mind from *yoga* is turned away,
Who fails to perfect be in *yoga*,
Which way, O Krishna, doth he go? 37

Is he, for having failed in both,[160]
Destroyed like a riven cloud,
Benighted on the path to Brahm,
Has he no prop, O mighty armed? 38

Be pleased, O Krishna, to dispel
This doubt by which I am assailed;
None other can, except thyself,
Succeed in chasing it away. 39

The Blessed Lord said:

O Pṛthā's son, in neither world
Destruction lies in store for him,
For none, my dear, e'er come to grief
Who worketh deeds of righteous men. 40

The man who once had failed in *yoga*,
Attains the world of righteous men,
And after being there a term,
'Mongst pious folks he is reborn.[161] 41

Or in a home of *yogins* wise
He doth perchance re-enter life;
But to attain a birth like this
On earth is very rare indeed. 42

---

[160] I.e., in securing *svarga* (heaven), through work on the one hand, and *mokṣa* (emancipation) through *yoga* on the other.

[161] Lit. in a family of holy and illustrious men.

तत्र तं बुद्धिसंयोगं लभते पौर्वदेहिकम्।
यतते च ततो भूयः संसिद्धौ कुरुनन्दन। ४३॥

tatra taṃ buddhisaṃyogaṃ labhate paurvadehikam|
yatate ca tato bhūyaḥ saṃsiddhau kurunandana| 43||

पूर्वाभ्यासेन तेनैव ह्रियते ह्यवशो ऽपि सः।
जिज्ञासुरपि योगस्य शब्दब्रह्मातिवर्तते॥ ४४॥

pūrvābhyāsena tenaiva hriyate hyavaśo 'pi saḥ|
jijñāsur api yogasya śabdabrahmātivartate|| 44||

प्रयत्नाद्यतमानस्तु योगी संशुद्धकिल्बिषः।
अनेकजन्मसंसिद्धस्ततो याति परां गतिम्॥ ४५॥

prayatnād yatamānas tu yogī saṃśuddhakilbiṣaḥ|
anekajanmasaṃsiddhas tato yāti parāṃ gatim|| 45||

तपस्विभ्यो ऽधिको योगी ज्ञानिभ्यो ऽपि मतो ऽधिकः।
कर्मिभ्यश्चाधिको योगी तस्माद्योगी भवार्जुन॥ ४६॥

tapasvibhyo 'dhiko yogī jñānibhyo 'pi mato 'dhikaḥ|
karmibhyaś cādhiko yogī tasmād yogī bhavārjuna|| 46||

योगिनामपि सर्वेषां मद्गतेनान्तरात्मना।
श्रद्धावान्भजते यो मां स मे युक्ततमो मतः॥ ४७॥

yoginām api sarveṣāṃ madgatenāntarātmanā|
śraddhāvān bhajate yo māṃ sa me yuktatamo mataḥ|| 47||

He there that knowledge re-acquires,
Which in the former life he had,
And thereupon, O Kuru's joy,
To gain perfection doth he strive. 43

By that same former practice[162] he
Resistlessly is swept away;[163]
Though merely wishing *yoga* to know,
Above the word divine[164] he soars. 44

The *yogin* who assiduous is,
Who's freed from sin and hath attained
Perfection after many births,
Achieves at last the goal supreme. 45

The *yogin* is far more esteemed
Than the ascetic or the wise,
Yea, even than the man of deeds;
Hence, Arjun, be a yogin thou! 46

Whoso 'mongst yogins, full of faith,
His inmost self in me reposed,
Doth worship me, I reckon him
The most attuned with me of all. 47

---

[162] I.e., by the *yoga*-practice of a former birth.
[163] Towards perfection.
[164] I.e., he rises above (the fruits of action laid down in the) Vedas.

Chapter Seven: The Yoga of Discernment (विज्ञानयोगः)

श्रीभगवानुवाच

मय्यासक्तमनाः पार्थ योगं युञ्जन्मदाश्रयः।
असंशयं समग्रं मां यथा ज्ञास्यसि तच्छृणु॥ १॥

śrībhagavān uvāca

mayy āsaktamanāḥ pārtha yogaṃ yuñjan madāśrayaḥ|
asaṃśayaṃ samagraṃ māṃ yathā jñāsyasi tac chṛṇu|| 1||

ज्ञानं ते ऽहं सविज्ञानमिदं वक्ष्याम्यशेषतः।
यज्ज्ञात्वा नेह भूयो ऽन्यज्ज्ञातव्यमवशिष्यते॥ २॥

jñānaṃ te 'haṃ savijñānam idaṃ vakṣyāmy aśeṣataḥ|
yaj jñātvā neha bhūyo 'nyaj jñātavyam avaśiṣyate|| 2||

मनुष्याणां सहस्रेषु कश्चिद्यतति सिद्धये।
यततामपि सिद्धानां कश्चिन्मां वेत्ति तत्त्वतः॥ ३॥

manuṣyāṇāṃ sahasreṣu kaścid yatati siddhaye|
yatatām api siddhānāṃ kaścin māṃ vetti tattvataḥ|| 3||

भूमिरापो ऽनलो वायुः खं मनो बुद्धिरेव च।
अहंकार इतीयं मे भिन्ना प्रकृतिरष्टधा॥ ४॥

bhūmir āpo 'nalo vāyuḥ khaṃ mano buddhir eva ca|
ahaṃkāra itīyaṃ me bhinnā prakṛtir aṣṭadhā|| 4||

अपरेयमितस्त्वन्यां प्रकृतिं विद्धि मे पराम्।
जीवभूतां महाबाहो ययेदं धार्यते जगत्॥ ५॥

apareyam itas tv anyāṃ prakṛtiṃ viddhi me parām|
jīvabhūtāṃ mahābāho yayedaṃ dhāryate jagat|| 5||

एतद्योनीनि भूतानि सर्वाणीत्युपधारय।
अहं कृत्स्नस्य जगतः प्रभवः प्रलयस्तथा॥ ६॥

etadyonīni bhūtāni sarvāṇīty upadhāraya|
ahaṃ kṛtsnasya jagataḥ prabhavaḥ pralayas tathā|| 6||

The Blessed Lord said:

In *yoga* engaged, in me reposed,
O Pārtha, thy mind intent on me,
Learn how, without a doubt, by thee
I might be known in full extent. 1

This knowledge and this wisdom[165] I
Shall now impart to thee in full;
With these equiped naught shall remain
For thee worth knowing here on earth. 2

'Mongst many thousands, one perchance
Endeavors to perfection gain;
Of those who strive and perfect are,
Scarce one truly knoweth me. 3

Earth, water, fire, air, space, and mind,
And reason and the ego-sense,
These are the eight-fold principles
Of which my nature[166] is composed. 4

The lower this, distinct therefrom,
There is my higher nature, know[167]—
The living soul, O mighty armed,[168]
That sustains all the universe. 5

Know thou that in these natures twain
All beings have indeed their birth;
From me the universe doth spring,
And will dissolve itself in me. 6

---

[165] *Vijñāna* as opposed to *jñāna*. *Vijñāna* is discriminative knowledge, acquired as the result of personal experience, not like *jñāna* which is acquired from books or teachers.

[166] *Prakṛti*: lit. matter-stuff, the substance of which the physical world is composed. It is this *prakṛti*, or nature, which is referred to in this line.

[167] My higher *prakṛti*—i.e., my very self as the supreme soul.

[168] I.e., the very spirit or soul which animates all living beings.

मत्तः परतरं नान्यत्किंचिदस्ति धनंजय।
मयि सर्वमिदं प्रोतं सूत्रे मणिगणा इव॥ ७॥

mattaḥ parataraṃ nānyat kiṃ cid asti dhanaṃjaya|
mayi sarvam idaṃ protaṃ sūtre maṇigaṇā iva|| 7||

रसो ऽहमप्सु कौन्तेय प्रभास्मि शशिसूर्ययोः।
प्रणवः सर्ववेदेषु शब्दः खे पौरुषं नृषु॥ ८॥

raso 'ham apsu kaunteya prabhāsmi śaśisūryayoḥ|
praṇavaḥ sarvavedeṣu śabdaḥ khe pauruṣaṃ nṛṣu|| 8||

पुण्यो गन्धः पृथिव्यां च तेजश्चास्मि विभावसौ।
जीवनं सर्वभूतेषु तपश्चास्मि तपस्विषु॥ ९॥

puṇyo gandhaḥ pṛthivyāṃ ca tejaś cāsmi vibhāvasau|
jīvanaṃ sarvabhūteṣu tapaś cāsmi tapasviṣu|| 9||

बीजं मां सर्वभूतानां विद्धि पार्थ सनातनम्।
बुद्धिर्बुद्धिमतामस्मि तेजस्तेजस्विनामहम्॥ १०॥

bījaṃ māṃ sarvabhūtānāṃ viddhi pārtha sanātanam|
buddhir buddhimatām asmi tejas tejasvinām aham|| 10||

बलं बलवतां चाहं कामरागविवर्जितम्।
धर्माविरुद्धो भूतेषु कामो ऽस्मि भरतर्षभ॥ ११॥

balaṃ balavatāṃ cāhaṃ kāmarāgavivarjitam|
dharmāviruddho bhūteṣu kāmo 'smi bharatarṣabha|| 11||

ये चैव सात्त्विका भावा राजसास्तामसाश्च ये।
मत्त एवेति तान्विद्धि न त्वहं तेषु ते मयि॥ १२॥

ye caiva sāttvikā bhāvā rājasās tāmasāś ca ye|
matta eveti tān viddhi na tv ahaṃ teṣu te mayi|| 12||

With me compared, O Dhanañjay,
There is naught higher that exists,
On me the universe is strung
As precious gems upon a thread. 7

In waters I the savour am,
In sun and moon I am the light,
And I am 'om' in all the Veda,
The sound in space, manhood in men.[169] 8

I am of earth the fragrance pure,
The brilliance of the burning fire,
The life am I in all that lives,
And in ascetics, penance I. 9

Know me to be, O Pṛthā's son,
The deathless seed in all that lives,
The wisdom of the wise am I,
And splendor of all splendid things. 10

I am the strength in those who're strong,
Exempt from passion and desire,
In all that lives I am desire,
Which is to virtue[170] unopposed. 11

Whatever natures may be pure,[171]
Darkened,[172] or with passion stained,[173]
Know thou they all proceed from me,
They are in me, not I in them. 12

---

[169]The vocative "O Kuntī's son" is omitted.
[170]*Dharma.*
[171]*Sāttvika.*
[172]*Tāmasika.*
[173]*Rājasika.*

त्रिभिर्गुणमयैर्भावैरेभिः सर्वमिदं जगत्।
मोहितं नाभिजानाति मामेभ्यः परमव्ययम्॥ १३॥

tribhir guṇamayair bhāvair ebhiḥ sarvam idaṃ jagat|
mohitaṃ nābhijānāti mām ebhyaḥ param avyayam|| 13||

दैवी ह्येषा गुणमयी मम माया दुरत्यया।
मामेव ये प्रपद्यन्ते मायामेतां तरन्ति ते॥ १४॥

daivī hy eṣā guṇamayī mama māyā duratyayā|
mām eva ye prapadyante māyām etāṃ taranti te|| 14||

न मां दुष्कृतिनो मूढाः प्रपद्यन्ते नराधमाः।
माययापहृतज्ञाना आसुरं भावमाश्रिताः॥ १५॥

na māṃ duṣkṛtino mūḍhāḥ prapadyante narādhamāḥ|
māyayāpahṛtajñānā āsuraṃ bhāvam āśritāḥ|| 15||

चतुर्विधा भजन्ते मां जनाः सुकृतिनोऽर्जुन।
आर्तो जिज्ञासुरर्थार्थी ज्ञानी च भरतर्षभ॥ १६॥

caturvidhā bhajante māṃ janāḥ sukṛtino 'rjuna|
ārto jijñāsur arthārthī jñānī ca bharatarṣabha|| 16||

तेषां ज्ञानी नित्ययुक्त एकभक्तिर्विशिष्यते।
प्रियो हि ज्ञानिनोऽत्यर्थमहं स च मम प्रियः॥ १७॥

teṣāṃ jñānī nityayukta ekabhaktir viśiṣyate|
priyo hi jñānino 'tyartham ahaṃ sa ca mama priyaḥ|| 17||

उदाराः सर्व एवैते ज्ञानी त्वात्मैव मे मतम्।
आस्थितः स हि युक्तात्मा मामेवानुत्तमां गतिम्॥ १८॥

udārāḥ sarva evaite jñānī tv ātmaiva me matam|
āsthitaḥ sa hi yuktātmā mām evānuttamāṃ gatim|| 18||

Deluded by these natures three,
Which from the *guṇas* are evolved,
The world entire doth not know me,
Transcending them, immutable.[174] 13

My god-like *māyā guṇa*-made,[175]
Cannot surmounted be with ease,
But those who refuge find in me,
Beyond this *māyā* wend their way. 14

Who are through *māyā* wisdomless,
And those who follow demons' ways,[176]
These seek me not, nor they who are
Deluded, wicked, evil men. 15

Of righteous men four kinds there are,
O Arjun, who do worship me,
The wise, O chief,[177] the suffering ones,
And those who wealth or knowledge seek. 16

Of these the wise, attuned always,
Who loves the one,[178] is far the best;
I to the wise am passing dear,
And he is very dear to me. 17

Noble indeed are all these men,
But as myself I deem the wise,
For he with steadfast mind resorts
To me alone, the highest goal.18

---

[174]I.e., the natures developed from the three *guṇas*.
[175]The divine *māyā* (illusion) inherent in me.
[176]The fiends referred to are the *asuras*, beings of low and devilish nature.
[177]Lit. O chief, or lord of the Bhāratas.
[178]I.e., to the one supreme being.

बहूनां जन्मनामन्ते ज्ञानवान्मां प्रपद्यते।
वासुदेवः सर्वमिति स महात्मा सुदुर्लभः॥ १९॥

bahūnāṃ janmanām ante jñānavān māṃ prapadyate|
vāsudevaḥ sarvam iti sa mahātmā sudurlabhaḥ|| 19||

कामैस्तैस्तैर्हृतज्ञानाः प्रपद्यन्ते ऽन्यदेवताः।
तं तं नियममास्थाय प्रकृत्या नियताः स्वया॥ २०॥

kāmais tais tair hṛtajñānāḥ prapadyante 'nyadevatāḥ|
taṃ taṃ niyamam āsthāya prakṛtyā niyatāḥ svayā|| 20||

यो यो यां यां तनुं भक्तः श्रद्धयार्चितुमिच्छति।
तस्य तस्याचलां श्रद्धां तामेव विदधाम्यहम्॥ २१॥

yo yo yāṃ yāṃ tanuṃ bhaktaḥ śraddhayārcitum icchati|
tasya tasyācalāṃ śraddhāṃ tām eva vidadhāmy aham|| 21||

स तया श्रद्धया युक्तस्तस्या राधनमीहते।
लभते च ततः कामान्मयैव विहितान्हि तान्॥ २२॥

sa tayā śraddhayā yuktas tasyā rādhanam īhate|
labhate ca tataḥ kāmān mayaiva vihitān hi tān|| 22||

अन्तवत्तु फलं तेषां तद्भवत्यल्पमेधसाम्।
देवान्देवयजो यान्ति मद्भक्ता यान्ति मामपि॥ २३॥

antavat tu phalaṃ teṣāṃ tadbhavaty alpamedhasām|
devān devayajo yānti madbhaktā yānti mām api|| 23||

अव्यक्तं व्यक्तिमापन्नं मन्यन्ते मामबुद्धयः।
परं भावमजानन्तो ममाव्ययमनुत्तमम्॥ २४॥

avyaktaṃ vyaktim āpannaṃ manyante mām abuddhayaḥ|
paraṃ bhāvam ajānanto mamāvyayam anuttamam|| 24||

The wise at close of countless births
Comes unto me, for he perceives
That Vāsudeva[179] is all in all,
Great souled is he and very rare! 19

Who through desire have been deprived
Of wisdom, follow other gods,
Observing various outward rites,
By their own natures thus constrained.[180] 20

Whatever god a devotee
In worship seeks, in earnest faith,
That selfsame faith of his do I
In worship of his god confirm. 21

Of faith as this possessed he seeks
The worship of his chosen god,
He gets from him whate'er he craves,
But what he gets he gets from me. 22

But fleeting the reward thus gained
By these small witted devotees,
They go to gods who worship gods,
My worshipers come unto me. 23

Unconscious of my higher state,
Immutable and unsurpassed,
By fools I am believed to be
The unrevealed[181] made manifest. 24

---

[179]A name of Kṛṣṇa. ["Son of Vasudeva." Sans. Ed.]
[180]Which are the result of the acts of their past lives.
[181]I.e., the ignorant take me to be no higher than what is indicated by my incarnations.

नाहं प्रकाशः सर्वस्य योगमायासमावृतः।
मूढो ऽयं नाभिजानाति लोको मामजमव्ययम्॥ २५॥

nāhaṃ prakāśaḥ sarvasya yogamāyāsamāvṛtaḥ|
mūḍho 'yaṃ nābhijānāti loko mām ajam avyayam|| 25||

वेदाहं समतीतानि वर्तमानानि चार्जुन।
भविष्याणि च भूतानि मां तु वेद न कश्चन॥ २६॥

vedāhaṃ samatītāni vartamānāni cārjuna|
bhaviṣyāṇi ca bhūtāni māṃ tu veda na kaścana|| 26||

इच्छाद्वेषसमुत्थेन द्वन्द्वमोहेन भारत।
सर्वभूतानि संमोहं सर्गे यान्ति परंतप॥ २७॥

icchādveṣasamutthena dvandvamohena bhārata|
sarvabhūtāni saṃmohaṃ sarge yānti paraṃtapa|| 27||

येषां त्वन्तगतं पापं जनानां पुण्यकर्मणाम्।
ते द्वन्द्वमोहनिर्मुक्ता भजन्ते मां दृढव्रताः॥ २८॥

yeṣāṃ tv antagataṃ pāpaṃ janānāṃ puṇyakarmaṇām|
te dvandvamohanirmuktā bhajante māṃ dṛḍhavratāḥ|| 28||

जरामरणमोक्षाय मामाश्रित्य यतन्ति ये।
ते ब्रह्म तद्विदुः कृत्स्नमध्यात्मं कर्म चाखिलम्॥ २९॥

jarāmaraṇamokṣāya mām āśritya yatanti ye|
te brahma tadviduḥ kṛtsnam adhyātmaṃ karma cākhilam|| 29||

साधिभूताधिदैवं मां साधियज्ञं च ये विदुः।
प्रयाणकाले ऽपि च मां ते विदुर्युक्तचेतसः॥ ३०॥

sādhibhūtādhidaivaṃ māṃ sādhiyajñaṃ ca ye viduḥ|
prayāṇakāle 'pi ca māṃ te vidur yuktacetasaḥ|| 30||

By *yoga-māyā*[182] deeply veiled,
I am not manifest to all;
This world, deluded, knows me not,
The birthless and the deathless one. 25

I know the beings that have been,
The beings too that now exist,
And such as shall hereafter be,
But none, O Arjun, knoweth me! 26

Deluded by the 'pairs' which spring
From longing and aversion both,
All beings, Bharat, at their birth
Deluded are, O Parantap. 27

But all such men whose deeds are pure,
In whom all sin is at an end,
Who by the 'pairs' are not beguiled,
With firm resolve they worship me. 28

Who taking refuge in me, strive
For freedom from decay and death,
They fully know the Adhyātman,[183]
The Brahm, the whole of action[184] too. 29

Who know me as the Adhibhūt,[185]
As Adhidaiv[186] and Adhiyajña,[187]
They even in the hour of death,
With minds attuned, know me in truth. 30

[182]The creative power of *yoga*, all things being the thought-forms of the one. (Mrs. Besant). [Śaṅkara defines *yoga-māyā* as "the acting of the three *guṇas* which is itself *māyā*." "By that am I veiled." Sans. Ed.]
[183]Reality underlying the individual self. See the Eighth Discourse. Note 4.
[184]*Karma.*
[185]I.e., as the supreme being in the physical world.
[186]I.e., as the supreme being amongst the gods; the supreme god.
[187]I.e., as the supreme sacrifice.

Chapter Eight: The Yoga of Brahman the Savior (तारकब्रह्मयोगः)

अर्जुन उवाच
किं तद्ब्रह्म किमध्यात्मं किं कर्म पुरुषोत्तम।
अधिभूतं च किं प्रोक्तमधिदैवं किमुच्यते॥ १॥

arjuna uvāca
kiṃ tad brahma kim adhyātmaṃ kiṃ karma puruṣottama|
adhibhūtaṃ ca kiṃ proktam adhidaivaṃ kim ucyate|| 1||

अधियज्ञः कथं को ऽत्र देहे ऽस्मिन्मधुसूदन।
प्रयाणकाले च कथं ज्ञेयो ऽसि नियतात्मभिः॥ २॥

adhiyajñaḥ kathaṃ ko 'tra dehe 'smin madhusūdana|
prayāṇakāle ca kathaṃ jñeyo 'si niyatātmabhiḥ|| 2||

श्रीभगवानुवाच
अक्षरं ब्रह्म परमं स्वभावो ऽध्यात्ममुच्यते।
भूतभावोद्भवकरो विसर्गः कर्मसंज्ञितः॥ ३॥

śrībhagavān uvāca
akṣaraṃ brahma paramaṃ svabhāvo 'dhyātmam ucyate|
bhūtabhāvodbhavakaro visargaḥ karmasaṃjñitaḥ|| 3||

अधिभूतं क्षरो भावः पुरुषश्चाधिदैवतम्।
अधियज्ञो ऽहमेवात्र देहे देहभृतां वर॥ ४॥

adhibhūtaṃ kṣaro bhāvaḥ puruṣaś cādhidaivatam|
adhiyajño 'ham evātra dehe dehabhṛtāṃ vara|| 4||

अन्तकाले च मामेव स्मरन्मुक्त्वा कलेवरम्।
यः प्रयाति स मद्भावं याति नास्त्यत्र संशयः॥ ५॥

antakāle ca mām eva smaran muktvā kalevaram|
yaḥ prayāti sa madbhāvaṃ yāti nāsty atra saṃśayaḥ|| 5||

यं यं वापि स्मरन्भावं त्यजत्यन्ते कलेवरम्।
तं तमेवैति कौन्तेय सदा तद्भावभावितः॥ ६॥

yaṃ yaṃ vāpi smaran bhāvaṃ tyajaty ante kalevaram|
taṃ tam evaiti kaunteya sadā tadbhāvabhāvitaḥ|| 6||

Arjun said:

O best of beings,[188] what is Brahm,
And action, and the Adhyātman,
And also that which has been named
The Adhibhūt and Adhidaiv? 1

And, Madhusūdan, who and how
Embodied[189] is the Adhiyajña?
How also by the self-controlled,
Thou in the hour of death art known? 2

The Blessed Lord said:

The deathless[190] and supreme is Brahm,
The ego[191] the Adhyātman is,
The offering which gives birth to things[192]
Is by the name of action known. 3

The Adhibhūt is all that dies,[193]
The Puruṣa[194] is the Adhidaiv,
O best of beings, I myself,
Embodied, am the Adhiyajña. 4

And who at death casts off the flesh,
On me alone his thoughts intent,
He to my being passeth o'er,
Of this no doubt at all can be. 5

But who at death puts off the flesh,
Intent on other deity,[195]
He to that deity goes forth,
On whom his thoughts had always dwelt. 6

---

[188]*Puruṣottama*: Best of Puruṣas. See note 7.

[189]Lit. in this body.

[190]Lit. imperishable (*akṣara*).

[191]I.e., the supreme Brahman, existing as the ego, as the innermost self, as the *pratyagātman*, in every individual body is the *adhyātman*. (Śaṅkara)

[192]I.e., the sacrifice which is the cause of the material world.

[193]I.e., the perishable physical existence.

[194]This word comes from the root $\sqrt{p\d{r}}$, "to fill," that by which everything is filled, or that which lies in the body (*pura*); hence, the individual sould or spirit.

[195]According to some commentators on "anything whatever," or any "idea" whatever occupying the thoughts.

तस्मात्सर्वेषु कालेषु मामनुस्मर युध्य च।
मय्यर्पितमनोबुद्धिर्मामेवैष्यस्यसंशयः॥ ७॥

tasmāt sarveṣu kāleṣu mām anusmara yudhya ca|
mayy arpitamanobuddhir mām evaiṣyasy asaṃśayaḥ|| 7||

अभ्यासयोगयुक्तेन चेतसा नान्यगामिना।
परमं पुरुषं दिव्यं याति पार्थानुचिन्तयन्॥ ८॥

abhyāsayogayuktena cetasā nānyagāminā|
paramaṃ puruṣaṃ divyaṃ yāti pārthānucintayan|| 8||

कविं पुराणमनुशासितारमणोरणीयांसमनुस्मरेद्यः।
सर्वस्य धातारमचिन्त्यरूपमादित्यवर्णं तमसः परस्तात्॥ ९॥

kaviṃ purāṇam anuśāsitāram aṇor aṇīyāṃsam anusmared yaḥ|
sarvasya dhātāram acintyarūpam ādityavarṇaṃ tamasaḥ parastāt|| 9||

प्रयाणकाले मनसाचलेन भक्त्या युक्तो योगबलेन चैव।
भ्रुवोर्मध्ये प्राणमावेश्य सम्यक्स तं परं पुरुषमुपैति दिव्यम्॥ १०॥

prayāṇakāle manasācalena bhaktyā yukto yogabalena caiva|
bhruvor madhye prāṇam āveśya samyak sa taṃ paraṃ puruṣam upaiti divyam|| 10||

यदक्षरं वेदविदो वदन्ति विशन्ति यद्यतयो वीतरागाः।
यदिच्छन्तो ब्रह्मचर्यं चरन्ति तत्ते पदं संग्रहेण प्रवक्ष्ये॥ ११॥

yad akṣaraṃ vedavido vadanti viśanti yad yatayo vītarāgāḥ|
yad icchanto brahmacaryaṃ caranti tat te padaṃ saṃgraheṇa pravakṣye|| 11||

सर्वद्वाराणि संयम्य मनो हृदि निरुध्य च।
मूर्ध्न्याधायात्मनः प्राणमास्थितो योगधारणाम्॥ १२॥

sarvadvārāṇi saṃyamya mano hṛdi nirudhya ca|
mūrdhny ādhāyātmanaḥ prāṇam āsthito yogadhāraṇām|| 12||

Therefore, remember me always,
And in this fight do thou engage,
With mind and reason fixed on me,
Thou doubtlessly shalt come to me. 7

With mind that wanders nowhere else,
By practice[196] e'er attuned with me,
And meditating always, Pārtha,
One finds the soul supreme,[197] divine. 8

Who thinks of him, the ancient and the sage,
Than atom smaller,[198] lord and stay of all,
Whose form cannot by man imagined be,
Refulgent as the sun, transcending gloom. 9

When putting off the flesh, the mind unswayed,
And in devotion fixed by pow'r of *yoga*,
The life-breath centered well betwixt the brows,
He goeth to that soul supreme divine. 10

That goal which Vedists say hath no decay,
Reached by ascetics rid of all desire,
For which men strive to lead the godly life,[199]
Of that I shall now briefly speak to thee. 11

Whoso, his body gates[200] all closed,
And mind within the heart confined,[201]
The life-breath held within the head,
In yoga- concentration fixed, 12

---

[196]I.e., by the practice of constantly meditating on me alone. In the original, the words are "attuned by constant practice."
[197]*Parama-puruṣa*—the highest *puruṣa*.
[198]Lit., minuter than the minutest, or subtler than the subtlest
[199]Lit. the life of *brahmacarya*.
[200]I.e., the sense organs.
[201]Means, withdrawing the heart from all external objects, directing the thoughts towards me alone.

ओमित्येकाक्षरं ब्रह्म व्याहरन्मामनुस्मरन्।
यः प्रयाति त्यजन्देहं स याति परमां गतिम्॥ १३॥

om ity ekākṣaraṃ brahma vyāharan mām anusmaran|
yaḥ prayāti tyajan dehaṃ sa yāti paramāṃ gatim|| 13||

अनन्यचेताः सततं यो मां स्मरति नित्यशः।
तस्याहं सुलभः पार्थ नित्ययुक्तस्य योगिनः॥ १४॥

ananyacetāḥ satataṃ yo māṃ smarati nityaśaḥ|
tasyāhaṃ sulabhaḥ pārtha nityayuktasya yoginaḥ|| 14||

मामुपेत्य पुनर्जन्म दुःखालयमशाश्वतम्।
नाप्नुवन्ति महात्मानः संसिद्धिं परमां गताः॥ १५॥

mām upetya punar janma duḥkhālayam aśāśvatam|
nāpnuvanti mahātmānaḥ saṃsiddhiṃ paramāṃ gatāḥ|| 15||

आ ब्रह्मभुवनाँल्लोकाः पुनरावर्तिनो ऽर्जुन।
मामुपेत्य तु कौन्तेय पुनर्जन्म न विद्यते॥ १६॥

ā brahmabhuvanā̃l lokāḥ punar āvartino 'rjuna|
mām upetya tu kaunteya punar janma na vidyate|| 16||

सहस्रयुगपर्यन्तमहर्यद्ब्रह्मणो विदुः।
रात्रिं युगसहस्रान्तां ते ऽहोरात्रविदो जनाः॥ १७॥

sahasrayugaparyantam ahar yad brahmaṇo viduḥ|
rātriṃ yugasahasrāntāṃ te 'horātravido janāḥ|| 17||

Repeats the one syllable "om,"
The Brahm, and meditates on me,
And leaves the body to depart,
He reacheth then the goal supreme. 13

And who with undivided mind
Upon me thinks unceasingly,
This yogin, e'er attuned with me,
With greatest ease finds me, O Pārtha! 14

These great souls who have come to me
And who perfection have attained,
Do not return to enter birth,
The home of woe, the transient state. 15

All worlds, including Brahmā's world,[202]
O Arjun, ever come and go,
But he who once has come to me,
Is ne'er reborn, O Kuntī's son. 16

The men who reckon day and night,[203]
They know a single day of his
A thousand ages[204] doth endure,
His night a thousand ages too. 17

---

[202]*Brahmā*, the *prajāpati*, the fashioner and architect of the universe.

[203]I.e., the persons who compute time. Another rendering of this line would seem to imply that only those who know Brahmā's day and night know earthly day and night as he knows them; they know much more than those whose knowledge is limited by the course of the sun and moon.

[204]Those "ages" or *yugas* are:

Kṛta-yuga	1,728,000	mortal years
Tretā-yuga	1,296,000	"
Dvāpara-yuga	864,000	"
Kali-yuga	432,000	"
Mahāyuga	4,320,000	"

A "day" of Brahmā equals 1,000 *mahāyugas* and a "night" of Brahmā also equals 1,000 *mahāyugas*. A day and night of Brahmā equal a *kalpa* (8,640,000,000 mortal years). 360 *kalpas* equal a "year" of Brahmā; 100 "years" of Brahmā equal a *mahākalpa*. At the end of a *mahākalpa*, Brahmā dies and the universe comes to an end.

अव्यक्ताद्व्यक्तयः सर्वाः प्रभवन्त्यहरागमे।
रात्र्यागमे प्रलीयन्ते तत्रैवाव्यक्तसंज्ञके॥ १८॥

avyaktād vyaktayaḥ sarvāḥ prabhavanty aharāgame|
rātryāgame pralīyante tatraivāvyaktasaṃjñake|| 18||

भूतग्रामः स एवायं भूत्वा भूत्वा प्रलीयते।
रात्र्यागमे ऽवशः पार्थ प्रभवत्यहरागमे॥ १९॥

bhūtagrāmaḥ sa evāyaṃ bhūtvā bhūtvā pralīyate|
rātryāgame 'vaśaḥ pārtha prabhavaty aharāgame|| 19||

परस्तस्मात्तु भावो ऽन्यो ऽव्यक्तो ऽव्यक्तात्सनातनः।
यः स सर्वेषु भूतेषु नश्यत्सु न विनश्यति॥ २०॥

parastasmāt tu bhāvo 'nyo 'vyakto 'vyaktāt sanātanaḥ|
yaḥ sa sarveṣu bhūteṣu naśyatsu na vinaśyati|| 20||

अव्यक्तो ऽक्षर इत्युक्तस्तमाहुः परमां गतिम्।
यं प्राप्य न निवर्तन्ते तद्धाम परमं मम॥ २१॥

avyakto 'kṣara ity uktas tam āhuḥ paramāṃ gatim|
yaṃ prāpya na nivartante tad dhāma paramaṃ mama|| 21||

पुरुषः स परः पार्थ भक्त्या लभ्यस्त्वनन्यया।
यस्यान्तःस्थानि भूतानि येन सर्वमिदं ततम्॥ २२॥

puruṣaḥ sa paraḥ pārtha bhaktyā labhyas tv ananyayā|
yasyāntaḥsthāni bhūtāni yena sarvam idaṃ tatam|| 22||

यत्र काले त्वनावृत्तिमावृत्तिं चैव योगिनः।
प्रयाता यान्ति तं कालं वक्ष्यामि भरतर्षभ॥ २३॥

yatra kāle tv anāvṛttim āvṛttiṃ caiva yoginaḥ|
prayātā yānti taṃ kālaṃ vakṣyāmi bharatarṣabha|| 23||

At dawn of day all things defined
Spring into life from the unseen;[205]
At fall of night they all dissolve[206]
Into the same unseen again. 18

This selfsame swarm of things create,
Again and yet again produced,
Dissolves unwilling,[207] Pārtha, at eve,
And reappears at birth of morn. 19

But higher far than this unseen
Is the unseen[208] who lives always,
The being who doth perish not,
When perished are all other things. 20

This unseen is th'eternal named,
And also called the highest goal,
Which having found, none e'er returns,[209]
And that is my supreme abode. 21

This highest spirit, Pṛthā's son,
In whom all creatures do abide,
By whom pervaded is the world,
Is reached by undivided love. 22

O Bharat's lord, I'll tell thee now
What are the "times"[210] when dying here,
The *yogins* go to come not back,
And when they go to come again. 23

---

[205]Lit. the unmanifested (*avyakta*), representing Prajāpati asleep, i.e., not actively engaged in the act of creation.

[206]I.e., when Prajāpati, at the coming of "night" goes to sleep, all manifested things dissolve into him again.

[207]In this cyclic return to birth the creatures have no "say" of their own, their return being governed by *karma*, actions done in former births.

[208]I.e., the imperishable (*akṣara*).

[209]I.e., to mundane existence.

[210]"Times" here means the paths indicated by the deities who preside over the divisions of time.

अग्निर्ज्योतिरहः शुक्लः षण्मासा उत्तरायणम्।
तत्र प्रयाता गच्छन्ति ब्रह्म ब्रह्मविदो जनाः॥ २४॥

agnir jyotir ahaḥ śuklaḥ ṣaṇmāsā uttarāyaṇam|
tatra prayātā gacchanti brahma brahmavido janāḥ|| 24||

धूमो रात्रिस्तथा कृष्णः षण्मासा दक्षिणायनम्।
तत्र चान्द्रमसं ज्योतिर्योगी प्राप्य निवर्तते॥ २५॥

dhūmo rātris tathā kṛṣṇaḥ ṣaṇmāsā dakṣiṇāyanam|
tatra cāndramasaṃ jyotir yogī prāpya nivartate|| 25||

शुक्लकृष्णे गती ह्येते जगतः शाश्वते मते।
एकया यात्यनावृत्तिमन्ययावर्तते पुनः॥ २६॥

śuklakṛṣṇe gatī hy ete jagataḥ śāśvate mate|
ekayā yāty anāvṛttim anyayāvartate punaḥ|| 26||

नैते सृती पार्थ जानन् योगी मुह्यति कश्चन।
तस्मात्सर्वेषु कालेषु योगयुक्तो भवार्जुन॥ २७॥

naite sṛtī pārtha jānanyogī muhyati kaścana|
tasmāt sarveṣu kāleṣu yogayukto bhavārjuna|| 27||

वेदेषु यज्ञेषु तपःसु चैव दानेषु यत्पुण्यफलं प्रदिष्टम्।
अत्येति तत्सर्वमिदं विदित्वा योगी परं स्थानमुपैति चाद्यम्॥ २८॥

vedeṣu yajñeṣu tapaḥsu caiva dāneṣu yat puṇyaphalaṃ pradiṣṭam|
atyeti tat sarvam idaṃ viditvā yogī paraṃ sthānam upaiti cādyam||
28||

Flame, fire,[211] the day, the bright fortnight,
The six months when the sun moves north,[212]
If they who know the Brahm depart
At "times" like these, they go to Brahm. 24

Smoke, night time, and the dark fortnight,
The six months when the sun moves south,[213]
The *yogin* who at such "times" dies,
The moonlight[214] gaining comes again. 25

This two-fold path, the bright and dark,
Is deemed the world's eternal track,
For by the one men come not back,
And by the other they return.[215] 26

O son of Pṛthā, knowing these,[216]
No *yogin* can deluded be.[217]
Therefore I say unceasingly,
O Arjun, steadfast be in *yoga*. 27

Whatever reward the Vedas ordain
For penances, sacrifice, or gifts,
The *yogin* knowing *this* beyond them goes,
And reaches the supreme and primal home. 28

---

[211]Flame and fire (also smoke in the next verse) also refer to the deities presiding over time, or to the deities of flame, fire and smoke respectively.
[212]The six months of the northern solstice.
[213]The six months of the southern solstice.
[214]The moon is one of the "heavens" of Hindu mythology.
[215]The bright path leads to *mokṣa*, the dark path to *saṃsāra*.
[216]I.e., these paths.
[217]Because he knows where these paths lead to.

Chapter Nine: The Yoga of the King of Secrets (राजगुह्ययोगः)

श्रीभगवानुवाच

इदं तु ते गुह्यतमं प्रवक्ष्याम्यनसूयवे।
ज्ञानं विज्ञानसहितं यज्ज्ञात्वा मोक्ष्यसे ऽशुभात्॥ १॥

śrībhagavān uvāca

idaṃ tu te guhyatamaṃ pravakṣyāmyanasūyave|
jñānaṃ vijñānasahitaṃ yaj jñātvā mokṣyase 'śubhāt|| 1||

राजविद्या राजगुह्यं पवित्रमिदमुत्तमम्।
प्रत्यक्षावगमं धर्म्यं सुसुखं कर्तुमव्ययम्॥ २॥

rājavidyā rājaguhyaṃ pavitram idam uttamam|
pratyakṣāvagamaṃ dharmyaṃ susukhaṃ kartum avyayam|| 2||

अश्रद्दधानाः पुरुषा धर्मस्यास्य परंतप।
अप्राप्य मां निवर्तन्ते मृत्युसंसारवर्त्मनि॥ ३॥

aśraddadhānāḥ puruṣā dharmasyāsya paraṃtapa|
aprāpya māṃ nivartante mṛtyusaṃsāravartmani|| 3||

मया ततमिदं सर्वं जगदव्यक्तमूर्तिना।
मत्स्थानि सर्वभूतानि न चाहं तेष्ववस्थितः॥ ४॥

mayā tatam idaṃ sarvaṃ jagad avyaktamūrtinā|
matsthāni sarvabhūtāni na cāhaṃ teṣv avasthitaḥ|| 4||

न च मत्स्थानि भूतानि पश्य मे योगमैश्वरम्।
भूतभृन्न च भूतस्थो ममात्मा भूतभावनः॥ ५॥

na ca matsthāni bhūtāni paśya me yogam aiśvaram|
bhūtabhṛn na ca bhūtastho mamātmā bhūtabhāvanaḥ|| 5||

यथाकाशस्थितो नित्यं वायुः सर्वत्रगो महान्।
तथा सर्वाणि भूतानि मत्स्थानीत्युपधारय॥ ६॥

yathākāśasthito nityaṃ vāyuḥ sarvatrago mahān|
tathā sarvāṇi bhūtāni matsthānītyupadhāraya|| 6||

The Blessed Lord said:

To thee who art from carping free,
The greatest secret I'll decare,
Wisdom[218] combined with knowledge[219] now,
Which knowing thou shalt freedom[220] gain. 1

A royal lore and mystery,
The best of sanctifiers this,
Of easy practice, plainly seen,[221]
Unperishing, not 'gainst the law.[222] 2

Those who have no faith in this lore,
O Parantap, not reaching me,
Come back again assuredly,
To tread this world of death anew. 3

By me, in my own subtle form,[223]
Pervaded is the universe,
In me indeed all creatures dwell,
But I dwell not in them at all. 4

Ah no! they do not dwell in me;
Behold and mark my mystic pow'r!
Though I'm the cause and stay of all,
Yet I myself do dwell in naught. 5

Just as the mighty atmosphere
Moves everywhere contained in space,
Know thou that in this very wise,
All things created dwell in me.[224] 6

---

[218] *Vijñāna.*
[219] *Jñāna.*
[220] I.e., from the evil of *saṃsāra.*
[221] I.e., directly or intuitively perceived.
[222] *Dharma*, which here implies self-knowledge.
[223] I.e., in my unmanifested form.
[224] The purport is that just as the atmosphere rests and moves in space without affecting it or its nature, so do all things rest in me, without affecting me.

सर्वभूतानि कौन्तेय प्रकृतिं यान्ति मामिकाम्।
कल्पक्षये पुनस्तानि कल्पादौ विसृजाम्यहम्॥ ७॥

sarvabhūtāni kaunteya prakṛtiṃ yānti māmikām|
kalpakṣaye punas tāni kalpādau visṛjāmy aham|| 7||

प्रकृतिं स्वामवष्टभ्य विसृजामि पुनः पुनः।
भूतग्राममिमं कृत्स्नमवशं प्रकृतेर्वशात्॥ ८॥

prakṛtiṃ svām avaṣṭabhya visṛjāmi punaḥ punaḥ|
bhūtagrāmam imaṃ kṛtsnam avaśaṃ prakṛtervaśāt|| 8||

न च मां तानि कर्माणि निबध्नन्ति धनंजय।
उदासीनवदासीनमसक्तं तेषु कर्मसु॥ ९॥

na ca māṃ tāni karmāṇi nibadhnanti dhanaṃjaya|
udāsīnavad āsīnam asaktaṃ teṣu karmasu|| 9||

मयाध्यक्षेण प्रकृतिः सूयते सचराचरम्।
हेतुनानेन कौन्तेय जगद्विपरिवर्तते॥ १०॥

mayādhyakṣeṇa prakṛtiḥ sūyate sacarācaram|
hetunānena kaunteya jagad viparivartate|| 10||

अवजानन्ति मां मूढा मानुषीं तनुमाश्रितम्।
परं भावमजानन्तो मम भूतमहेश्वरम्॥ ११॥

avajānanti māṃ mūḍhā mānuṣīṃ tanum āśritam|
paraṃ bhāvam ajānanto mama bhūtamaheśvaram|| 11||

मोघाशा मोघकर्माणो मोघज्ञाना विचेतसः।
राक्षसीमासुरीं चैव प्रकृतिं मोहिनीं श्रिताः॥ १२॥

moghāśā moghakarmāṇo moghajñānā vicetasaḥ|
rākṣasīm āsurīṃ caiva prakṛtiṃ mohinīṃ śritāḥ|| 12||

When ends an age[225] all beings go
Into my nature,[226] Kuntī's son,
And when another age[227] begins,
I send them forth from me again. 7

Resorting to my nature[228] I
Do send forth o'er and o'er again,
This swarm of all created things,
Controlled by nature helplessly. 8

Nor do these actions fetter me,
For I, O Dhanañjay, remain
As one without the least concern,
And to those actions unattached. 9

Through me, the supervisor, nature doth
Bring forth what moves and moveth not;
It is because I supervise,
That the world revolves, O Kuntī's son. 10

The witless ones hold me in scorn,
As one who's clothed in human form,
Discerning not my higher state
As sovereign paramount of all. 11

Their hopes are vain, their deeds are vain,
Their wisdom's vain, they have no sense;
To the deceitful nature they
Of fiends and demons[229] wedded are. 12

---

[225]*Kalpa*. The beginning of a *kalpa* is the time of production and the end of a *kalpa* that of dissolution of created beings.
[226]*Prakṛti*. My *prakṛti*, the lower *prakṛti* consisting of undifferentiated matter.
[227]Again, *kalpa*.
[228]*Prakṛti*.
[229]*Rākṣasas* and *asuras*.

महात्मानस्तु मां पार्थ दैवीं प्रकृतिमाश्रिताः।
भजन्त्यनन्यमनसो ज्ञात्वा भूतादिमव्ययम्॥ १३॥

mahātmānas tu māṃ pārtha daivīṃ prakṛtim āśritāḥ|
bhajanty ananyamanaso jñātvā bhūtādim avyayam|| 13||

सततं कीर्तयन्तो मां यतन्तश्च दृढव्रताः।
नमस्यन्तश्च मां भक्त्या नित्ययुक्ता उपासते॥ १४॥

satataṃ kīrtayanto māṃ yatantaś ca dṛḍhavratāḥ|
namasyantaś ca māṃ bhaktyā nityayuktā upāsate|| 14||

ज्ञानयज्ञेन चाप्यन्ये यजन्तो मामुपासते।
एकत्वेन पृथक्त्वेन बहुधा विश्वतोमुखम्॥ १५॥

jñānayajñena cāpy anye yajanto mām upāsate|
ekatvena pṛthaktvena bahudhā viśvatomukham|| 15||

अहं क्रतुरहं यज्ञः स्वधाहम् अहमौषधम्।
मन्त्रो ऽहमहमेवाज्यमहमग्निरहं हुतम्॥ १६॥

ahaṃ kratur ahaṃ yajñaḥ svadhāham aham auṣadham|
mantro 'ham aham evājyam aham agniraham hutam|| 16||

पिताहमस्य जगतो माता धाता पितामहः।
वेद्यं पवित्रमोंकार ऋक् साम यजुरेव च॥ १७॥

pitāham asya jagato mātā dhātā pitāmahaḥ|
vedyaṃ pavitram oṃkāra ṛk sāma yajureva ca|| 17||

गतिर्भर्ता प्रभुः साक्षी निवासः शरणं सुहृत्।
प्रभवः प्रलयः स्थानं निधानं बीजमव्ययम्॥ १८॥

gatirbhartā prabhuḥ sākṣī nivāsaḥ śaraṇaṃ suhṛt|
prabhavaḥ pralayaḥ sthānaṃ nidhānaṃ bījam avyayam|| 18||

Whereas the great-souled, Pṛthā's son,
Possess a godlike nature, and
Know me, the deathless source of all,
And worship me with single mind.[230] 13

Engaged always in praising me,
And striving ever,[231] firm in vows,
Always attuned and reverent,
They truly worship me with love. 14

By offering wisdom-sacrifice,[232]
Yet other men do worship me;
The one, the many, everywhere,
In countless forms made manifest. 15

I am the prayer,[233] the sacrifice,[234]
For manes food, I healing herb,
The chant, the sacrificial ghee,
The fire as well, the offering burnt; 16

The father of this world I am,
Creator, mother, and grandsire,
The knowable, the cleanser I,
The sacred "om," the triple Veda;[235] 17

The goal I am, the lord, the home,[236]
Sustainer, seer, shelter, friend,
The source, the end, the stay am I,
The treasure house,[237] the deathless seed.; 18

---

[230] I.e., with unwavering mind.
[231] For *brahma-jñāna*.
[232] "The homage of intellectual worship."
[233] In the original, *kratu*, a Vedic sacrifice.
[234] In the original, *yajña*, a sacrifice laid down in the Smṛtis.
[235] The *Ṛk*, the *Sāman* and the *Yajus*.
[236] I.e., the abode or the place where all things dwell.
[237] I.e., the receptacle, the place of deposit where things are preserved.

तपाम्यहमहं वर्षं निगृह्णाम्युत्सृजामि च।
अमृतं चैव मृत्युश्च सदसच्चाहमर्जुन॥ १९॥

tapāmy aham ahaṃ varṣaṃ nigṛhṇāmy utsṛjāmi ca|
amṛtaṃ caiva mṛtyuś ca sadasac cāham arjuna|| 19||

त्रैविद्या मां सोमपाः पूतपापा यज्ञैरिष्ट्वा स्वर्गतिं प्रार्थयन्ते।
ते पुण्यमासाद्य सुरेन्द्रलोकमश्नन्ति दिव्यान्दिवि देवभोगान्॥ २०॥

traividyā māṃ somapāḥ pūtapāpā yajñair iṣṭvā svargatiṃ prārthayante|
te puṇyam āsādya surendralokam aśnanti divyān divi devab-
hogān|| 20||

ते तं भुक्त्वा स्वर्गलोकं विशालं क्षीणे पुण्ये मर्त्यलोकं विशन्ति।
एवं त्रयीधर्ममनुप्रपन्ना गतागतं कामकामा लभन्ते॥ २१॥

te taṃ bhuktvā svargalokaṃ viśālaṃ kṣīṇe puṇye martyalokaṃ
viśanti|
evaṃ trayīdharmam anuprapannā gatāgataṃ kāmakāmā lab-
hante|| 21||

अनन्याश्चिन्तयन्तो मां ये जनाः पर्युपासते।
तेषां नित्याभियुक्तानां योगक्षेमं वहाम्यहम्॥ २२॥

ananyāś cintayanto māṃ ye janāḥ paryupāsate|
teṣāṃ nityābhiyuktānāṃ yogakṣemaṃ vahāmy aham|| 22||

ये ऽप्यन्यदेवताभक्ता यजन्ते श्रद्धयान्विताः।
ते ऽपि मामेव कौन्तेय यजन्त्यविधिपूर्वकम्॥ २३॥

ye 'py anyadevatābhaktā yajante śraddhayānvitāḥ|
te 'pi mām eva kaunteya yajanty avidhipūrvakam|| 23||

अहं हि सर्वयज्ञानां भोक्ता च प्रभुरेव च।
न तु मामभिजानन्ति तत्त्वेनातश्च्यवन्ति ते॥ २४॥

ahaṃ hi sarvayajñānāṃ bhoktā ca prabhur eva ca|
na tu mām abhijānanti tattvenātaś cyavanti te|| 24||

The giver of the heat I am,
I send forth rain, I hold it back,
I'm deathlessness[238] and I am death,
Sat and *asat*,[239] O Pṛthā's son. 19

Who know the Vedas, who drink the soma juice,
Sin-purged, who pray for heaven adoring me,[240]
Great Indra's holy world they reach at last,
And there enjoy the pleasures of the gods. 20

Having enjoyed that spacious heavenly world,
Their merit spent, they come to earth once more,
Desiring things, obeying Vedic law,
For their reward they have to come and go.[241] 21

For those who worship me alone,
And think of none except myself,
Who always are attuned with me,
Both gain and safety I secure.[242] 22

The devotees of other gods,
Who worship them in faith sincere,
These also, know, O Kuntī's son,
Though wrongly,[243] yet they worship me. 23

Of every sacrifice I am
The lord and the enjoyer both,
But me they know not as I am,[244]
And for this reason do they fail.[245] 24

---

[238]Immortality
[239]Existence and non-existence—"the final pair of opposites beyond which is only the one" (Mrs. Besant).
[240]Offering sacrifices to me.
[241]I.e., they attain only to transitory states involving going and coming.
[242]Gain, i.e., what they have not; safety, i.e., perservation of what they already have.
[243]Because in outer form they worship othr gods.
[244]I.e., not as I am in reality.
[245]To attain *mokṣa*.

यान्ति देवव्रता देवान्पितॄन्यान्ति पितृव्रताः।
भूतानि यान्ति भूतेज्या यान्ति मद्याजिनो ऽपि माम्॥ २५॥

yānti devavratā devān pitṝn yānti pitṛvratāḥ|
bhūtāni yānti bhūtejyā yānti madyājino 'pi mām|| 25||

पत्रं पुष्पं फलं तोयं यो मे भक्त्या प्रयच्छति।
तदहं भक्त्युपहृतमश्नामि प्रयतात्मनः॥ २६॥

patraṃ puṣpaṃ phalaṃ toyaṃ yo me bhaktyā prayacchati|
tad ahaṃ bhaktyupahṛtam aśnāmi prayatātmanaḥ|| 26||

यत्करोषि यदश्नासि यज्जुहोषि ददासि यत्।
यत्तपस्यसि कौन्तेय तत्कुरुष्व मदर्पणम्॥ २७॥

yat karoṣi yad aśnāsi yaj juhoṣi dadāsi yat|
yat tapasyasi kaunteya tat kuruṣva madarpaṇam|| 27||

शुभाशुभफलैरेवं मोक्ष्यसे कर्मबन्धनैः।
संन्यासयोगयुक्तात्मा विमुक्तो मामुपैष्यसि॥ २८॥

śubhāśubhaphalair evaṃ mokṣyase karmabandhanaiḥ|
saṃnyāsayogayuktātmā vimukto mām upaiṣyasi|| 28||

समो ऽहं सर्वभूतेषु न मे द्वेष्यो ऽस्ति न प्रियः।
ये भजन्ति तु मां भक्त्या मयि ते तेषु चाप्यहम्॥ २९॥

samo 'haṃ sarvabhūteṣu na me dveṣyo 'sti na priyaḥ|
ye bhajanti tu māṃ bhaktyā mayi te teṣu cāpy aham|| 29||

अपि चेत्सुदुराचारो भजते मामनन्यभाक्।
साधुरेव स मन्तव्यः सम्यग्व्यवसितो हि सः॥ ३०॥

api cet sudurācāro bhajate mām ananyabhāk|
sādhur eva sa mantavyaḥ samyag vyavasito hi saḥ|| 30||

They go to gods who worship gods,
Who *manes* seek to *manes*[246] go,
Who worship *bhūtas* go to *bhūtas*,[247]
My worshipers come unto me. 25

Whoever offers me in love
A leaf or water, flow'r or fruit,
Such gift of love do I accept
From those who in their hearts are pure. 26

Whate'er thy work, whate'er thy food,
Whate'er thy sacrifice, thy alms,
Whate'er the penance thou must do,
That dedicate to me, O Pārtha. 27

Deliv'rance thus shalt thou attain
From bonds of action, good or ill;
Renouncing all,[248] a freed man thou
Shalt come to me assuredly. 28

The same am I to all that lives,
To me none hateful is or dear,[249]
But they who worship me in love,
They dwell in me, and I in them. 29

If even one immersed in sin
Should worship me wholeheartedly,
He must a righteous man be deemed,
For his resolve is right indeed.[250] 30

---

[246]*Manes*, ancestral spirits in Roman religion, but used here for *pitṝn*, the forefathers or ancestors. [Sans. Ed.]

[247]Elementals, or nature-spirits.

[248]Lit. attuned to me by the *yoga* of renunciation.

[249]This verse is apparently incompatible with the beautiful verses at the end of the Twelfth Discourse. The true purport of the verse is to indicate the perfect impartiality of God in his dealings with men.

[250]Because he worships the one supreme being.

क्षिप्रं भवति धर्मात्मा शश्वच्छान्तिं निगच्छति।
कौन्तेय प्रतिजानीहि न मे भक्तः प्रणश्यति॥ ३१॥

kṣipraṃ bhavati dharmātmā śaśvacchāntiṃ nigacchati|
kaunteya pratijānīhi na me bhaktaḥ praṇaśyati|| 31||

मां हि पार्थ व्यपाश्रित्य ये ऽपि स्युः पापयोनयः।
स्त्रियो वैश्यास्तथा शूद्रास्ते ऽपि यान्ति परां गतिम्॥ ३२॥

māṃ hi pārtha vyapāśritya ye 'pi syuḥ pāpayonayaḥ|
striyo vaiśyās tathā śūdrās te 'pi yānti parāṃ gatim|| 32||

किं पुनर्ब्राह्मणाः पुण्या भक्ता राजर्षयस्तथा।
अनित्यमसुखं लोकमिमं प्राप्य भजस्व माम्॥ ३३॥

kiṃ punar brāhmaṇāḥ puṇyā bhaktā rājarṣayas tathā|
anityam asukhaṃ lokam imaṃ prāpya bhajasva mām|| 33||

मन्मना भव मद्भक्तो मद्याजी मां नमस्कुरु।
मामेवैष्यसि युक्त्वैवमात्मानं मत्परायणः॥ ३४॥

manmanā bhava madbhakto madyājī māṃ namaskuru|
mām evaiṣyasi yuktvaivam ātmānaṃ matparāyaṇaḥ|| 34||

Ere long a saint he doth become,[251]
And findeth everlasting peace;
O Kuntī's son, do thou proclaim,
My lover he is never lost! 31

O Pārtha, those who refuge take
In me, though born of sinful wombs,
The *vaiśyas*, *śūdras*, womenfolk,
They too attain the goal supreme. 32

Much more the holy brahmins then,
And royal saints, my votaries;
Hence in this joyless, passing world,
Do thou, O Arjun, worship me. 33

Thy heart, thy love bestow on me,
Thy sacrifice and homage too,
Thus with the self attuned, thou shalt
Come unto me, thy goal supreme. 34

---

[251] A saint: i.e., a holy soul.

Chapter Ten: The Yoga of Expansion (विभूतियोगः)

श्रीभगवानुवाच

भूय एव महाबाहो शृणु मे परमं वचः।
यत् ते ऽहं प्रीयमाणाय वक्ष्यामि हितकाम्यया॥ १॥

śrībhagavān uvāca

bhūya eva mahābāho śṛṇu me paramaṃ vacaḥ|
yat te 'haṃ prīyamāṇāya vakṣyāmi hitakāmyayā|| 1||

न मे विदुः सुरगणाः प्रभवं न महर्षयः।
अहमादिर्हि देवानां महर्षीणां च सर्वशः॥ २॥

na me viduḥ suragaṇāḥ prabhavaṃ na maharṣayaḥ|
aham ādirhi devānāṃ maharṣīṇāṃ ca sarvaśaḥ|| 2||

यो मामजमनादिं च वेत्ति लोकमहेश्वरम्।
असंमूढः स मर्त्येषु सर्वपापैः प्रमुच्यते॥ ३॥

yo māṃ ajam anādiṃ ca vetti lokamaheśvaram|
asaṃmūḍhaḥ sa martyeṣu sarvapāpaiḥ pramucyate|| 3||

बुद्धिर्ज्ञानमसंमोहः क्षमा सत्यं दमः शमः।
सुखं दुःखं भवो ऽभावो भयं चाभयमेव च॥ ४॥

buddhir jñānam asaṃmohaḥ kṣamā satyaṃ damaḥ śamaḥ|
sukhaṃ duḥkhaṃ bhavo 'bhāvo bhayaṃ cābhayam eva ca|| 4||

अहिंसा समता तुष्टिस्तपो दानं यशो ऽयशः।
भवन्ति भावा भूतानां मत्त एव पृथग्विधाः॥ ५॥

ahiṃsā samatā tuṣṭis tapo dānaṃ yaśo 'yaśaḥ|
bhavanti bhāvā bhūtānāṃ matta eva pṛthagvidhāḥ|| 5||

महर्षयः सप्त पूर्वे चत्वारो मनवस्तथा।
मद्भावा मानसा जाता येषां लोक इमाः प्रजाः॥ ६॥

maharṣayaḥ sapta pūrve catvāro manavastathā|
madbhāvā mānasā jātā yeṣāṃ loka imāḥ prajāḥ|| 6||

The Blessed Lord said:

O mighty armed! give ear again
To my supernal word,
Which I will utter for thy good,
Who my beloved art. 1[252]

Neither the host of shining ones,
Nor mighty *ṛṣis* know
My origin, for I have made
The gods and *ṛṣis* both. 2

Beginning have I not, nor end,
I am the world's great lord,
Who knows me thus, he knows the truth,
And is from all sin freed. 3

Forgiveness, reason, truth and calm,
And non-delusion too,
Restraint and wisdom, joy and pain,
Fear, courage, birth and death, 4

Content, composure, harmlessness,
Gifts, pleasure, fame and shame,
These several moods of living things
Come forth from me alone. 5

The ancient four,[253] the Manus too,[254]
The seven *ṛṣis* great,[255]
Were from my mind and nature born,
And from them sprang the world. 6

---

[252]Verses 1-11 have an alternative meter for aesthetic purposes. Sir Edwin Arnold does the same in his translation on the grounds that the poem is gaining momentum. It's reasonable considering that verses 8 to 11 are considered by many to the kernel of the whole text.

[253]The four virgin youths, the highest in the hierarchy of this earth.

[254]Fourteen in number. Each appointed to preside over a cycle of 4,320,000 years.

[255]Like Bhṛgu, born like the other two groups from the mind of Brahmā to inaugurate Brahmā's day-creation.

एतां विभूतिं योगं च मम यो वेत्ति तत्त्वतः।
सो ऽविकम्पेन योगेन युज्यते नात्र संशयः॥ ७॥

etāṃ vibhūtiṃ yogaṃ ca mama yo vetti tattvataḥ|
so 'vikampena yogena yujyate nātra saṃśayaḥ|| 7||

अहं सर्वस्य प्रभवो मत्तः सर्वं प्रवर्तते।
इति मत्वा भजन्ते मां बुधा भावसमन्विताः॥ ८॥

ahaṃ sarvasya prabhavo mattaḥ sarvaṃ pravartate|
iti matvā bhajante māṃ budhā bhāvasamanvitāḥ|| 8||

मच्चित्ता मद्गतप्राणा बोधयन्तः परस्परम्।
कथयन्तश्च मां नित्यं तुष्यन्ति च रमन्ति च॥ ९॥

maccittā madgataprāṇā bodhayantaḥ parasparam|
kathayantaś ca māṃ nityaṃ tuṣyanti ca ramanti ca|| 9||

तेषां सततयुक्तानां भजतां प्रीतिपूर्वकम्।
ददामि बुद्धियोगं तं येन मामुपयान्ति ते॥ १०॥

teṣāṃ satatayuktānāṃ bhajatāṃ prītipūrvakam|
dadāmi buddhiyogaṃ taṃ yena mām upayānti te|| 10||

तेषामेवानुकम्पार्थमहमज्ञानजं तमः।
नाशयाम्यात्मभावस्थो ज्ञानदीपेन भास्वता॥ ११॥

teṣām evānukampārtham aham ajñānajaṃ tamaḥ|
nāśayāmy ātmabhāvastho jñānadīpena bhāsvatā|| 11||

अर्जुन उवाच

परं ब्रह्म परं धाम पवित्रं परमं भवान्।
पुरुषं शाश्वतं दिव्यमादिदेवमजं विभुम्॥ १२॥

arjuna uvāca

paraṃ brahma paraṃ dhāma pavitraṃ paramaṃ bhavān|
puruṣaṃ śāśvataṃ divyam ādidevam ajaṃ vibhum|| 12||

Whoso in very truth doth know
This yoga and power of mine,
Unfaltering is the yoga he has,
Of this no doubt can be. 7

I am the source of all, from me
All creatures are evolved;
In rapt emotion, thinking thus,
The wise do worship me. 8

Minds fixed in me, lives given to me,
Each praising me to each,
Of me conversing always, they
With joy and peace are filled. 9

To those who ever are attuned,
And worship me with love,
That knowledge[256] do I freely give,
Whereby they come to me. 10

And all for love of them,
Indwelling in their very hearts,
With wisdom's light resplendent I
Their darkness[257] do dispel. 11

Arjun said:

The Brahm supreme, the goal supreme,
Supremely holy art thou lord;
Th'eternal being, the divine,
First of gods, unborn, the lord! 12

---

[256] *Buddhi-yoga*, discriminating knowledge.
[257] In the original, darkness born of ignorance.

आहुस्त्वामृषयः सर्वे देवर्षिर्नारदस्तथा।
असितो देवलो व्यासः स्वयं चैव ब्रवीषि मे॥ १३॥

āhus tvām ṛṣayaḥ sarve devarṣir nāradas tathā|
asito devalo vyāsaḥ svayaṃ caiva bravīṣi me|| 13||

सर्वमेतदृतं मन्ये यन्मां वदसि केशव।
न हि ते भगवन्व्यक्तिं विदुर्देवा न दानवाः॥ १४॥

sarvam etad ṛtaṃ manye yan māṃ vadasi keśava|
na hi te bhagavan vyaktiṃ vidur devā na dānavāḥ|| 14||

स्वयमेवात्मनात्मानं वेत्थ त्वं पुरुषोत्तम।
भूतभावन भूतेश देवदेव जगत्पते॥ १५॥

svayam evātmanātmānaṃ vettha tvaṃ puruṣottama|
bhūtabhāvana bhūteśa devadeva jagatpate|| 15||

वक्तुमर्हस्यशेषेण दिव्या ह्यात्मविभूतयः।
याभिर्विभूतिभिर्लोकानिमांस्त्वं व्याप्य तिष्ठसि॥ १६॥

vaktum arhasy aśeṣeṇa divyā hy ātmavibhūtayaḥ|
yābhir vibhūtibhir lokān imāṃs tvaṃ vyāpya tiṣṭhasi|| 16||

कथं विद्यामहं योगिंस्त्वां सदा परिचिन्तयन्।
केषु केषु च भावेषु चिन्त्यो ऽसि भगवन्मया॥ १७॥

kathaṃ vidyām ahaṃ yogiṃs tvāṃ sadā paricintayan|
keṣu keṣu ca bhāveṣu cintyo 'si bhagavan mayā|| 17||

विस्तरेणात्मनो योगं विभूतिं च जनार्दन।
भूयः कथय तृप्तिर्हि शृण्वतो नास्ति मे ऽमृतम्॥ १८॥

vistareṇātmano yogaṃ vibhūtiṃ ca janārdana|
bhūyaḥ kathaya tṛptir hi śṛṇvato nāsti me 'mṛtam|| 18||

Thus all the *ṛṣis* thee acclaim,
Asita and Devala, also Vyāsa,
And Nārad too the sage divine,
And thine own lips confirm the same. 13

What thou hast said to me I deem,
O Keśav, as the very truth,
Thy manifested forms, O lord,
Nor gods nor demons[258] ever know. 14

O best of beings, only thou
Dost know thyself by thine own self;
The source of all, the lord of all,
World-ruler and the god of gods. 15

Without reserve be pleased to tell
Of thine own godlike[259] glory now;
The glory wherewith thou doth dwell,
Pervading all the universe. 16

By constant meditation how,
O yogin, can I know thyself?
What are the aspects,[260] lord, in which
I ought to meditate on thee? 17

O Janārdan, tell me again,
In fullness of thy pow'r[261] and *yoga*,
For of the nectar of thy words
Mine ears can never drink enough. 18

[258]The *dānavas*, or evil spirits.

[259]I.e., divine.

[260]Since to know thee fully is impossible, in what special manifestations of thine ought I to meditate on thee?

[261] *Vibhūti*, translated as glory in this book.

श्रीभगवानुवाच
हन्त ते कथयिष्यामि दिव्या ह्यात्मविभूतयः।
प्राधान्यतः कुरुश्रेष्ठ नास्त्यन्तो विस्तरस्य मे॥ १९॥

śrībhagavān uvāca
hanta te kathayiṣyāmi divyā hy ātmavibhūtayaḥ|
prādhānyataḥ kuruśreṣṭha nāsty anto vistarasya me|| 19||

अहमात्मा गुडाकेश सर्वभूताशयस्थितः।
अहमादिश्च मध्यं च भूतानामन्त एव च॥ २०॥

aham ātmā guḍākeśa sarvabhūtāśayasthitaḥ|
aham ādiśca madhyaṃ ca bhūtānām anta eva ca|| 20||

आदित्यानामहं विष्णुर्ज्योतिषां रविरंशुमान्।
मरीचिर्मरुतामस्मि नक्षत्राणामहं शशी॥ २१॥

ādityānām ahaṃ viṣṇur jyotiṣāṃ ravir aṃśumān|
marīcir marutām asmi nakṣatrāṇām ahaṃ śaśī|| 21||

वेदानां सामवेदोऽस्मि देवानामस्मि वासवः।
इन्द्रियाणां मनश्चास्मि भूतानामस्मि चेतना॥ २२॥

vedānāṃ sāmavedo 'smi devānām asmi vāsavaḥ|
indriyāṇāṃ manaś cāsmi bhūtānām asmi cetanā|| 22||

रुद्राणां शंकरश्चास्मि वित्तेशो यक्षरक्षसाम्।
वसूनां पावकश्चास्मि मेरुः शिखरिणामहम्॥ २३॥

rudrāṇāṃ śaṃkaraś cāsmi vitteśo yakṣarakṣasām|
vasūnāṃ pāvakaś cāsmi meruḥ śikhariṇām aham|| 23||

पुरोधसां च मुख्यं मां विद्धि पार्थ बृहस्पतिम्।
सेनानीनामहं स्कन्दः सरसामस्मि सागरः॥ २४॥

purodhasāṃ ca mukhyaṃ māṃ viddhi pārtha bṛhaspatim|
senānīnām ahaṃ skandaḥ sarasām asmi sāgaraḥ|| 24||

The Blessed Lord said:

Yea, best of Kurus, I'll unfold
My glories in their prominence,[262]
There is indeed no limit set
To all the glories I possess. 19

I am the self, O Guḍākeś,
In every being's heart enshrined;
Of every living creature I
Beginning am, and mean, and end. 20

Of the Ādityas[263] Viṣṇu I,
Of shining orbs the radiant sun,
Of Maruts I Marīci[264] am,
'Midst constellations I the moon. 21

Of Vedas I'm the Sāman Veda,
I'm Vāsava of the shining ones,
And of the senses I am mind,
And consciousness in all that lives. 22

And I of Rudras Śaṅkara am,[265]
Of jinns and ogre hosts, wealth-lord,[266]
Of Vasus I'm the god of fire,[267]
And Meru of all mountain peaks.[268] 23

Of household priests, O Pṛthā's son,
I am the chief Bṛhaspati,[269]
And of commanders I am Skanda,[270]
And ocean vast of all the lakes. 24

---

[262] I.e., the salient features of my glories.

[263] The Ādityas or sun-gods, are twelve in number, of whom the chief bears the name of Viṣṇu.

[264] The wind-gods, forty-nine in number, Marīci being the chief.

[265] The Rudras are terror-gods, eleven in number, of whom Śaṅkara is the chief.

[266] Kubera, the lord of wealth, is the chief of the Yakṣas and Rākṣasas, jinn and goblins.

[267] The Vasus are eight in number, of whom the fire-god, Agni, is the chief.

[268] Meru is the highest mountain peak in Hindu mythological geography.

[269] The household priest of Indra.

[270] The second son of Śiva, commanding the armies of the Devas.

महर्षीणां भृगुरहं गिरामस्म्येकमक्षरम्।
यज्ञानां जपयज्ञो ऽस्मि स्थावराणां हिमालयः॥ २५॥

maharṣīṇāṃ bhṛgur ahaṃ girām asmy ekam akṣaram|
yajñānāṃ japayajño 'smi sthāvarāṇāṃ himālayaḥ|| 25||

अश्वत्थः सर्ववृक्षाणां देवर्षीणां च नारदः।
गन्धर्वाणां चित्ररथः सिद्धानां कपिलो मुनिः॥ २६॥

aśvatthaḥ sarvavṛkṣāṇāṃ devarṣīṇāṃ ca nāradaḥ|
gandharvāṇāṃ citrarathaḥ siddhānāṃ kapilo muniḥ|| 26||

उच्चैःश्रवसमश्वानां विद्धि माममृतोद्भवम्।
ऐरावतं गजेन्द्राणां नराणां च नराधिपम्॥ २७॥

uccaiḥśravasam aśvānāṃ viddhi mām amṛtodbhavam|
airāvataṃ gajendrāṇāṃ narāṇāṃ ca narādhipam|| 27||

आयुधानामहं वज्रं धेनूनामस्मि कामधुक्।
प्रजनश्चास्मि कन्दर्पः सर्पाणामस्मि वासुकिः॥ २८॥

āyudhānām ahaṃ vajraṃ dhenūnām asmi kāmadhuk|
prajanaś cāsmi kandarpaḥ sarpāṇām asmi vāsukiḥ|| 28||

अनन्तश्चास्मि नागानां वरुणो यादसामहम्।
पितॄणामर्यमा चास्मि यमः संयमतामहम्॥ २९॥

anantaś cāsmi nāgānāṃ varuṇo yādasām aham|
pitṝṇām aryamā cāsmi yamaḥ saṃyamatām aham|| 29||

Of mighty *ṛṣis* Bhṛgu I,
Of words the one-syllabled "om,"
Of sacrifices I am *japa*,[271]
Of fixed things Himālaya. 25

I am the banyan[272] of the trees,
And Nārad[273] of the heavenly saints,
Of Gandharvas I am Chitrarath,[274]
And of perfect sages, Kapil wise.[275] 26

Amongst the horses know thou me,
The *amṛt*-born Ucchaiḥśravas,[276]
Of lordly tuskers Airāvat,[277]
And king am I of all mankind. 27

Of weapons I'm the thunderbolt,
Of cows I am the Kāmadhuk,
I am Kandarpa[278] who procreates,
And of the serpents Vāsuki.[279] 28

And of the *nāgas* I am Ananta,[280]
Of water dwellers Varuṇa[281] I,
Of *pitṛs* I am Aryaman,[282]
Of regulators I am Yam.[283] 29

---

[271]*Japa* is the best of sacrifices; it consists of silent meditation on the deity with the help of reciting some sacred *mantra* with or without the help of beads.

[272]*Aśvattha*, the *ficus religiosa*.

[273]The greatest celestial *ṛṣi*; he also excells in music.

[274]The chief of the Gandharvas, celestial musicians.

[275]The great sage who propounded the *Sāṅkhya* philosophy.

[276]Indra's horse, brought up at the churning of the ocean by the Devas and the Asuras (demons) combined.

[277]Indra's elephant.

[278]Love, the motive for progeny, not merely carnal passion.

[279]The seven-headed serpent which in Hindu mythology carries the earth upon one of its hoods.

[280]The king of venom-less snakes.

[281]Varuṇa is the sea-god.

[282]Aryaman is the king of the *manes*.

[283]Yama is the god of death, the Hindu Pluto.

प्रह्लादश्चास्मि दैत्यानां कालः कलयतामहम्।
मृगाणां च मृगेन्द्रोऽहं वैनतेयश्च पक्षिणाम्॥ ३०॥

prahlādaś cāsmi daityānāṃ kālaḥ kalayatām aham|
mṛgāṇāṃ ca mṛgendro 'haṃ vainateyaś ca pakṣiṇām|| 30||

पवनः पवतामस्मि रामः शस्त्रभृतामहम्।
झषाणां मकरश्चास्मि स्रोतसामस्मि जाह्नवी॥ ३१॥

pavanaḥ pavatām asmi rāmaḥ śastrabhṛtām aham|
jhaṣāṇāṃ makaraś cāsmi srotasām asmi jāhnavī|| 31||

सर्गाणामादिरन्तश्च मध्यं चैवाहमर्जुन।
अध्यात्मविद्या विद्यानां वादः प्रवदतामहम्॥ ३२॥

sargāṇām ādir antaś ca madhyaṃ caivāham arjuna|
adhyātmavidyā vidyānāṃ vādaḥ pravadatām aham|| 32||

अक्षराणामकारोऽस्मि द्वन्द्वः सामासिकस्य च।
अहमेवाक्षयः कालो धाताहं विश्वतोमुखः॥ ३३॥

akṣarāṇām akāro 'smi dvandvaḥ sāmāsikasya ca|
aham evākṣayaḥ kālo dhātāhaṃ viśvatomukhaḥ|| 33||

मृत्युः सर्वहरश्चाहमुद्भवश्च भविष्यताम्।
कीर्तिः श्रीर्वाक् च नारीणां स्मृतिर्मेधा धृतिः क्षमा॥ ३४॥

mṛtyuḥ sarvaharaś cāham udbhavaśca bhaviṣyatām|
kīrtiḥ śrīr vāk ca nārīṇāṃ smṛtir medhā dhṛtiḥ kṣamā|| 34||

Of *daityas* know Prahlād[284] I am,
Of reckoners I'm time itself,
Of beasts I am the king of beasts,[285]
And Vainateya[286] of the birds. 30

Of purifiers I'm the wind,
Of weapon wielders Rām[287] himself,
Of aquatic beasts the Makara,[288]
And of the rivers Jāhnavī.[289] 31

Of all creations I'm the source,
The middle and the terminal,
Of sciences self-knowledge I,
And *vāda*[290] 'mongst the arguments. 32

Of letters I the alpha am,
And *dvandva*[291] of conjunctive forms,
I also am eternal time,
And the supporter facing all.[292] 33

And I am all-devouring death,
And source of all that is to be,
'Mongst females[293] I'm Forgiveness, Speech,
Fame, Mem'ry, Fortune, Courage, Mind. 34

---

[284] Prahlāda was the virtuous son of the demon king Hiraṇyakaśipu. The king hated Hari or Viṣṇu whom the son loved. For this reason the king severely oppressed the boy and ultimately tried to kill him. Viṣṇu, for the boy's sake, became incarnate as a man-lion and killed the father.

[285] I.e., the lion.

[286] I.e., the *garuḍa* or eagle on whom Viṣṇu rides.

[287] The hero of the Rāmāyaṇa.

[288] The shark.

[289] I.e., the Ganges, the daughter of the *ṛṣi* Jāhnu.

[290] Arguments are of three kinds: *jalpa*, *vitaṇḍa*, and *vāda*. *Jalpa* is the form of argument by which an adversary is silenced by over-bearing reply. *Vitaṇḍa* is silly carping at the adversary's arguments, and *vāda* is arguing with the object of ascertaining the truth of a proposition.

[291] *Dvandva* is the copulative compound in Sanskrit grammar.

[292] The four-faced demi-urge.

[293] I.e., feminine perfections or the female deities presiding over those qualities.

बृहत्साम तथा साम्नां गायत्री छन्दसामहम्।
मासानां मार्गशीर्षो ऽहमृतूनां कुसुमाकरः॥ ३५॥

bṛhatsāma tathā sāmnāṃ gāyatrī chandasām aham|
māsānāṃ mārgaśīrṣo 'ham ṛtūnāṃ kusumākaraḥ|| 35||

द्यूतं छलयतामस्मि तेजस्तेजस्विनामहम्।
जयो ऽस्मि व्यवसायो ऽस्मि सत्त्वं सत्त्ववतामहम्॥ ३६॥

dyūtaṃ chalayatām asmi tejas tejasvinām aham|
jayo 'smi vyavasāyo 'smi sattvaṃ sattvavatām aham|| 36||

वृष्णीनां वासुदेवो ऽस्मि पाण्डवानां धनंजयः।
मुनीनामप्यहं व्यासः कवीनामुशना कविः॥ ३७॥

vṛṣṇīnāṃ vāsudevo 'smi pāṇḍavānāṃ dhanaṃjayaḥ|
munīnām apy ahaṃ vyāsaḥ kavīnām uśanā kaviḥ|| 37||

दण्डो दमयतामस्मि नीतिरस्मि जिगीषताम्।
मौनं चैवास्मि गुह्यानां ज्ञानं ज्ञानवतामहम्॥ ३८॥

daṇḍo damayatām asmi nītir asmi jigīṣatām|
maunaṃ caivāsmi guhyānāṃ jñānaṃ jñānavatām aham|| 38||

यच्चापि सर्वभूतानां बीजं तदहमर्जुन।
न तदस्ति विना यत्स्यान्मया भूतं चराचरम्॥ ३९॥

yac cāpi sarvabhūtānāṃ bījaṃ tad aham arjuna|
tad asti vinā yat syān mayā bhūtaṃ carācaram|| 39||

नान्तो ऽस्ति मम दिव्यानां विभूतीनां परंतप।
एष तूद्देशतः प्रोक्तो विभूतेर्विस्तरो मया॥ ४०॥

nānto 'sti mama divyānāṃ vibhūtīnāṃ paraṃtapa|
eṣa tūddeśataḥ prokto vibhūter vistaro mayā|| 40||

Of Sāmans[294] I'm the chiefest chant,
Of meters I'm the *gāyatrī*,[295]
Kārtik[296] I am of all the months,
Of seasons flower-laden spring.[297] 35

Of those who cheat I gamb'ling am,
And splendor of the splendid I,
I victory am, I'm industry,
And goodness of the good I am. 36

And of the Vṛṣṇis, Vāsudeva,
And of the Pāṇḍavas, Dhanañjay,
Amongst the sages I am Vyāsa,[298]
Of poets Uśanas the bard.[299] 37

Of chastisers I'm the punishing rod,
Of victory contrivers, Policy,
Of secret things I silence am,
And wisdom of the wise am I. 38[300]

And, Arjun, whatso'er the seed
Of living creatures that I am;
No moving or unmoving thing
Can have existence but for me. 39

O foe tormentor, Parantap,
My heavenly glories endless are,
A sample only have I given
Of my own glory's vast extent. 40

---

[294]I.e., the hymns of the *Sāma Veda*; the chief of those hymns is in praise of Indra, the king of the gods.
[295]A well-known Vedic metre here praised as the best.
[296]*Mārgaśīrṣa*, November.
[297]*Vasanta*, April-May, the season of flowers.
[298]The *ṛṣi* who codified the Vedas.
[299]Uśanas, the son of Bhṛgu, the priest and preceptor of the Daityas.
[300]Editor's interpolation for a missing couplet.

यद्यद्विभूतिमत्सत्त्वं श्रीमदूर्जितमेव वा।
तत्तदेवावगच्छ त्वं मम तेजोंशसंभवम्॥ ४१॥

yad yad vibhūtimat sattvaṃ śrīmadūrjitam eva vā|
tat tad evāvagaccha tvaṃ mama tejoṃśasaṃbhavam|| 41||

अथ वा बहुनैतेन किं ज्ञातेन तवार्जुन।
विष्टभ्याहमिदं कृत्स्नमेकांशेन स्थितो जगत्॥ ४२॥

atha vā bahunaitena kiṃ jñātena tavārjuna|
viṣṭabhyāham idaṃ kṛtsnam ekāṃśena sthito jagat|| 42||

Whatever is of glory, strength,
Of beauty too, know all to be
A showing forth of but a part
Of my own splendor infinite. 41

But, Arjun, what can it avail
To thee, this knowledge vast of me?
By but a fraction of myself
I stand supporting all these worlds. 42

Chapter Eleven: Seeing the Cosmic Form (विश्वरूपदर्शनयोगः)

अर्जुन उवाच

मदनुग्रहाय परमं गुह्यमध्यात्मसंज्ञितम्।
यत्त्वयोक्तं वचस्तेन मोहोऽयं विगतो मम॥ १॥

arjuna uvāca

madanugrahāya paramaṃ guhyam adhyātmasaṃjñitam|
yat tvayoktaṃ vacas tena moho 'yaṃ vigato mama|| 1||

भवाप्ययौ हि भूतानां श्रुतौ विस्तरशो मया।
त्वत्तः कमलपत्राक्ष माहात्म्यमपि चाव्ययम्॥ २॥

bhavāpyayau hi bhūtānāṃ śrutau vistaraśo mayā|
tvattaḥ kamalapatrākṣa māhātmyam api cāvyayam|| 2||

एवमेतद्यथात्थ त्वमात्मानं परमेश्वर।
द्रष्टुमिच्छामि ते रूपमैश्वरं पुरुषोत्तम॥ ३॥

evam etad yathāttha tvam ātmānaṃ parameśvara|
draṣṭum icchāmi te rūpam aiśvaraṃ puruṣottama|| 3||

मन्यसे यदि तच्छक्यं मया द्रष्टुमिति प्रभो।
योगेश्वर ततो मे त्वं दर्शयात्मानमव्ययम्॥ ४॥

manyase yadi tac chakyaṃ mayā draṣṭum iti prabho|
yogeśvara tato me tvaṃ darśayātmānam avyayam|| 4||

श्रीभगवानुवाच

पश्य मे पार्थ रूपाणि शतशोऽथ सहस्रशः।
नानाविधानि दिव्यानि नानावर्णाकृतीनि च॥ ५॥

śrībhagavān uvāca

paśya me pārtha rūpāṇi śataśo 'tha sahasraśaḥ|
nānāvidhāni divyāni nānāvarṇākṛtīni ca|| 5||

पश्यादित्यान् वसून् रुद्रान् अश्विनौ मरुतस्तथा।
बहून्यदृष्टपूर्वाणि पश्याश्चर्याणि भारत॥ ६॥

paśyādityān vasūn rudrān aśvinau marutas tathā|
bahūny adṛṣṭapūrvāṇi paśyāścaryāṇi bhārata|| 6||

Arjun said:

The greatest secret, Adhyātman,
Which for my good thou hast revealed
In thy discourse to me, O lord,
All my delusion[301] hath dispelled. 1

In fullness I have heard from thee
Of all creation's births and deaths,
And also, O thou lotus-eyed,
Of thy eternal majesty. 2

O lord supreme, what thou hast said
About thyself is true indeed,
But still, O best of beings, I
Would fain behold thy form divine. 3

If thinkest thou, O lord, that I
Can bear the sight, then graciously
Do thou, O yogin's lord, reveal
To me thine own eternal self. 4

The Blessed Lord said:

O son of Pṛthā! now behold
My forms divine in varied shapes,
In many colors, many kinds,
By hundreds and by thousands too. 5

The Ādityas, the Vasus see,
The Rudras, Maruts, Aśvins twain;[302]
Uncounted wonders ne'er yet seen,
Do thou behold, O Bhārat, now. 6

---

[301]I.e., my delusion, or want of discrimination regarding the self and the non-self.
[302]The twin-gods of dawn.

इहैकस्थं जगत्कृत्स्नं पश्याद्य सचराचरम्।
मम देहे गुडाकेश यच्चान्यद्द्रष्टुम् इच्छसि॥ ७॥

ihaikasthaṃ jagat kṛtsnaṃ paśyādya sacarācaram|
mama dehe guḍākeśa yac cānyad draṣṭum icchasi|| 7||

न तु मां शक्यसे द्रष्टुमनेनैव स्वचक्षुषा।
दिव्यं ददामि ते चक्षुः पश्य मे योगमैश्वरम्॥ ८॥

na tu māṃ śakyase draṣṭum anenaiva svacakṣuṣā|
divyaṃ dadāmi te cakṣuḥ paśya me yogam aiśvaram|| 8||

संजय उवाच
एवमुक्त्वा ततो राजन्महायोगेश्वरो हरिः।
दर्शयामास पार्थाय परमं रूपमैश्वरम्॥ ९॥

saṃjaya uvāca

evam uktvā tato rājan mahāyogeśvaro hariḥ|
darśayāmāsa pārthāya paramaṃ rūpam aiśvaram|| 9||

अनेकवक्त्रनयनमनेकाद्भुतदर्शनम्।
अनेकदिव्याभरणं दिव्यानेकोद्यतायुधम्॥ १०॥

anekavaktranayanam anekādbhutadarśanam|
anekadivyābharaṇaṃ divyānekodyatāyudham|| 10||

दिव्यमाल्याम्बरधरं दिव्यगन्धानुलेपनम्।
सर्वाश्चर्यमयं देवमनन्तं विश्वतोमुखम्॥ ११॥

divyamālyāmbaradharaṃ divyagandhānulepanam|
sarvāścaryamayaṃ devam anantaṃ viśvatomukham|| 11||

दिवि सूर्यसहस्रस्य भवेद्युगपदुत्थिता।
यदि भाः सदृशी सा स्याद्भासस्तस्य महात्मनः॥ १२॥

divi sūryasahasrasya bhaved yugapad utthitā|
yadi bhāḥ sadṛśī sā syād bhāsas tasya mahātmanaḥ|| 12||

The whole world see thou gathered here
Within my body, Guḍākeś,
All moving and unmoving things,
And aught besides thou fain would see. 7

Indeed thou cannot see me thus
With thy unseeing human eye,
I give thee now an eye divine;
Behold therefore my sov'ran yoga! 8

Sañjay said:

Thus having spoken forthwith, king,
Hari, the mighty lord of yoga
Revealed himself to Pṛthā's son,
In his supreme and sov'ran form. 9

Of countless mouths and countless eyes,
Of countless wondrous sights possessed,
Of countless heavenly ornaments,
Of countless heavenly weapons raised; 10

Bedecked with heavenly wreaths and robes,
Anointed with unguents divine,
All-wonderful and splendor-clothed,
Unbounded, facing every side. 11

The splendor of a thousand suns,
If all at once could light the sky,
It then perchance may shadow forth
The splendor of that mighty one. 12

तत्रैकस्थं जगत्कृत्स्नं प्रविभक्तमनेकधा।
अपश्यद्देवदेवस्य शरीरे पाण्डवस्तदा॥ १३॥

tatraikasthaṃ jagat kṛtsnaṃ pravibhaktam anekadhā|
apaśyad devadevasya śarīre pāṇḍavas tadā|| 13||

ततः स विस्मयाविष्टो हृष्टरोमा धनंजयः।
प्रणम्य शिरसा देवं कृताञ्जलिरभाषत॥ १४॥

tataḥ sa vismayāviṣṭo hṛṣṭaromā dhanaṃjayaḥ|
praṇamya śirasā devaṃ kṛtāñjalir abhāṣata|| 14||

अर्जुन उवाच

पश्यामि देवांस्तव देव देहे
सर्वांस्तथा भूतविशेषसंघान्।
ब्रह्माणमीशं कमलासनस्थम्
ऋषींश्च सर्वानुरगांश्च दिव्यान्॥ १५॥

arjuna uvāca

paśyāmi devāṃs tava deva dehe
sarvāṃs tathā bhūtaviśeṣasaṃghān|
brahmāṇam īśaṃ kamalāsanastham
ṛṣīṃś ca sarvān uragāṃś ca divyān|| 15||

अनेकबाहूदरवक्त्रनेत्रं
पश्यामि त्वा सर्वतो ऽनन्तरूपम्।
नान्तं न मध्यं न पुनस्तवादिं
पश्यामि विश्वेश्वर विश्वरूप॥ १६॥

anekabāhūdaravaktranetraṃ
paśyāmi tvā sarvato 'nantarūpam|
nāntaṃ na madhyaṃ na punas tavādiṃ
paśyāmi viśveśvara viśvarūpa|| 16||

There in the body of the god
Of gods, the son of Pāṇḍu saw
The whole world gathered into one,
And split up too in many parts. 13

Then Dhanañjay, amazement filled,
Thrilled through and through, his hair on end,
Before the lord bowed low his head,
And with joined palms him thus addressed. 14

Arjun said:

The gods within thy body see I lord,
And hosts of other beings of their kind,
Brahma, the god upon his lotus-throne,
And all the *ṛṣis* and celestial snakes. 15

I see thee everywhere unbounded form
With countless stomachs, mouths and arms and eyes;
Source, middle, end of thee I do not see,
O lord of all, O universal form! 16

किरीटिनं गदिनं चक्रिणं च
तेजोराशिं सर्वतो दीप्तिमन्तम्।
पश्यामि त्वां दुर्निरीक्ष्यं समन्ताद्
दीप्तानलार्कद्युतिमप्रमेयम्॥ १७॥

kirīṭinaṃ gadinaṃ cakriṇaṃ ca
tejorāśiṃ sarvato dīptimantam|
paśyāmi tvāṃ durnirīkṣyaṃ samantād
dīptānalārkadyutim aprameyam|| 17||

त्वमक्षरं परमं वेदितव्यं
त्वमस्य विश्वस्य परं निधानम्।
त्वमव्ययः शाश्वतधर्मगोप्ता
सनातनस्त्वं पुरुषो मतो मे॥ १८॥

tvam akṣaraṃ paramaṃ veditavyaṃ
tvam asya viśvasya paraṃ nidhānam|
tvam avyayaḥ śāśvatadharmagoptā
sanātanas tvaṃ puruṣo mato me|| 18||

अनादिमध्यान्तमनन्तवीर्यम्
अनन्तबाहुं शशिसूर्यनेत्रम्।
पश्यामि त्वां दीप्तहुताशवक्त्रं
स्वतेजसा विश्वमिदं तपन्तम्॥ १९॥

anādimadhyāntam anantavīryam
anantabāhuṃ śaśisūryanetram|
paśyāmi tvāṃ dīptahutāśavaktraṃ
svatejasā viśvam idaṃ tapantam|| 19||

A mass of brilliance shining on all sides,
With discus, crown and mace I thee behold,
Blazing all round like burning fire or sun,
Hard to behold and measureless indeed. 17

Unperishing and worthy to be known
As the supreme, the world's supreme support,
Eternal virtue's changeless guardian thou,
I look upon thee as the primal soul. 18

I see no source nor end, nor mean of thee,
Of endless power, possessed of many arms,
The sun and moon thy eyes, the fire thy face,
Thy radiance giving warmth to all the worlds. 19

द्यावापृथिव्योरिदमन्तरं हि
व्याप्तं त्वयैकेन दिशश्च सर्वाः।
दृष्ट्वाद्भुतं रूपमिदं तवोग्रं
लोकत्रयं प्रव्यथितं महात्मन्॥ २०॥

dyāvāpṛthivyor idam antaraṃ hi
vyāptaṃ tvayaikena diśaś ca sarvāḥ|
dṛṣṭvādbhutaṃ rūpam idaṃ tavograṃ
lokatrayaṃ pravyathitaṃ mahātman|| 20||

अमी हि त्वा सुरसंघा विशन्ति
केचिद्भीताः प्राञ्जलयो गृणन्ति।
स्वस्तीत्युक्त्वा महर्षिसिद्धसंघाः
स्तुवन्ति त्वां स्तुतिभिः पुष्कलाभिः॥ २१॥

amī hi tvā surasaṃghā viśanti
kecid bhītāḥ prāñjalayo gṛṇanti|
svastīty uktvā maharṣisiddhasaṃghāḥ
stuvanti tvāṃ stutibhiḥ puṣkalābhiḥ|| 21||

रुद्रादित्या वसवो ये च साध्या
विश्वे ऽश्विनौ मरुतश्चोष्मपाश्च।
गन्धर्वयक्षासुरसिद्धसंघा
वीक्षन्ते त्वां विस्मिताश्चैव सर्वे॥ २२॥

rudrādityā vasavo ye ca sādhyā
viśve 'śvinau marutaś coṣmapāś ca|
gandharvayakṣāsurasiddhasaṃghā
vīkṣante tvāṃ vismitāś caiva sarve|| 22||

The vast expanse that spreads 'twixt earth and heaven,
All space as well is filled with thee alone,
The three worlds quake with fear, O great-souled one,
At sight of thy most awful wondrous form. 20

Lo! into thee these hosts of *suras*[303] go,
Some with joined palms extolling thee with awe,
Whilst bands of *siddhas*[304] and *ṛṣis* great
Cry, 'hail to thee!' in vibrant hymns of praise. 21

The Ādityas, Rudras, Vasus and Sādhyas,
Aśvins, Viśvas, Maruts and Uṣmapas,
Gandharvas and demons, Yakṣas and Siddhas,
In awe struck legions are beholding thee. 22

---

[303] Gods.
[304] *Siddhas*: sages such as Kapila.

रूपं महत्ते बहुवक्त्रनेत्रं
महाबाहो बहुबाहूरुपादम्।
बहूदरं बहुदंष्ट्राकरालं
दृष्ट्वा लोकाः प्रव्यथितास्तथाहम्॥ २३॥

rūpaṃ mahat te bahuvaktranetraṃ
mahābāho bahubāhūrupādam|
bahūdaraṃ bahudaṃṣṭrākarālaṃ
dṛṣṭvā lokāḥ pravyathitās tathāham|| 23||

नभःस्पृशं दीप्तमनेकवर्णं
व्यात्ताननं दीप्तविशालनेत्रम्।
दृष्ट्वा हि त्वां प्रव्यथितान्तरात्मा
धृतिं न विन्दामि शमं च विष्णो॥ २४॥

nabhaḥspṛśaṃ dīptam anekavarṇaṃ
vyāttānanaṃ dīptaviśālanetram|
dṛṣṭvā hi tvāṃ pravyathitāntarātmā
dhṛtiṃ na vindāmi śamaṃ ca viṣṇo|| 24||

दंष्ट्राकरालानि च ते मुखानि
दृष्ट्वैव कालानलसंनिभानि।
दिशो न जाने न लभे च शर्म
प्रसीद देवेश जगन्निवास॥ २५॥

daṃṣṭrākarālāni ca te mukhāni
dṛṣṭvaiva kālānalasaṃnibhāni|
diśo na jāne na labhe ca śarma
prasīda deveśa jagannivāsa|| 25||

Thy mighty form with countless mouths and eyes,
With countless arms and countless thighs and feet,
And countless stomachs, countless fang-set mouths,
The worlds beholding quake, and so do I. 23

Stretched high as heaven, radiant and rainbow-hued,
With gaping mouths, and large and fiery eyes,
I having seen this sight, my heart doth quake,
No courage have I, Viṣṇu, and no peace. 24

At sight of these thy mouths with fearful fangs,
Which so resemble time's devouring flames,
No peace have I, I know not where I am,
Have mercy lord of gods, the world's abode! 25

अमी च त्वां धृतराष्ट्रस्य पुत्राः
सर्वे सहैवावनिपालसंघैः।
भीष्मो द्रोणः सूतपुत्रस्तथासौ
सहास्मदीयैरपि योधमुख्यैः॥ २६॥

amī ca tvāṃ dhṛtarāṣṭrasya putrāḥ
sarve sahaivāvanipālasaṃghaiḥ|
bhīṣmo droṇaḥ sūtaputras tathāsau
sahāsmadīyair api yodhamukhyaiḥ|| 26||

वक्त्राणि ते त्वरमाणा विशन्ति
दंष्ट्राकरालानि भयानकानि।
केचिद्विलग्ना दशनान्तरेषु
संदृश्यन्ते चूर्णितैरुत्तमाङ्गैः॥ २७॥

vaktrāṇi te tvaramāṇā viśanti
daṃṣṭrākarālāni bhayānakāni|
kecid vilagnā daśanāntareṣu
saṃdṛśyante cūrṇitair uttamāṅgaiḥ|| 27||

यथा नदीनां बहवो ऽम्बुवेगाः
समुद्रमेवाभिमुखा द्रवन्ति।
तथा तवामी नरलोकवीरा
विशन्ति वक्त्राण्यभिविज्वलन्ति॥ २८॥

yathā nadīnāṃ bahavo 'mbuvegāḥ
samudram evābhimukhā dravanti|
tathā tavāmī naralokavīrā
viśanti vaktrāṇy abhivijvalanti|| 28||

The sons of Dhṛtarāṣṭra, and with them,
This host of mighty kings and Bhīsma and Droṇa,
And Karṇa also, the chariot driver's son,
And all the chiefest warriors on our side, 26

At headlong speed they are all rushing on
Into those awful mouths with fearful fangs;
Some with their heads to powder crushed are seen,
Stuck fast within the gaps between thy fangs. 27

As river torrents flow with furious speed
Towards the ocean's dark unfathomed depths,
So hurl themselves within thy flaming mouths
These mighty heroes of the world of men. 28

यथा प्रदीप्तं ज्वलनं पतंगा
विशन्ति नाशाय समृद्धवेगाः।
तथैव नाशाय विशन्ति लोका-
स्तवापि वक्त्राणि समृद्धवेगाः॥ २९॥

yathā pradīptaṃ jvalanaṃ pataṃgā
viśanti nāśāya samṛddhavegāḥ|
tathaiva nāśāya viśanti lokās
tavāpi vaktrāṇi samṛddhavegāḥ|| 29||

लेलिह्यसे ग्रसमानः समन्ताल्
लोकान् समग्रान् वदनैर्ज्वलद्भिः।
तेजोभिरापूर्य जगत्समग्रं
भासस्तवोग्राः प्रतपन्ति विष्णो॥ ३०॥

lelihyase grasamānaḥ samantāl
lokān samagrān vadanair jvaladbhiḥ|
tejobhir āpūrya jagat samagraṃ
bhāsas tavogrāḥ pratapanti viṣṇo|| 30||

आख्याहि मे को भवानुग्ररूपो
नमो ऽस्तु ते देववर प्रसीद।
विज्ञातुमिच्छामि भवन्तमाद्यं
न हि प्रजानामि तव प्रवृत्तिम्॥ ३१॥

ākhyāhi me ko bhavān ugrarūpo
namo 'stu te devavara prasīda|
vijñātum icchāmi bhavantam ādyaṃ
na hi prajānāmi tava pravṛttim|| 31||

As moths at nightfall fly with urgent speed
Into a burning flame to fall destroyed,
So all these creatures with impetuous haste,
Within thy mouths rush in to meet their doom. 29

With thy great flaming mouths on every side,
Thou licketh up all men, devouring them,
And thy fierce splendor filling all the worlds
Is Viṣṇu, burning them with blazing rays. 30

Tell me who art thou, lord, so fierce in form?
I bow to thee; have mercy, god supreme!
I fain would know thee, O primeval one,
For all thy actions are beyond my ken. 31

श्रीभगवानुवाच

कालो ऽस्मि लोकक्षयकृत्प्रवृद्धो
लोकान्समाहर्तुमिह प्रवृत्तः।
ऋते ऽपि त्वा न भविष्यन्ति सर्वे
ये ऽवस्थिताः प्रत्यनीकेषु योधाः॥ ३२॥

śrībhagavān uvāca

kālo 'smi lokakṣayakṛt pravṛddho
lokān samāhartum iha pravṛttaḥ|
ṛte 'pi tvā na bhaviṣyanti sarve
ye 'vasthitāḥ pratyanīkeṣu yodhāḥ|| 32||

तस्मात्त्वमुत्तिष्ठ यशो लभस्व
जित्वा शत्रून्भुङ्क्ष्व राज्यं समृद्धम्।
मयैवैते निहताः पूर्वमेव
निमित्तमात्रं भव सव्यसाचिन्॥ ३३॥

tasmāt tvam uttiṣṭha yaśo labhasva
jitvā śatrūn bhuṅkṣva rājyaṃ samṛddham|
mayaivaite nihatāḥ pūrvam eva
nimittamātraṃ bhava savyasācin|| 33||

द्रोणं च भीष्मं च जयद्रथं च
कर्णं तथान्यानपि योधवीरान्।
मया हतांस् त्वं जहि मा व्यथिष्ठा
युध्यस्व जेतासि रणे सपत्नान्॥ ३४॥

droṇaṃ ca bhīṣmaṃ ca jayadrathaṃ ca
karṇaṃ tathānyān api yodhavīrān|
mayā hatāṃstvaṃ jahi mā vyathiṣṭhā
yudhyasva jetāsi raṇe sapatnān|| 34||

The Blessed Lord said:

I am the world effacer, mighty Time,
Made manifest to overthrow these worlds.
Without thy aid none shall indeed survive
Of all the warriors now for battle met. 32

Therefore do thou arise and win renown,
Thy foes o'ercome, this spacious realm enjoy;
By me they are already all destroyed,
Be my mere instrument, Ambidextrous one.[305] 33

Thy *guru* Droṇa, Bhīṣma and Jayadrath,
And Karṇa, and many other warriors brave,
These slain by me already, do thou slay.
Fear not, but fight. Thou shalt o'ercome thy foes. 34

---

[305] I.e., Arjuna, who could shoot with his left hand as well as with his right.

संजय उवाच

एतच्छ्रुत्वा वचनं केशवस्य
कृताञ्जलिर्वेपमानः किरीटी।
नमस्कृत्वा भूय एवाह कृष्णं
सगद्गदं भीतभीतः प्रणम्य॥ ३५॥

saṃjaya uvāca

etac chrutvā vacanaṃ keśavasya
kṛtāñjalir vepamānaḥ kirīṭī|
namaskṛtvā bhūya evāha kṛṣṇaṃ
sagadgadaṃ bhītabhītaḥ praṇamya|| 35||

अर्जुन उवाच

स्थाने हृषीकेश तव प्रकीर्त्या
जगत्प्रहृष्यत्यनुरज्यते च।
रक्षांसि भीतानि दिशो द्रवन्ति
सर्वे नमस्यन्ति च सिद्धसंघाः॥ ३६॥

arjuna uvāca

sthāne hṛṣīkeśa tava prakīrtyā
jagat prahṛṣyaty anurajyate ca|
rakṣāṃsi bhītāni diśo dravanti
sarve namasyanti ca siddhasaṃghāḥ|| 36||

कस्माच्च ते न नमेरन्महात्मन्
गरीयसे ब्रह्मणो ऽप्यादिकर्त्रे।
अनन्त देवेश जगन्निवास
त्वमक्षरं सदसत्तत्परं यत्॥ ३७॥

kasmāc ca te na nameran mahātman
garīyase brahmaṇo 'pyādikartre|
ananta deveśa jagannivāsa
tvam akṣaraṃ sadasat tatparaṃ yat|| 37||

Sañjay said:

Thus having heard the speech by Keśav made,
As suppliant, bowing low with folded hands,
Arjun, the crowned one, all trembling still,
In stammering words, awe-struck, to Krishna said: 35

Arjun said:

O Hṛṣīkeś! in thy renown the world
Most rightly doth rejoice and hymn thy praise;
The *rāksasas* to every quarter flee
In fear, the hosts of *siddhas* bow to thee. 36

How should they otherwise, O high-souled one,
Than Brahmā greater, and the primal cause,
Infinite, lord of gods, the world's abode,
Beyond *sat* and *asat*, permanent, supreme.[306] 37

---

[306] In the original, "what is beyond them"—beyond *sat* and *asat*.

त्वमादिदेवः पुरुषः पुराण-
स्त्वमस्य विश्वस्य परं निधानम्।
वेत्तासि वेद्यं च परं च धाम
त्वया ततं विश्वमनन्तरूप॥ ३८॥

tvam ādidevaḥ puruṣaḥ purāṇas
tvam asya viśvasya paraṃ nidhānam|
vettāsi vedyaṃ ca paraṃ ca dhāma
tvayā tataṃ viśvam anantarūpa|| 38||

वायुर्यमो ऽग्निर्वरुणः शशाङ्कः
प्रजापतिस्त्वं प्रपितामहश्च।
नमो नमस्ते ऽस्तु सहस्रकृत्वः
पुनश्च भूयो ऽपि नमो नमस्ते॥ ३९॥

vāyur yamo 'gnir varuṇaḥ śaśāṅkaḥ
prajāpatis tvaṃ prapitāmahaś ca|
namo namaste 'stu sahasrakṛtvaḥ
punaś ca bhūyo 'pi namo namas te|| 39||

नमः पुरस्तादथ पृष्ठतस्ते
नमो ऽस्तु ते सर्वत एव सर्व।
अनन्तवीर्यामितविक्रमस्त्वं
सर्वं समाप्नोषि ततो ऽसि सर्वः॥ ४०॥

namaḥ purastād atha pṛṣṭhatas te
namo 'stu te sarvata eva sarva|
anantavīryāmitavikramas tvaṃ
sarvaṃ samāpnoṣi tato 'si sarvaḥ|| 40||

The primal god, the ancient being thou,
And of the universe receptacle supreme,[307]
Knower and known, the highest dwelling place,
By thee, O endless-formed, the worlds are filled. 38

Thou Vāyu art, Yam, Agni, and the moon,
Varuṇa, Prajāpati, the great grandsire,
All hail to thee, a thousand times all hail,
And once again, and yet again, all hail! 39

All hail to thee before, all hail behind!
All hail to thee from every side, thou all!
In power boundless, measureless in strength,
Thou fillest all and therefore thou art all. 40

[307] That in which the universe rests secure during a deluge.

सखेति मत्वा प्रसभं यदुक्तं
हे कृष्ण हे यादव हे सखेति।
अजानता महिमानं तवेदं
मया प्रमादात्प्रणयेन वापि॥ ४१॥

sakheti matvā prasabhaṃ yad uktaṃ
he kṛṣṇa he yādava he sakheti|
ajānatā mahimānaṃ tavedaṃ
mayā pramādāt praṇayena vāpi|| 41||

यच्चावहासार्थमसत्कृतो ऽसि
विहारशय्यासनभोजनेषु।
एको ऽथ वाप्यच्युत तत्समक्षं
तत्क्षामये त्वामहमप्रमेयम्॥ ४२॥

yac cāvahāsārtham asatkṛto 'si
vihāraśayyāsanabhojaneṣu|
eko 'tha vāpy acyuta tat samakṣaṃ
tat kṣāmaye tvām aham aprameyam|| 42||

पितासि लोकस्य चराचरस्य
त्वमस्य पूज्यश्च गुरुर्गरीयान्।
न त्वत्समो ऽस्त्यभ्यधिकः कुतो ऽन्यो
लोकत्रये ऽप्यप्रतिमप्रभाव॥ ४३॥

pitāsi lokasya carācarasya
tvam asya pūjyaś ca gurur garīyān|
na tvatsamo 'sty abhyadhikaḥ kuto 'nyo
lokatraye 'py apratimaprabhāva|| 43||

If rashly deeming thee as but a friend,
Of this thy greatness knowing naught till now,
Through carelessness or through my love for thee,
I've called thee Yādav, Krishna, or my friend. 41

Whatever disrespect I've shown to thee
In jest, at play, reposing or at meals,
O sinless one, alone or with my friends,
I pardon crave for this, O boundless one. 42

World's father thou, of all that's fixed or moves,
The greatest guru thou, most worshipful,
No peer hast thou; who can excel thee, lord,
Whose might is unsurpassed in all the world? 43

तस्मात्प्रणम्य प्रणिधाय कायं
प्रसादये त्वामहमीशमीड्यम्।
पितेव पुत्रस्य सखेव सख्युः
प्रियः प्रियायार्हसि देव सोढुम्॥ ४४॥

tasmāt praṇamya praṇidhāya kāyaṃ
prasādaye tvām aham īśam īḍyam|
piteva putrasya sakheva sakhyuḥ
priyaḥ priyāyārhasi deva soḍhum|| 44||

अदृष्टपूर्वं हृषितो ऽस्मि दृष्ट्वा
भयेन च प्रव्यथितं मनो मे।
तदेव मे दर्शय देव रूपं
प्रसीद देवेश जगन्निवास॥ ४५॥

adṛṣṭapūrvaṃ hṛṣito 'smi dṛṣṭvā
bhayena ca pravyathitaṃ mano me|
tad eva me darśaya deva rūpaṃ
prasīda deveśa jagannivāsa|| 45||

किरीटिनं गदिनं चक्रहस्त-
मिच्छामि त्वां द्रष्टुमहं तथैव।
तेनैव रूपेण चतुर्भुजेन
सहस्रबाहो भव विश्वमूर्ते॥ ४६॥

kirīṭinaṃ gadinaṃ cakrahastam
icchāmi tvāṃ draṣṭum ahaṃ tathaiva|
tenaiva rūpeṇa caturbhujena
sahasrabāho bhava viśvamūrte|| 46||

Therefore with body bent as suppliant,
I beg forgiveness, lord most worshipful,
As father with his son, as friend with friend,
As lover with his love, do thou forbear. 44

I having seen what was unseen before,
My heart is glad, yet is alarmed with fear,
Show me again, O lord, thy homely form,
Have mercy god of gods, all world's abode! 45

Crowned, sceptered, with the discus in thy hand,
Thus would I see thee in thy form of old;
Once more put on thy four-armed form for me,
O thousand-armed, O universal form! 46

श्रीभगवानुवाच

मया प्रसन्नेन तवार्जुनेदं
रूपं परं दर्शितमात्मयोगात्।
तेजोमयं विश्वमनन्तमाद्यं
यन्मे त्वदन्येन न दृष्टपूर्वम्॥ ४७॥

śrībhagavān uvāca

mayā prasannena tavārjunedaṃ
rūpaṃ paraṃ darśitam ātmayogāt|
tejomayaṃ viśvam anantam ādyaṃ
yan me tvadanyena na dṛṣṭapūrvam|| 47||

न वेद यज्ञाध्ययनैर्न दानै-
र्न च क्रियाभिर्न तपोभिरुग्रैः।
एवंरूपः शक्य अहं नृलोके
द्रष्टुं त्वदन्येन कुरुप्रवीर॥ ४८॥

na veda yajñādhyayanair na dānair
na ca kriyābhir na tapobhir ugraiḥ|
evaṃrūpaḥ śakya ahaṃ nṛloke
draṣṭuṃ tvadanyena kurupravīra|| 48||

मा ते व्यथा मा च विमूढभावो
दृष्ट्वा रूपं घोरमीदृङ्ममेदम्।
व्यपेतभीः प्रीतमनाः पुनस्त्वं
तदेव मे रूपमिदं प्रपश्य॥ ४९॥

mā te vyathā mā ca vimūḍhabhāvo
dṛṣṭvā rūpaṃ ghoram īdṛṅ mamedam|
vyapetabhīḥ prītamanāḥ punas tvaṃ
tad eva me rūpam idaṃ prapaśya|| 49||

The Blessed Lord said:

For love of thee, Arjun, thus have I shown
This form supreme by mine own mystic power,
Most glorious, universal, endless, first,
That none except thyself hath ever seen. 47

Nor study of the Veda, nor sacrifice,
Nor gifts, nor works, nor fierce austerities,
Can win a vision of this form on earth,
Which thou, O Kuru's chief, alone hath seen. 48

Be not afraid, nor be at all perplexed
At seeing this my terror striking form,
Exempt from fear, thy heart again at ease,
Once more behold me in my form of old. 49

संजय उवाच

इत्यर्जुनं वासुदेवस्तथोक्त्वा
स्वकं रूपं दर्शयामास भूयः।
आश्वासयामास च भीतमेनं
भूत्वा पुनः सौम्यवपुर्महात्मा॥ ५०॥

saṃjaya uvāca

ity arjunaṃ vāsudevas tathoktvā
svakaṃ rūpaṃ darśayāmāsa bhūyaḥ|
āśvāsayāmāsa ca bhītam enaṃ
bhūtvā punaḥ saumyavapur mahātmā|| 50||

अर्जुन उवाच

दृष्ट्वेदं मानुषं रूपं तव सौम्यं जनार्दन।
इदानीमस्मि संवृत्तः सचेताः प्रकृतिं गतः॥ ५१॥

arjuna uvāca

dṛṣṭvedaṃ mānuṣaṃ rūpaṃ tava saumyaṃ janārdana|
idānīm asmi saṃvṛttaḥ sacetāḥ prakṛtiṃ gataḥ|| 51||

श्रीभगवानुवाच

सुदुर्दर्शमिदं रूपं दृष्टवानसि यन्मम।
देवा अप्यस्य रूपस्य नित्यं दर्शनकाङ्क्षिणः॥ ५२॥

śrībhagavān uvāca

sudurdarśam idaṃ rūpaṃ dṛṣṭavān asi yan mama|
devā apy asya rūpasya nityaṃ darśanakāṅkṣiṇaḥ|| 52||

नाहं वेदैर्न तपसा न दानेन न चेज्यया।
शक्य एवंविधो द्रष्टुं दृष्टवानसि मां यथा॥ ५३॥

nāhaṃ vedair na tapasā na dānena na cejyayā|
śakya evaṃvidho draṣṭuṃ dṛṣṭavān asi māṃ yathā|| 53||

Sanjay said:

To Arjun having thus addressed himself,
He, Vāsudeva, reshowed his former form,
And in his gentle guise, the high-souled one
Brought peace to him who had been sore afraid. 50

Arjun said:

Seeing again, O Janārdan,
This gentle human form of thine,
My peace of mind I have regained,
And to my normal self returned. 51

The Blessed Lord said:

'Tis very hard to see this form
Which thou hast been vouchsafed to see,
The gods themselves in very truth,
Forever long to see this form. 52

Nor by the Veda, nor penances,
Nor charities, nor sacrifice,
Can I be seen as thou hast seen,
In this my universal form. 53

भक्त्या त्वनन्यया शक्य अहमेवंविधो ऽर्जुन।
ज्ञातुं द्रष्टुं च तत्त्वेन प्रवेष्टुं च परंतप॥ ५४॥

bhaktyā tvananyayā śakya aham evaṃvidho 'rjuna|
jñātuṃ draṣṭuṃ ca tattvena praveṣṭuṃ ca paraṃtapa|| 54||

मत्कर्मकृन्मत्परमो मद्भक्तः सङ्गवर्जितः।
निर्वैरः सर्वभूतेषु यः स मामेति पाण्डव॥ ५५॥

matkarmakṛn matparamo madbhaktaḥ saṅgavarjitaḥ|
nirvairaḥ sarvabhūteṣu yaḥ sa mām eti pāṇḍava|| 55||

But I may yet be known like this,
By love on me alone bestowed,
And known and seen too as I am,
And entered into, Parantap. 54

Who works for me, his highest goal,
Who loveth me, attachments freed,
Who hateth none, O Pṛthā's son,
He comes to me assuredly. 55

Chapter Twelve: The Yoga of Bhakti (भक्तियोगः)

अर्जुन उवाच

एवं सततयुक्ता ये भक्तास्त्वां पर्युपासते।
ये चाप्यक्षरमव्यक्तं तेषां के योगवित्तमाः॥ १॥

arjuna uvāca

evaṃ satatayuktā ye bhaktāstvāṃ paryupāsate|
ye cāpyakṣaram avyaktaṃ teṣāṃ ke yogavittamāḥ|| 1||

श्रीभगवानुवाच

मय्यावेश्य मनो ये मां नित्ययुक्ता उपासते।
श्रद्धया परयोपेतास्ते मे युक्ततमा मताः॥ २॥

śrībhagavān uvāca

mayy āveśya mano ye māṃ nityayuktā upāsate|
śraddhayā parayopetās te me yuktatamā matāḥ|| 2||

ये त्वक्षरमनिर्देश्यमव्यक्तं पर्युपासते।
सर्वत्रगमचिन्त्यं च कूटस्थमचलं ध्रुवम्॥ ३॥

ye tv akṣaram anirdeśyam avyaktaṃ paryupāsate|
sarvatragam acintyaṃ ca kūṭastham acalaṃ dhruvam|| 3||

संनियम्येन्द्रियग्रामं सर्वत्र समबुद्धयः।
ते प्राप्नुवन्ति मामेव सर्वभूतहिते रताः॥ ४॥

saṃniyamyendriyagrāmaṃ sarvatra samabuddhayaḥ|
te prāpnuvanti mām eva sarvabhūtahite ratāḥ|| 4||

क्लेशो ऽधिकतरस्तेषामव्यक्तासक्तचेतसाम्।
अव्यक्ता हि गतिर्दुःखं देहवद्भिरवाप्यते॥ ५॥

kleśo 'dhikataras teṣām avyaktāsaktacetasām|
avyaktā hi gatir duḥkhaṃ dehavadbhir avāpyate|| 5||

ये तु सर्वाणि कर्माणि मयि संन्यस्य मत्पराः।
अनन्येनैव योगेन मां ध्यायन्त उपासते॥ ६॥

ye tu sarvāṇi karmāṇi mayi saṃnyasya matparāḥ|
ananyenaiva yogena māṃ dhyāyanta upāsate|| 6||

Arjun said:

Who knows *yoga* best—the devotees
Who worship thee, attuned always,
Or those who meditate upon
Th'eternal and the unrevealed?[308] 1

The Blessed Lord said:

Who with their minds on me intent,
And with the highest faith endued,
Always attuned, do worship me,
Of *yogins* I deem these the best.[309] 2

Yet they who th'eternal seek,
The undefined, the unrevealed,
Th'omnipresent, th'unthinkable,
Th'ineffable, th'immutable; 3

Restraining all their senses well,
And equal minded in all things,
Rejoicing in the good of all,
These also surely come to me. 4

The travail greater is of those
With minds set on the unrevealed,[310]
For such a goal[311] is hard to reach
By man in his embodied state.[312] 5

But as for those who worship me,
Consigning every act to me,
For whom I am the highest goal,
Who meditate on me alone, 6

---

[308]More correctly, the imperishable (*akṣara*) and the unmanifested (*avyakta*).
[309]Or, the better versed in *yoga* I deem.
[310]The unmanifested.
[311]I.e., the goal of the unmanifested.
[312]Lit. by the embodied.

तेषामहं समुद्धर्ता मृत्युसंसारसागरात्।
भवामि नचिरात्पार्थ मय्यावेशितचेतसाम्॥ ७॥

teṣām ahaṃ samuddhartā mṛtyusaṃsārasāgarāt|
bhavāmi na cirāt pārtha mayy āveśitacetasām|| 7||

मय्येव मन आधत्स्व मयि बुद्धिं निवेशय।
निवसिष्यसि मय्येव अत ऊर्ध्वं न संशयः॥ ८॥

mayy eva mana ādhatsva mayi buddhiṃ niveśaya|
nivasiṣyasi mayy eva ata ūrdhvaṃ na saṃśayaḥ|| 8||

अथ चित्तं समाधातुं न शक्नोषि मयि स्थिरम्।
अभ्यासयोगेन ततो मामिच्छाप्तुं धनंजय॥ ९॥

atha cittaṃ samādhātuṃ na śaknoṣi mayi sthiram|
abhyāsayogena tato mām icchāptuṃ dhanaṃjaya|| 9||

अभ्यासे ऽप्यसमर्थो ऽसि मत्कर्मपरमो भव।
मदर्थमपि कर्माणि कुर्वन् सिद्धिमवाप्स्यसि॥ १०॥

abhyāse 'pyasamartho 'si matkarmaparamo bhava|
madartham api karmāṇi kurvan siddhim avāpsyasi|| 10||

अथैतदप्यशक्तो ऽसि कर्तुं मद्योगमाश्रितः।
सर्वकर्मफलत्यागं ततः कुरु यतात्मवान्॥ ११॥

athaitad apy aśakto 'si kartuṃ madyogam āśritaḥ|
sarvakarmaphalatyāgaṃ tataḥ kuru yatātmavān|| 11||

श्रेयो हि ज्ञानमभ्यासाज्ज्ञानाद्ध्यानं विशिष्यते।
ध्यानात्कर्मफलत्यागस्त्यागाच्छान्तिरनन्तरम्॥ १२॥

śreyo hi jñānam abhyāsāj jñānād dhyānaṃ viśiṣyate|
dhyānāt karmaphalatyāgas tyāgāc chāntir anantaram|| 12||

Of these, whose hearts are fixed on me,
Ere long the savior I become
From that deep sea, O Pṛthā's son,
Of ceaseless rounds of births and deaths.[313] 7

Thy mind in me alone repose,
And let thy reason enter me,[314]
For thus thou shalt assuredly
In me alone hereafter dwell. 8

But if thou canst not fix thy mind
With steadfastness on me alone,
By *yoga* of constant effort then,
Seek thou to reach me, Dhanañjay. 9

Should effort be too much for thee,
Then on my service be intent;
Performing actions for my sake,
Perfection thou shalt surely gain. 10

If even this thou canst not do,
Thyself attuning with me then,
And self-controlling, set aside
All the reward which action brings. 11

Than effort, wisdom better is,
And meditation better still;
Renouncing fruits is best of all,
And such surrender bringeth peace. 12

---

[313] I.e., *saṃsāra*.
[314] I.e., let thy *buddhi* constantly think upon me as the supreme goal.

अद्वेष्टा सर्वभूतानां मैत्रः करुण एव च।
निर्ममो निरहंकारः समदुःखसुखः क्षमी॥ १३॥

adveṣṭā sarvabhūtānāṃ maitraḥ karuṇa eva ca|
nirmamo nirahaṃkāraḥ samaduḥkhasukhaḥ kṣamī|| 13||

संतुष्टः सततं योगी यतात्मा दृढनिश्चयः।
मय्यर्पितमनोबुद्धिर्यो मद्भक्तः स मे प्रियः॥ १४॥

saṃtuṣṭaḥ satataṃ yogī yatātmā dṛḍhaniścayaḥ|
mayy arpitamanobuddhir yo madbhaktaḥ sa me priyaḥ|| 14||

यस्मान्नोद्विजते लोको लोकान्नोद्विजते च यः।
हर्षामर्षभयोद्वेगैर्मुक्तो यः स च मे प्रियः॥ १५॥

yasmān nodvijate loko lokān nodvijate ca yaḥ|
harṣāmarṣabhayodvegair mukto yaḥ sa ca me priyaḥ|| 15||

अनपेक्षः शुचिर्दक्ष उदासीनो गतव्यथः।
सर्वारम्भपरित्यागी यो मद्भक्तः स मे प्रियः॥ १६॥

anapekṣaḥ śucir dakṣa udāsīno gatavyathaḥ|
sarvārambhaparityāgī yo madbhaktaḥ sa me priyaḥ|| 16||

यो न हृष्यति न द्वेष्टि न शोचति न काङ्क्षति।
शुभाशुभपरित्यागी भक्तिमान् यः स मे प्रियः॥ १७॥

yo na hṛṣyati na dveṣṭi na śocati na kāṅkṣati|
śubhāśubhaparityāgī bhaktimān yaḥ sa me priyaḥ|| 17||

समः शत्रौ च मित्रे च तथा मानापमानयोः।
शीतोष्णसुखदुःखेषु समः सङ्गविवर्जितः॥ १८॥

samaḥ śatrau ca mitre ca tathā mānāpamānayoḥ|
śītoṣṇasukhaduḥkheṣu samaḥ saṅgavivarjitaḥ|| 18||

Who's friendly and compassionate,
Who hateth none, who selfless is,
Forgiving, free from ego-sense,
In pain and pleasure equipoised, 13

Devoted and content always,
Of purpose firm and self-controlled,
His mind and reason giv'n to me,
My lover, he is dear to me. 14

The man from whom the world shrinks not,
Who shrinks not from the world in turn,
Who has no envy, fear nor joy,
Nor sorrow, he is dear to me. 15

Who has no wants and who is pure,
Untroubled,[315] clever,[316] unconcerned,[317]
His undertakings who resigns,
My lover, he is dear to me. 16

Who feels no joy,[318] who feels no hate,[319]
Who doth not grieve or wish for aught,
Renouncing good and evil both,[320]
He, full of love, is dear to me. 17

Who treats alike both friend and foe,
Who is the same in fame and shame,
In heat and cold, in joy and pain,
Who from attachments is exempt, 18

[315] I.e., indifferent to worldly things.
[316] I.e., proficient or expert in carrying out scriptural ordinances.
[317] Or passionless.
[318] On obtaining what is pleasant.
[319] On obtaining what is unpleasant.
[320] Because both meritorious and sinful deeds are equally effective in causing *saṃsāra*.

तुल्यनिन्दास्तुतिर्मौनी संतुष्टो येन केनचित्।
अनिकेतः स्थिरमतिर्भक्तिमान् मे प्रियो नरः॥ १९॥

tulyanindāstutir maunī saṃtuṣṭo yena kena cit|
aniketaḥ sthiramatir bhaktimān me priyo naraḥ|| 19||

ये तु धर्म्यामृतमिदं यथोक्तं पर्युपासते।
श्रद्दधाना मत्परमा भक्तास्ते ऽतीव मे प्रियाः॥ २०॥

ye tu dharmyāmṛtam idaṃ yathoktaṃ paryupāsate|
śraddadhānā matparamā bhaktās te 'tīva me priyāḥ|| 20||

Who praise and blame alike regards,
Who is content whate'er befall,
Who's silent,[321] homeless, firm in mind,[322]
This man, love-filled, is dear to me. 19

These lovers who with faith endued
Partake of this life-giving lore,[323]
Of whom I am the goal supreme,
They are exceeding dear to me. 20

---

[321]I.e., who governs his tongue.
[322]I.e., steady-minded.
[323]The *bhakti-yoga*, as herein taught.

Chapter Thirteen: The Yoga of Nature and Self (प्रकृतिपुरुषविवेकयोगः)

श्रीभगवानुवाच
इदं शरीरं कौन्तेय क्षेत्रमित्यभिधीयते।
एतद्यो वेत्ति तं प्राहुः क्षेत्रज्ञ इति तद्विदः॥ १॥

śrībhagavān uvāca

idaṃ śarīraṃ kaunteya kṣetram ity abhidhīyate|
etad yo vetti taṃ prāhuḥ kṣetrajña iti tad vidaḥ|| 1||

क्षेत्रज्ञं चापि मां विद्धि सर्वक्षेत्रेषु भारत।
क्षेत्रक्षेत्रज्ञयोर्ज्ञानं यत्तज्ज्ञानं मतं मम॥ २॥

kṣetrajñaṃ cāpi māṃ viddhi sarvakṣetreṣu bhārata|
kṣetrakṣetrajñayor jñānaṃ yat taj jñānaṃ mataṃ mama|| 2||

तत्क्षेत्रं यच्च यादृक् च यद्विकारि यतश्च यत्।
स च यो यत्प्रभावश्च तत्समासेन मे शृणु॥ ३॥

tat kṣetraṃ yac ca yādṛk ca yad vikāri yataś ca yat|
sa ca yo yat prabhāvaś ca tat samāsena me śṛṇu|| 3||

ऋषिभिर्बहुधा गीतं छन्दोभिर्विविधैः पृथक्।
ब्रह्मसूत्रपदैश्चैव हेतुमद्भिर्विनिश्चितैः॥ ४॥

ṛṣibhir bahudhā gītaṃ chandobhir vividhaiḥ pṛthak|
brahmasūtrapadaiś caiva hetumadbhir viniścitaiḥ|| 4||

महाभूतान्यहंकारो बुद्धिरव्यक्तमेव च।
इन्द्रियाणि दशैकं च पञ्च चेन्द्रियगोचराः॥ ५॥

mahābhūtāny ahaṃkāro buddhir avyaktam eva ca|
indriyāṇi daśaikaṃ ca pañca cendriyagocarāḥ|| 5||

इच्छा द्वेषः सुखं दुःखं संघातश्चेतना धृतिः।
एतत्क्षेत्रं समासेन सविकारमुदाहृतम्॥ ६॥

icchā dveṣaḥ sukhaṃ duḥkhaṃ saṃghātaś cetanā dhṛtiḥ|
etat kṣetraṃ samāsena savikāram udāhṛtam|| 6||

The Blessed Lord said:

This body, O thou Kuntī's son,
Is designated as the field;
Field-knower, so the sages say,
Is he by whom the field is known.[324] 1

In every field, O Bharat's son,
Learn thou that I the knower am;
Field-knowledge, and of him who knows,
Is knowledge true it seems to me.[325] 2

What is that field, its origin,
Its nature, transformations too?
Who is the knower, what his power?
Of this in brief now hear from me. 3

Distinctly and in many ways
Have *ṛṣi* sung in diverse hymns
And passages[326] which treat of Brahm,
Conclusive and well reasoned out. 4

The elements,[327] the ego-sense,[328]
And reason and the unrevealed,[329]
The senses ten, the single sense,
And of the senses, objects five.[330] 5

Aversion, longing, pleasure, pain,
The body, courage, consciousness;
The field with all its changes thus,
In fewest words has been described. 6

[324]"Field" and "Field-knower" are the *kṣetra* and the *kṣetra-jña* of the original. *Kṣetra* is matter, body, habitat, field, soil, or that which is enjoyed. *Kṣetra-jña* is the soul, or spirit, the knower, the conscious dweller, or he who enjoys the field. Briefly, *kṣetra* is matter, and *kṣetra-jña* is the soul or spirit.

[325]Lit. I deem the knowledge of the *kṣetra* and the *kṣetra-jña* to be *the* knowledge.

[326]*Brahma-sūtra*, these are aphoristic sentences which treat of the knowledge of Brahman,

[327]The elements here referred to are the "great" or "subtle" elements (earth, water, fire, air, and space) as distinguished from the "gross" elements, which are the objects of the senses.

[328]Egoism (*ahaṅkāra*): self-consciousness—the consciousness of the ego, which is the root or cause of the elements.

[329]The unrevealed or unmanifested (*avyakta*), is the primordial matter-stuff (*prakṛti*) of which the great elements, *buddhi*, and *ahaṅkāra* are the eight constituents.

[330]The five objects of the senses are sound, touch, color (or form), taste, and smell.

अमानित्वमदम्भित्वमहिंसा क्षान्तिरार्जवम्।
आचार्योपासनं शौचं स्थैर्यमात्मविनिग्रहः॥ ७॥

amānitvam adambhitvam ahiṃsā kṣāntir ārjavam|
ācāryopāsanaṃ śaucaṃ sthairyam ātmavinigrahaḥ|| 7||

इन्द्रियार्थेषु वैराग्यमनहंकार एव च।
जन्ममृत्युजराव्याधिदुःखदोषानुदर्शनम्॥ ८॥

indriyārtheṣu vairāgyam anahaṃkāra eva ca|
janmamṛtyujarāvyādhiduḥkhadoṣānudarśanam|| 8||

असक्तिरनभिष्वङ्गः पुत्रदारगृहादिषु।
नित्यं च समचित्तत्वमिष्टानिष्टोपपत्तिषु॥ ९॥

asaktir anabhiṣvaṅgaḥ putradāragṛhādiṣu|
nityaṃ ca samacittatvam iṣṭāniṣṭopapattiṣu|| 9||

मयि चानन्ययोगेन भक्तिरव्यभिचारिणी।
विविक्तदेशसेवित्वमरतिर्जनसंसदि॥ १०॥

mayi cānanyayogena bhaktir avyabhicāriṇī|
viviktadeśasevitvam aratir janasaṃsadi|| 10||

अध्यात्मज्ञाननित्यत्वं तत्त्वज्ञानार्थदर्शनम्।
एतज्ज्ञानमिति प्रोक्तमज्ञानं यदतो ऽन्यथा॥ ११॥

adhyātmajñānanityatvaṃ tattvajñānārthadarśanam|
etaj jñānam iti proktam ajñānaṃ yad ato 'nyathā|| 11||

ज्ञेयं यत्तत्प्रवक्ष्यामि यज्ज्ञात्वामृतमश्नुते।
अनादिमत्परं ब्रह्म न सत्तन्नासदुच्यते॥ १२॥

jñeyaṃ yat tat pravakṣyāmi yaj jñātvāmṛtam aśnute|
anādimat paraṃ brahma na sat tan nāsad ucyate|| 12||

Uprightness, patience, modesty,
Humility and harmlessness,
The guru's service, steadfastness,
And purity and self-control, 7

Indiff'rence to the things of sense,
And absence of all egoism,
With insight of the ill in birth,
In pain of sickness, death and age, 8

Detachment, also want of love
For son, for wife, or for the home,
And constant equanimity
In wanted and unwanted things; 9

Unswerving love for me by *yoga*,
Without a thought of aught besides,
Resort to lonely spots, dislike
For men's society; 10

And in self-knowledge constancy,
Direct perception of the truth[331]—
These are, indeed, as wisdom known;
All else is grossest ignorance.[332] 11

Him I'll describe who should be known,[333]
Whom knowing man immortal grows,
The Brahm supreme, who ne'er began,
Who as *asat* and *sat* is known. 12

[331]Intuitive perception of the end of the knowledge of truth—this being *mokṣa*.
[332]Lit. all that is opposed to this is ignorance.
[333]I.e., I will describe that (him—the Brahman—the supreme soul) the knowledge of which follows from the practice of the virtues described in verses 7-11.

सर्वतः पाणिपादं तत्सर्वतो ऽक्षिशिरोमुखम्।
सर्वतः श्रुतिमल्लोके सर्वमावृत्य तिष्ठति॥ १३॥

sarvataḥ pāṇipādaṃ tat sarvato 'kṣiśiromukham|
sarvataḥ śrutimal loke sarvam āvṛtya tiṣṭhati|| 13||

सर्वेन्द्रियगुणाभासं सर्वेन्द्रियविवर्जितम्।
असक्तं सर्वभृच्चैव निर्गुणं गुणभोक्तृ च॥ १४॥

sarvendriyaguṇābhāsaṃ sarvendriyavivarjitam|
asaktaṃ sarvabhṛc caiva nirguṇaṃ guṇabhoktṛ ca|| 14||

बहिरन्तश्च भूतानामचरं चरमेव च।
सूक्ष्मत्वात्तदविज्ञेयं दूरस्थं चान्तिके च तत्॥ १५॥

bahir antaś ca bhūtānām acaraṃ caram eva ca|
sūkṣmatvāt tad avijñeyaṃ dūrasthaṃ cāntike ca tat|| 15||

अविभक्तं च भूतेषु विभक्तमिव च स्थितम्।
भूतभर्तृ च तज्ज्ञेयं ग्रसिष्णु प्रभविष्णु च॥ १६॥

avibhaktaṃ ca bhūteṣu vibhaktam iva ca sthitam|
bhūtabhartṛ ca taj jñeyaṃ grasiṣṇu prabhaviṣṇu ca|| 16||

ज्योतिषामपि तज्ज्योतिस्तमसः परमुच्यते।
ज्ञानं ज्ञेयं ज्ञानगम्यं हृदि सर्वस्य विष्ठितम्॥ १७॥

jyotiṣām api taj jyotis tamasaḥ param ucyate|
jñānaṃ jñeyaṃ jñānagamyaṃ hṛdi sarvasya viṣṭhitam|| 17||

इति क्षेत्रं तथा ज्ञानं ज्ञेयं चोक्तं समासतः।
मद्भक्त एतद्विज्ञाय मद्भावायोपपद्यते॥ १८॥

iti kṣetraṃ tathā jñānaṃ jñeyaṃ coktaṃ samāsataḥ|
madbhakta etad vijñāya madbhāvāyopapadyate|| 18||

He everywhere hath hands and feet,
On all sides faces, heads and eyes,
And he hath ears on every side,
World-dweller he, embracing all.[334] 13

He hath no senses, yet he shines
With all the faculties of sense;[335]
Though unattached, yet stay of all,[336]
Though guna-less, yet sensing them.[337] 14

Within all beings and without,
Though motionless, yet movable,
Through subtlety he's undiscerned,
He's close at hand, yet far away. 15

Though undivided, yet he lives
As if divided in all things;
He should be known as stay of all,
Creator and destroyer both.[338] 16

He's radiance of radiant things,
He's said to be beyond all gloom;
As knowledge, object, and its goal,
He is in every heart enshrined. 17

Thus have the field and wisdom too,
And wisdom's object[339] here been sketched,
My lover, knowing this full well,
Is fitted for mine own estate. 18

---

[334]The purport of this verse is that the soul (God) is omnipresent and omnipotent.
[335]Though the soul has no sense-organs yet it can see, hear, etc.
[336]Though really having no relation to anything, yet appearing to be so related through *māyā*.
[337]Though devoid of the *guṇas*, yet the soul is the enjoyer of the *guṇas*, which as sense-objects are capable of giving pleasure and pain.
[338]Lit. devourer and causer.
[339]The knowable, or "that which should be known," v.12.

प्रकृतिं पुरुषं चैव विद्ध्यनादी उभावपि।
विकारांश्च गुणांश्चैव विद्धि प्रकृतिसंभवान्॥ १९॥

prakṛtiṃ puruṣaṃ caiva viddhy anādī ubhāv api|
vikārāṃś ca guṇāṃś caiva viddhi prakṛtisaṃbhavān|| 19||

कार्यकारणकर्तृत्वे हेतुः प्रकृतिरुच्यते।
पुरुषः सुखदुःखानां भोक्तृत्वे हेतुरुच्यते॥ २०॥

kāryakāraṇakartṛtve hetuḥ prakṛtir ucyate|
puruṣaḥ sukhaduḥkhānāṃ bhoktṛtve hetur ucyate|| 20||

पुरुषः प्रकृतिस्थो हि भुङ्क्ते प्रकृतिजान् गुणान्।
कारणं गुणसङ्गो ऽस्य सदसद्योनिजन्मसु॥ २१॥

puruṣaḥ prakṛtistho hi bhuṅkte prakṛtijān guṇān|
kāraṇaṃ guṇasaṅgo 'sya sadasadyonijanmasu|| 21||

उपद्रष्टानुमन्ता च भर्ता भोक्ता महेश्वरः।
परमात्मेति चाप्युक्तो देहे ऽस्मिन्पुरुषः परः॥ २२॥

upadraṣṭānumantā ca bhartā bhoktā maheśvaraḥ|
paramātmeti cāpy ukto dehe 'smin puruṣaḥ paraḥ|| 22||

य एवं वेत्ति पुरुषं प्रकृतिं च गुणैः सह।
सर्वथा वर्तमानो ऽपि न स भूयो ऽभिजायते॥ २३॥

ya evaṃ vetti puruṣaṃ prakṛtiṃ ca guṇaiḥ saha|
sarvathā vartamāno 'pi na sa bhūyo 'bhijāyate|| 23||

ध्यानेनात्मनि पश्यन्ति केचिदात्मानमात्मना।
अन्ये सांख्येन योगेन कर्मयोगेन चापरे॥ २४॥

dhyānenātmani paśyanti kecid ātmānam ātmanā|
anye sāṃkhyena yogena karmayogena cāpare|| 24||

Know thou that matter and the soul
Are both alike beginning-less;
All changes[340] also, do thou learn,
And *guṇas*,[341] are of matter born. 19

The body[342] and the senses[343] both
In matter solely have their source;
Experience of all pleasure, pain,
Is functioned by the soul alone.[344] 20

The soul in matter shrined enjoys
The *guṇas* that are matter-born;
Attachment to the *guṇas* leads
To birth in good and evil wombs. 21

As permitter and observer,
Supporter and enjoyer too,
The self supreme, the mighty lord,
Thus is the Paramātmā known. 22

The man who knoweth thus the soul,
And matter with its *guṇas* three,
He never shall be born again,
Whatever may his conduct be. 23

The self[345] by self[346] within the self,[347]
By meditation some behold,
Whilst some by the *Sāṅkhya yoga*,
And others by *Karma yoga* see. 24

---

[340]Modifications or developments, meaning the body, senses, etc.

[341]Meaning pleasure, pain, etc.; changes and *guṇas* together may be taken to mean the body, the feelings, and the senses.

[342]Lit. effect, i.e., the body.

[343]Lit. instruments, i.e., the senses.

[344]Lit. the soul is the cause or source for experiencing pleasure and pain. The purport is that the production of the physical body and of the senses is accomplished by matter (*prakṛti*); on the other hand, the faculty of enjoying or experiencing pleasure and pain is due entirely to the soul.

[345]I.e., the individual self.

[346]I.e., the mind.

[347]I.e., the body.

अन्ये त्वेवमजानन्तः श्रुत्वान्येभ्य उपासते।
ते ऽपि चातितरन्त्येव मृत्युं श्रुतिपरायणाः॥ २५॥

anye tv evam ajānantaḥ śrutvānyebhya upāsate|
te 'pi cātitaranty eva mṛtyuṃ śrutiparāyaṇāḥ|| 25||

यावत्संजायते किंचित्सत्त्वं स्थावरजङ्गमम्।
क्षेत्रक्षेत्रज्ञसंयोगात्तद्विद्धि भरतर्षभ॥ २६॥

yāvat saṃjāyate kiṃ cit sattvaṃ sthāvarajaṅgamam|
kṣetrakṣetrajñasaṃyogāt tad viddhi bharatarṣabha|| 26||

समं सर्वेषु भूतेषु तिष्ठन्तं परमेश्वरम्।
विनश्यत्स्वविनश्यन्तं यः पश्यति स पश्यति॥ २७॥

samaṃ sarveṣu bhūteṣu tiṣṭhantaṃ parameśvaram|
vinaśyatsv avinaśyantaṃ yaḥ paśyati sa paśyati|| 27||

समं पश्यन् हि सर्वत्र समवस्थितमीश्वरम्।
न हिनस्त्यात्मनात्मानं ततो याति परां गतिम्॥ २८॥

samaṃ paśyan hi sarvatra samavasthitam īśvaram|
na hinasty ātmanātmānaṃ tato yāti parāṃ gatim|| 28||

प्रकृत्यैव च कर्माणि क्रियमाणानि सर्वशः।
यः पश्यति तथात्मानमकर्तारं स पश्यति॥ २९॥

prakṛtyaiva ca karmāṇi kriyamāṇāni sarvaśaḥ|
yaḥ paśyati tathātmānam akartāraṃ sa paśyati|| 29||

यदा भूतपृथग्भावमेकस्थमनुपश्यति।
तत एव च विस्तारं ब्रह्म संपद्यते तदा॥ ३०॥

yadā bhūtapṛthagbhāvam ekastham anupaśyati|
tata eva ca vistāraṃ brahma saṃpadyate tadā|| 30||

Yet others, ignorant of this,
From hearsay only worship me,
And clinging fast to what they've heard,
They too in safety cross o'er death. 25

Whatever being comes to birth,
Immovable or movable,
O best of Bhārats, know it springs
From matter's union with the soul.[348] 26

Who doth behold the same great lord,
Dwelling in all creature shapes,
The deathless one in those that die,
Who seeth thus, he sees indeed. 27

For whoso sees the lord supreme
Abiding everywhere alike,
Doth not destroy the self by self,[349]
And thus attains the highest bliss. 28

And he who sees that every act
By nature is alone performed,
And that the self is actionless,
He verily doth see aright. 29

When he perceives this varied show
Exists in him, the One, alone,
And from the One it emanates,
He then attains the state of Brahm. 30

---

[348]Of *kṣetra* and *kṣetra-jña*.

[349]Destroying the self by the self is to deprive oneself of true knowledge, i.e., of the real nature of the soul. This knowledge is impossible of attainment in the presence of ingorance and of false knowledge. When these are removed it is only then that the sage—the seer—attains to the highest goal within the reach of man, viz. *Brahma-nirvāṇa*.

अनादित्वान्निर्गुणत्वात्परमात्मायमव्ययः।
शरीरस्थो ऽपि कौन्तेय न करोति न लिप्यते॥ ३१॥

anāditvān nirguṇatvāt paramātmāyam avyayaḥ|
śarīrastho 'pi kaunteya na karoti na lipyate|| 31||

यथा सर्वगतं सौक्ष्म्यादाकाशं नोपलिप्यते।
सर्वत्रावस्थितो देहे तथात्मा नोपलिप्यते॥ ३२॥

yathā sarvagataṃ saukṣmyād ākāśaṃ nopalipyate|
sarvatrāvasthito dehe tathātmā nopalipyate|| 32||

यथा प्रकाशयत्येकः कृत्स्नं लोकमिमं रविः।
क्षेत्रं क्षेत्री तथा कृत्स्नं प्रकाशयति भारत। ३३॥

yathā prakāśayaty ekaḥ kṛtsnaṃ lokam imaṃ raviḥ|
kṣetraṃ kṣetrī tathā kṛtsnaṃ prakāśayati bhārata| 33||

क्षेत्रक्षेत्रज्ञयोरेवमन्तरं ज्ञानचक्षुषा।
भूतप्रकृतिमोक्षं च ये विदुर्यान्ति ते परम्॥ ३४॥

kṣetrakṣetrajñayor evam antaraṃ jñānacakṣuṣā|
bhūtaprakṛtimokṣaṃ ca ye vidur yānti te param|| 34||

Beginning-less and *guṇa*-less,
The self supreme who waneth not,
Though he's embodied, Kuntī's son,
He acteth not nor is he stained. 31

Just as the all-pervading space,
Through subtlety remains unsoiled,
So too untainted is the self,
Though he embodied dwells in all. 32

E'en as the sun illuminates,
O Bharat's son, the earth throughout,
So too, the knower of the field,
Illuminates the total field. 33

They who with wisdom's eye can part[350]
The field from him who knows the field,
Who matter's dissolution see,[351]
They reach unto the self supreme. 34

---

[350] I.e., can distinguish between.

[351] Lit. "destruction of the nature of all entities" (Telang); "destruction of the cause of beings" (Mahādev Śāstri). Matter, being the physical cause from which all beings are produced, its destruction, i.e., the realization of its non-existence, results from self-knowledge.

Chapter Fourteen: The Yoga of the Three Guṇa (गुणत्रयविभागयोगः)

श्रीभगवानुवाच
परं भूयः प्रवक्ष्यामि ज्ञानानां ज्ञानमुत्तमम्।
यज्ज्ञात्वा मुनयः सर्वे परां सिद्धिमितो गताः॥ १॥

śrībhagavān uvāca

paraṃ bhūyaḥ pravakṣyāmi jñānānāṃ jñānam uttamam|
yaj jñātvā munayaḥ sarve parāṃ siddhim ito gatāḥ|| 1||

इदं ज्ञानमुपाश्रित्य मम साधर्म्यमागताः।
सर्गे ऽपि नोपजायन्ते प्रलये न व्यथन्ति च॥ २॥

idaṃ jñānam upāśritya mama sādharmyam āgatāḥ|
sarge 'pi nopajāyante pralaye na vyathanti ca|| 2||

मम योनिर्महद्ब्रह्म तस्मिन् गर्भं दधाम्यहम्।
संभवः सर्वभूतानां ततो भवति भारत॥ ३॥

mama yonir mahadbrahma tasmin garbhaṃ dadhāmy aham|
saṃbhavaḥ sarvabhūtānāṃ tato bhavati bhārata|| 3||

सर्वयोनिषु कौन्तेय मूर्तयः संभवन्ति याः।
तासां ब्रह्म महद्योनिरहं बीजप्रदः पिता॥ ४॥

sarvayoniṣu kaunteya mūrtayaḥ saṃbhavanti yāḥ|
tāsāṃ brahma mahadyonir ahaṃ bījapradaḥ pitā|| 4||

सत्त्वं रजस्तम इति गुणाः प्रकृतिसंभवाः।
निबध्नन्ति महाबाहो देहे देहिनमव्ययम्॥ ५॥

sattvaṃ rajas tama iti guṇāḥ prakṛtisaṃbhavāḥ|
nibadhnanti mahābāho dehe dehinam avyayam|| 5||

तत्र सत्त्वं निर्मलत्वात्प्रकाशकमनामयम्।
सुखसङ्गेन बध्नाति ज्ञानसङ्गेन चानघ॥ ६॥

tatra sattvaṃ nirmalatvāt prakāśakam anāmayam|
sukhasaṅgena badhnāti jñānasaṅgena cānagha|| 6||

The Blessed Lord said:

Yet once again I shall proclaim
The highest wisdom and the best,[352]
Which having gained, all sages have
The perfect state beyond attained.[353] 1

Who refuged in this wisdom have
Attained to unity[354] with me,
They are not born when worlds are born,
Nor suffer[355] when they are destroyed.[356] 2

Great Brahm[357] is but a womb for me,
In which I do the seed disperse;
From thence, O Bharat's son, proceeds
The birth of all created things. 3

And from whatever wombs are born
These varied forms,[358] O Kuntī's son,
Great Brahm is verily their womb,
And their seed-giving father I. 4

Sattva and *rajas*, *tamas* too,
The *guṇas* three of matter born,
Within the body these bind fast
The deathless self who dwells within. 5

Of these the *sattva*, void of stain,
And therefore full of life and health,
Binds fast with love of happiness,
And love of wisdom, Sinless one. 6

---

[352] I.e., the best of all wisdoms.

[353] I.e., have reached perfection (emancipation) beyond the bonds of the body.

[354] Unity here means identity.

[355] I.e., are not destroyed.

[356] I.e., they are not born at the time of the creation of a world, or destroyed at its dissolution; they are not affected even at the time of Brahmā's dissolution.

[357] Brahman, here, stands for the lower *prakṛti*.

[358] Forms, or bodies which proceed from the wombs of Devas, Gandharvas, Yakṣas, Rākṣasas, man and animals—all these spring from *prakṛti*.

रजो रागात्मकं विद्धि तृष्णासङ्गसमुद्भवम्।
तन्निबध्नाति कौन्तेय कर्मसङ्गेन देहिनम्॥ ७॥

rajo rāgātmakaṃ viddhi tṛṣṇāsaṅgasamudbhavam|
tan nibadhnāti kaunteya karmasaṅgena dehinam|| 7||

तमस्त्वज्ञानजं विद्धि मोहनं सर्वदेहिनाम्।
प्रमादालस्यनिद्राभिस्तन्निबध्नाति भारत॥ ८॥

tamas tv ajñānajaṃ viddhi mohanaṃ sarvadehinām|
pramādālasyanidrābhis tan nibadhnāti bhārata|| 8||

सत्त्वं सुखे संजयति रजः कर्मणि भारत।
ज्ञानमावृत्य तु तमः प्रमादे संजयत्युत॥ ९॥

sattvaṃ sukhe saṃjayati rajaḥ karmaṇi bhārata|
jñānam āvṛtya tu tamaḥ pramāde saṃjayaty uta|| 9||

रजस्तमश्चाभिभूय सत्त्वं भवति भारत।
रजः सत्त्वं तमश्चैव तमः सत्त्वं रजस्तथा॥ १०॥

rajas tamaś cābhibhūya sattvaṃ bhavati bhārata|
rajaḥ sattvaṃ tamaś caiva tamaḥ sattvaṃ rajas tathā|| 10||

सर्वद्वारेषु देहेऽस्मिन्प्रकाश उपजायते।
ज्ञानं यदा तदा विद्याद्विवृद्धं सत्त्वमित्युत॥ ११॥

sarvadvāreṣu dehe 'smin prakāśa upajāyate|
jñānaṃ yadā tadā vidyādvivṛddhaṃ sattvam ity uta|| 11||

लोभः प्रवृत्तिरारम्भः कर्मणाम् अशमः स्पृहा।
रजस्येतानि जायन्ते विवृद्धे भरतर्षभ॥ १२॥

lobhaḥ pravṛttir ārambhaḥ karmaṇām aśamaḥ spṛhā|
rajasy etāni jāyante vivṛddhe bharatarṣabha|| 12||

Rajas, the passion-nature, know
Is spring of craving and desire;
With bonds of action, Kuntī's son,
It binds the self who dwells within. 7

But *tamas*, born of ignorance,
Deluding all embodied selves,
Doth fetter them, O Bharat's son,
With stupor, sloth and heedlessness. 8

Sattva unites with happiness,
Rajas to action, Bharat's son;
Whilst *tamas*, veiling wisdom's light,
Doth wed the self to heedlessness. 9

When *tamas*, Bhārat, is o'ercome,
Along with *rajas*, *sattva* reigns;
Rajas or *tamas* reigns in turn
When are the other two eclipsed. 10

When wisdom's light[359] shoots forth its beams
From all the gates the body has,
Then one indeed may apprehend
That *sattva* is predominant. 11

Greed, energy, desire, unrest,
The undertaking too of deeds,
O best of Bhārats, these arise
When *rajas* gains ascendancy. 12

---

[359] I.e., intelligence or understanding.

अप्रकाशो ऽप्रवृत्तिश्च प्रमादो मोह एव च।
तमस्येतानि जायन्ते विवृद्धे कुरुनन्दन॥ १३॥

aprakāśo 'pravṛttiś ca pramādo moha eva ca|
tamasy etāni jāyante vivṛddhe kurunandana|| 13||

यदा सत्त्वे प्रवृद्धे तु प्रलयं याति देहभृत्।
तदोत्तमविदां लोकानमलान्प्रतिपद्यते॥ १४॥

yadā sattve pravṛddhe tu pralayaṃ yāti dehabhṛt|
tadottamavidāṃ lokān amalān pratipadyate|| 14||

रजसि प्रलयं गत्वा कर्मसङ्गिषु जायते।
तथा प्रलीनस्तमसि मूढयोनिषु जायते॥ १५॥

rajasi pralayaṃ gatvā karmasaṅgiṣu jāyate|
tathā pralīnas tamasi mūḍhayoniṣu jāyate|| 15||

कर्मणः सुकृतस्याहुः सात्त्विकं निर्मलं फलम्।
रजसस्तु फलं दुःखमज्ञानं तमसः फलम्॥ १६॥

karmaṇaḥ sukṛtasyāhuḥ sāttvikaṃ nirmalaṃ phalam|
rajasas tu phalaṃ duḥkham ajñānaṃ tamasaḥ phalam|| 16||

सत्त्वात्संजायते ज्ञानं रजसो लोभ एव च।
प्रमादमोहौ तमसो भवतो ऽज्ञानमेव च॥ १७॥

sattvāt saṃjāyate jñānaṃ rajaso lobha eva ca|
pramādamohau tamaso bhavato 'jñānam eva ca|| 17||

ऊर्ध्वं गच्छन्ति सत्त्वस्था मध्ये तिष्ठन्ति राजसाः।
जघन्यगुणवृत्तस्था अधो गच्छन्ति तामसाः॥ १८॥

ūrdhvaṃ gacchanti sattvasthā madhye tiṣṭhanti rājasāḥ|
jaghanyaguṇavṛttasthā adho gacchanti tāmasāḥ|| 18||

Obscurity and heedlessness,
Stagnation and delusion too,
O Kuru's joy, all these arise
When *tamas* gains ascendancy. 13

Should the embodied self depart
When *sattva* is predominant,
He reaches then those spotless realms
Where they who know the highest dwell. 14

But should he go when *rajas* reigns
He is reborn 'mongst those who act;
And should he die when tamas reigns,
He's born again in senseless wombs.[360] 15

Of all good actions it is said
The fruit is *sattvic*, free from taint,
Whilst pain the fruit of rajas is,
And that of tamas ignorance. 16

From *sattva* wisdom is produced,
And avarice from *rajas* springs,
From *tamas* ignorance comes forth,
And heedlessness and error too. 17

Who follow *sattva* upwards go,
The *rājasik* midway remain,
The *tāmasik* who tread the path
Of the last *guṇa*, downwards go.[361] 18

---

[360]I.e., in the wombs of the senseless, or non-intelligent, such as the lower animals.

[361]Upwards go: i.e., are born as Devas, Gandharvas, etc.; midway remain, are born as men; downwards go, are born as brutes.

नान्यं गुणेभ्यः कर्तारं यदा द्रष्टानुपश्यति।
गुणेभ्यश्च परं वेत्ति मद्भावं सो ऽधिगच्छति॥ १९॥

nānyaṃ guṇebhyaḥ kartāraṃ yadā draṣṭānupaśyati|
guṇebhyaś ca paraṃ vetti madbhāvaṃ so 'dhigacchati|| 19||

गुणानेतानतीत्य त्रीन् देही देहसमुद्भवान्।
जन्ममृत्युजरादुःखैर्विमुक्तो ऽमृतमश्नुते॥ २०॥

guṇān etān atītya trīn dehī dehasamudbhavān|
janmamṛtyujarāduḥkhair vimukto 'mṛtam aśnute|| 20||

अर्जुन उवाच

कैर्लिङ्गैस्त्रीन् गुणानेतानतीतो भवति प्रभो।
किमाचारः कथं चैतांस्त्रीन् गुणानतिवर्तते॥ २१॥

arjuna uvāca

kair liṅgais trīn guṇān etān atīto bhavati prabho|
kimācāraḥ kathaṃ caitāṃs trīn guṇān ativartate|| 21||

श्रीभगवानुवाच

प्रकाशं च प्रवृत्तिं च मोहमेव च पाण्डव।
न द्वेष्टि संप्रवृत्तानि न निवृत्तानि काङ्क्षति॥ २२॥

śrībhagavān uvāca

prakāśaṃ ca pravṛttiṃ ca moham eva ca pāṇḍava|
na dveṣṭi saṃpravṛttāni na nivṛttāni kāṅkṣati|| 22||

उदासीनवदासीनो गुणैर्यो न विचाल्यते।
गुणा वर्तन्त इत्येव यो ऽवतिष्ठति नेङ्गते॥ २३॥

udāsīnavadāsīno guṇair yo na vicālyate|
guṇā vartanta ity eva yo 'vatiṣṭhati neṅgate|| 23||

And when a seer sees at length
No agent but the *guṇas* three,
And knoweth him who these transcends,
To my estate he then attains. 19

When the embodied self has passed
Beyond these body-makers[362] three,
'Tis freed from birth, age, death and pain,
And immortality attains. 20

Arjun said:

What are the marks of him, O lord,
Who hath beyond the *guṇas* crossed?
What is his conduct, how doth he
Beyond the *guïas* wend his way? 21

The Blessed Lord said:

Who hateth not delusion, light,
Nor energy when these prevail,
Who craveth not for them at all
O Pāṇḍav, when they've ceased to be; 22

Who seated like one unconcerned,
Is never by the *guṇas* moved;
Who knowing that the *guṇas* act,
Remaineth firm, immovable. 23

[362] According to the commentators, bodies are developments of the *guṇas*.

समदुःखसुखः स्वस्थः समलोष्टाश्मकाञ्चनः।
तुल्यप्रियाप्रियो धीरस्तुल्यनिन्दात्मसंस्तुतिः॥ २४॥

samaduḥkhasukhaḥ svasthaḥ samaloṣṭāśmakāñcanaḥ|
tulyapriyāpriyo dhīras tulyanindātmasaṃstutiḥ|| 24||

मानापमानयोस्तुल्यस्तुल्यो मित्रारिपक्षयोः।
सर्वारम्भपरित्यागी गुणातीतः स उच्यते॥ २५॥

mānāpamānayos tulyas tulyo mitrāripakṣayoḥ|
sarvārambhaparityāgī guṇātītaḥ sa ucyate|| 25||

मां च यो ऽव्यभिचारेण भक्तियोगेन सेवते।
स गुणान्समतीत्यैतान्ब्रह्मभूयाय कल्पते॥ २६॥

māṃ ca yo 'vyabhicāreṇa bhaktiyogena sevate|
sa guṇān samatītyaitān brahmabhūyāya kalpate|| 26||

ब्रह्मणो हि प्रतिष्ठाहममृतस्याव्ययस्य च।
शाश्वतस्य च धर्मस्य सुखस्यैकान्तिकस्य च॥ २७॥

brahmaṇo hi pratiṣṭhāham amṛtasyāvyayasya ca|
śāśvatasya ca dharmasya sukhasyaikāntikasya ca|| 27||

Who's centered in the self,[363] who looks alike,
On joy and pain, clod, stone and gold,
On praise and blame, dislikes and likes,
And who with wisdom is endued, 24

Who is the same in fame and shame,
Who treats alike both friend and foe,
His undertakings who resigns,
Is said to have the *guṇas* crossed. 25

And whoso serveth me alone,
With *yoga* of love unfailingly,
He going past these *guṇas* three,
Is fit to be transformed to Brahm. 26

For in me is the dwelling place
Of Brahm, the changeless, deathless one,
And of eternal righteousness,
And of the bliss that never wains. 27

[363]I.e., whose mind is not distracted by external things.

Chapter Fifteen: The Yoga of the Supreme Person (पुरुषोत्तमयोगः)

श्रीभगवानुवाच

ऊर्ध्वमूलमधःशाखमश्वत्थं प्राहुर् अव्ययम्।
छन्दांसि यस्य पर्णानि यस्तं वेद स वेदवित्॥ १॥

śrībhagavān uvāca

ūrdhvamūlam adhaḥśākham aśvatthaṃ prāhuravyayam|
chandāṃsi yasya parṇāni yastaṃ veda sa vedavit|| 1||

अधश्चोर्ध्वं प्रसृतास्तस्य शाखा
गुणप्रवृद्धा विषयप्रवालाः।
अधश्च मूलान्यनुसंततानि
कर्मानुबन्धीनि मनुष्यलोके॥ २॥

adhaś cordhvaṃ prasṛtās tasya śākhā
guṇapravṛddhā viṣayapravālāḥ|
adhaś ca mūlāny anusaṃtatāni
karmānubandhīni manuṣyaloke|| 2||

न रूपमस्येह तथोपलभ्यते
नान्तो न चादिर्न च संप्रतिष्ठा।
अश्वत्थमेनं सुविरूढमूलम्
असङ्गशस्त्रेण दृढेन छित्त्वा॥ ३॥

na rūpam asyeha tathopalabhyate
nānto na cādirna ca saṃpratiṣṭhā|
aśvattham enaṃ suvirūḍhamūlam
asaṅgaśastreṇa dṛḍhena chittvā|| 3||

ततः पदं तत्परिमार्गितव्यं
यस्मिन् गता न निवर्तन्ति भूयः।
तमेव चाद्यं पुरुषं प्रपद्ये
यतः प्रवृत्तिः प्रसृता पुराणी॥ ४॥

tataḥ padaṃ tatparimārgitavyaṃ
yasmin gatā na nivartanti bhūyaḥ|
tam eva cādyaṃ puruṣaṃ prapadye
yataḥ pravṛttiḥ prasṛtā purāṇī|| 4||

The Blessed Lord said:

With shoots below and roots above,
'Tis said the deathless *pipal*[364] grows,
Its leaves are hymns; who knoweth it
Is in the Veda truly versed. 1

Upwards and downwards,[365] *guṇa*-fed,[366] its leaves
Which have sense objects for their buds, extend,
And pendulous in the world of men distend
Its many branches, which are the bonds of deeds.[367] 2

Its form[368] as such is unperceived on earth,
Its origin, its end, its rooting place;
When this strong-rooted *pipal* is cut down
With axe of non-attachment, keen and strong, 3

That goal[369] beyond can then indeed be sought,
From whence, who reach it, come again no more.
"I refuge seek in that primeval soul,
From whom did emanate the ancient stream."[370] 4

---

[364]The *pipal* tree—the *ficus religiosa*—is here emblematical of the course of worldly life (*saṃsāra*). The supreme being—the ultimate cause of all things—is represented as its roots. Hence, these are said to be above. Its branches, which are below, are the successive orders of created beings in an evolutional series. Its leaves are the Vedic hymns, for as the leaves of a tree are essential to its life, so are the Vedic ordinances conducive to the preservation of the tree of *saṃsāra*, by enjoining various rites which result in material enjoyments, or even lead, according to some authorities, to salvation.

[365]Upwards and downwards, i.e., from the highest to the lowest of created beings.

[366]*Guṇa*-fed, i.e., sustained by the *guṇas* manifesting themselves as the body, senses, etc.

[367]The descending aerial roots are the desires for various enjoyments.

[368]I.e., its real significance is not known to those who live and move in this world. The man who knows the tree thus, i.e., as described, is said to know the Vedas because knowledge of it is in effect knowledge of the Vedas, which is that *saṃsāra* springs from the supreme being, is kept up by the Vedic rites, and destroyed by knowledge of the supreme (Telang).

[369]Viṣṇu's abode.

[370]The stream of *saṃsāra*.

निर्मानमोहा जितसङ्गदोषा
अध्यात्मनित्या विनिवृत्तकामाः।
द्वन्द्वैर्विमुक्ताः सुखदुःखसंज्ञै-
र्गच्छन्त्यमूढाः पदमव्ययं तत्॥ ५॥

nirmānamohā jitasaṅgadoṣā
adhyātmanityā vinivṛttakāmāḥ|
dvandvair vimuktāḥ sukhaduḥkhasaṃjñair
gacchanty amūḍhāḥ padam avyayaṃ tat|| 5||

न तद्भासयते सूर्यो न शशाङ्को न पावकः।
यद्गत्वा न निवर्तन्ते तद्धाम परमं मम॥ ६॥

na tad bhāsayate sūryo na śaśāṅko na pāvakaḥ|
yad gatvā na nivartante tad dhāma paramaṃ mama|| 6||

ममैवांशो जीवलोके जीवभूतः सनातनः।
मनःषष्ठानीन्द्रियाणि प्रकृतिस्थानि कर्षति॥ ७॥

mamaivāṃśo jīvaloke jīvabhūtaḥ sanātanaḥ|
manaḥṣaṣṭhānīndriyāṇi prakṛtisthāni karṣati|| 7||

शरीरं यदवाप्नोति यच्चाप्युत्क्रामतीश्वरः।
गृहीत्वैतानि संयाति वायुर्गन्धानिवाशयात्॥ ८॥

śarīraṃ yad avāpnoti yac cāpyutkrāmatīśvaraḥ|
gṛhītvaitāni saṃyāti vāyur gandhān ivāśayāt|| 8||

श्रोत्रं चक्षुः स्पर्शनं च रसनं घ्राणमेव च।
अधिष्ठाय मनश्चायं विषयानुपसेवते॥ ९॥

śrotraṃ cakṣuḥ sparśanaṃ ca rasanaṃ ghrāṇam eva ca|
adhiṣṭhāya manaś cāyaṃ viṣayān upasevate|| 9||

उत्क्रामन्तं स्थितं वापि भुञ्जानं वा गुणान्वितम्।
विमूढा नानुपश्यन्ति पश्यन्ति ज्ञानचक्षुषः॥ १०॥

utkrāmantaṃ sthitaṃ vāpi bhuñjānaṃ vā guṇānvitam|
vimūḍhā nānupaśyanti paśyanti jñānacakṣuṣaḥ|| 10||

Who no delusions have, who are not proud,
Who have attachment's evil overcome;
The freed from lust and "pairs,"[371] the self-absorbed,
The men of wisdom reach that deathless[372] goal. 5

The sun shines not upon that goal,
Nor moon nor fire illumine it;
That is mine own supernal home,
From whence, once there, none e'er returns. 6

A portion of myself transformed
As living soul in this mortal world,[373]
The senses and the mind attracts,
In matter veiled,[374] towards itself. 7

Whene'er the soul[375] a form acquires,
Whenever he departs therefrom,
He taketh these with him and goes,
As takes the wind perfume from flow'rs.[376] 8

Presiding o'er the sense of sight,
And o'er the sense of touch and taste,
And over hearing and the mind,
He doth enjoy all things of sense. 9

Who are deluded see him not,
When he who's to the *guṇas* wed
Enjoys himself, or goes, or stays;
They see him who are wisdom-eyed. 10

---

[371]Such as pleasure and pain (omitted).

[372]Lit. indestructible.

[373]Lit. in the world of life. [Or, "As live soul in this world of life. Sans. Ed.]

[374]In the Sāṅkhya philosophy the sense-organs, the mind, etc., form part of matter—hence "matter-veiled."

[375]Lit. lord (*īśvara*), here meaning the individual embodied soul. [Śaṅkara: the lord, the master of the cluster of body, etc., that is, the living being (*jīva*). Sans. Ed.]

[376]Lit. from their retreats.

यतन्तो योगिनश्चैनं पश्यन्त्यात्मन्यवस्थितम्।
यतन्तो ऽप्यकृतात्मानो नैनं पश्यन्त्यचेतसः॥ ११॥

yatanto yoginaś cainaṃ paśyanty ātmany avasthitam|
yatanto 'pyakṛtātmāno nainaṃ paśyanty acetasaḥ|| 11||

यदादित्यगतं तेजो जगद्भासयते ऽखिलम्।
यच्चन्द्रमसि यच्चाग्नौ तत्तेजो विद्धि मामकम्॥ १२॥

yad ādityagataṃ tejo jagad bhāsayate 'khilam|
yac candramasi yac cāgnau tat tejo viddhi māmakam|| 12||

गामाविश्य च भूतानि धारयाम्यहमोजसा।
पुष्णामि चौषधीः सर्वाः सोमो भूत्वा रसात्मकः॥ १३॥

gām āviśya ca bhūtāni dhārayāmy aham ojasā|
puṣṇāmi cauṣadhīḥ sarvāḥ somo bhūtvā rasātmakaḥ|| 13||

अहं वैश्वानरो भूत्वा प्राणिनां देहमाश्रितः।
प्राणापानसमायुक्तः पचाम्यन्नं चतुर्विधम्॥ १४॥

ahaṃ vaiśvānaro bhūtvā prāṇināṃ deham āśritaḥ|
prāṇāpānasamāyuktaḥ pacāmy annaṃ caturvidham|| 14||

सर्वस्य चाहं हृदि संनिविष्टो मत्तः स्मृतिर्ज्ञानमपोहनं च।
वेदैश्च सर्वैरहमेव वेद्यो वेदान्तकृद्वेदविदेव चाहम्॥ १५॥

sarvasya cāhaṃ hṛdi saṃniviṣṭo mattaḥ smṛtir jñānam apohanaṃ ca|
vedaiś ca sarvair aham eva vedyo vedāntakṛd vedavid eva cāham|| 15||

द्वाविमौ पुरुषौ लोके क्षरश्चाक्षर एव च।
क्षरः सर्वाणि भूतानि कूटस्थो ऽक्षर उच्यते॥ १६॥

dvāv imau puruṣau loke kṣaraś cākṣara eva ca|
kṣaraḥ sarvāṇi bhūtāni kūṭastho 'kṣara ucyate|| 16||

By strenuous effort devotees
Perceive him dwelling in their selves;[377]
The wisdomless, the self-untrained,[378]
Though striving hard, perceive him not. 11

The light which dwelling in the sun
Illumines all the world below,
Which shineth in the moon and fire,
That light, know thou, is mine indeed. 12

I, filling all the earth, support
All beings by my energy;
Transformed into the watery moon,[379]
I nourish every living herb. 13

Transformed into the inner fire,[380]
In living creatures do I dwell,
United with the breath of life,[381]
The four-fold food[382] do I digest. 14

And I am shrined in every heart, from me
Both memory and knowledge come and go;[383]
'Tis I who in the Veda am to be known,
Veda-knower I, and author of Vedānt. 15

This world two groups of beings[384] holds,
Th'enduring and the perishing;[385]
The perishing all creatures are,
The enduring that which lasts for aye. 16

---

[377]Selves, here, stands for bodies.
[378]Self, in this line, stands for mind.
[379]The moon is believed to be a source of moisture, hence it nourishes plants.
[380]*Vaiśvānara*, the digestive heat of the stomach.
[381]I.e., *prāṇa* and *apāna*.
[382]Foods are classified into four varieties: those that have to be chewed, sucked, licked, and drunk.
[383]I.e., the memory of what was experienced in past lives and knowledge of things transcending ordinary limits of space, time, or visible nature (Mahādeva Śāstrī).
[384]*puruṣas*.
[385]*Akṣara* (imperishable) and *kṣara* (perishable).

उत्तमः पुरुषस्त्वन्यः परमात्मेत्युदाहृतः।
यो लोकत्रयमाविश्य बिभर्त्यव्यय ईश्वरः॥ १७॥

uttamaḥ puruṣas tv anyaḥ paramātmety udāhṛtaḥ|
yo lokatrayam āviśya bibharty avyaya īśvaraḥ|| 17||

यस्मात्क्षरमतीतो ऽहमक्षरादपि चोत्तमः।
अतो ऽस्मि लोके वेदे च प्रथितः पुरुषोत्तमः॥ १८॥

yasmāt kṣaram atīto 'ham akṣarād api cottamaḥ|
ato 'smi loke vede ca prathitaḥ puruṣottamaḥ|| 18||

यो मामेवमसंमूढो जानाति पुरुषोत्तमम्।
स सर्वविद्भजति मां सर्वभावेन भारत॥ १९॥

yo mām evam asaṃmūḍho jānāti puruṣottamam|
sa sarvavid bhajati māṃ sarvabhāvena bhārata|| 19||

इति गुह्यतमं शास्त्रमिदमुक्तं मयानघ।
एतद्बुद्ध्वा बुद्धिमान्स्यात्कृतकृत्यश्च भारत॥ २०॥

iti guhyatamaṃ śāstram idam uktaṃ mayānagha|
etad buddhvā buddhimān syāt kṛtakṛtyaś ca bhārata|| 20||

There also is the soul supreme,
The highest self—his other name—,
Th'eternal lord who doth uphold
And permeate the triple-world. 17

Since I transcend what perisheth,
And do excel what changes not,
Therefore the Veda an' all the world.
Proclaim me as the soul supreme. 18

Who, undeluded, knoweth me
In this wise as the soul supreme,
He, knowing all, doth worship me
With his whole being, Bharat's son. 19

O sinless one, thus have I taught
This most mysterious science now,
Which knowing, Bhārat, man becomes
Awakened, and his work is done. 20

Chapter Sixteen: The Yoga of Excellences (दैवासुरसम्पद्विभागयोगः)

श्रीभगवानुवाच

अभयं सत्त्वसंशुद्धिर्ज्ञानयोगव्यवस्थितिः।
दानं दमश्च यज्ञश्च स्वाध्यायस्तप आर्जवम्॥

śrībhagavān uvāca

abhayaṃ sattvasaṃśuddhir jñānayogavyavasthitiḥ|
dānaṃ damaś ca yajñaś ca svādhyāyas tapa ārjavam||

अहिंसा सत्यमक्रोधस्त्यागः शान्तिरपैशुनम्।
दया भूतेष्वलोलुप्त्वं मार्दवं ह्रीरचापलम्॥ २॥

ahiṃsā satyam akrodhas tyāgaḥ śāntir apaiśunam|
dayā bhūteṣv aloluptvaṃ mārdavaṃ hrīr acāpalam|| 2||

तेजः क्षमा धृतिः शौचमद्रोहो नातिमानिता।
भवन्ति संपदं दैवीमभिजातस्य भारत॥ ३॥

tejaḥ kṣamā dhṛtiḥ śaucam adroho nātimānitā|
bhavanti saṃpadaṃ daivīm abhijātasya bhārata|| 3||

दम्भो दर्पो ऽतिमानश्च क्रोधः पारुष्यमेव च।
अज्ञानं चाभिजातस्य पार्थ संपदमासुरीम्॥ ४॥

dambho darpo 'timānaś ca krodhaḥ pāruṣyam eva ca|
ajñānaṃ cābhijātasya pārtha saṃpadam āsurīm|| 4||

दैवी संपद्विमोक्षाय निबन्धायासुरी मता।
मा शुचः संपदं दैवीम् अभिजातो ऽसि पाण्डव॥ ५॥

daivī saṃpad vimokṣāya nibandhāyāsurī matā|
mā śucaḥ saṃpadaṃ daivīm abhijāto 'si pāṇḍava|| 5||

द्वौ भूतसर्गौ लोके ऽस्मिन्दैव आसुर एव च।
दैवो विस्तरशः प्रोक्त आसुरं पार्थ मे शृणु॥ ६॥

dvau bhūtasargau loke 'smin daiva āsura eva ca|
daivo vistaraśaḥ prokta āsuraṃ pārtha me śṛṇu|| 6||

The Blessed Lord said:

Heart's purity and fearlessness,
In *yoga* of wisdom[386] steadfastness,
Gifts, sacrifice and self-restraint,
Uprightness, penance, studiousness,[387] 1

Truth, harmlessness and wrathlessness,
Renunciation, straightness,[388] peace,
Compassion,[389] meekness, modesty,
Uncovetousness and constancy,[390] 2

Forgiveness, vigor, fortitude,
Spitelessness,[391] cleanliness, lack of pride,
O Bhārat, these belong to him
Who comes to birth with godlike gifts. 3

Wrath, ignorance, hypocrisy,
Conceit, and pride, and insolence,
O Pārtha, these belong to him
Who's born with gifts demoniac. 4

The godlike gifts are deemed to be
The means by which is freedom gained,
The others but enslave; grieve not,
For thou art born with gifts divine. 5

Two kinds of creatures[392] dwell in earth,
The godlike and demoniac.[393]
The first I have described at length,
Now of the second shall I speak. 6

---

[386] *Jñāna-yoga.*
[387] Study of the scriptures.
[388] i.e., absence of crookedness.
[389] Lit. compassion to all living things.
[390] I.e., unfickleness,
[391] Absence of hatred.
[392] Or, two creations of beings.
[393] *Asuric.*

प्रवृत्तिं च निवृत्तिं च जना न विदुरासुराः।
न शौचं नापि चाचारो न सत्यं तेषु विद्यते॥ ७॥

pravṛttiṃ ca nivṛttiṃ ca janā na vidur āsurāḥ|
śaucaṃ nāpi cācāro na satyaṃ teṣu vidyate|| 7||

असत्यमप्रतिष्ठं ते जगदाहुरनीश्वरम्।
अपरस्परसंभूतं किमन्यत्कामहैतुकम्॥ ८॥

asatyam apratiṣṭhaṃ te jagad āhur anīśvaram|
aparasparasaṃbhūtaṃ kim anyat kāmahaitukam|| 8||

एतां दृष्टिमवष्टभ्य नष्टात्मानो ऽल्पबुद्धयः।
प्रभवन्त्युग्रकर्माणः क्षयाय जगतो ऽहिताः॥ ९॥

etāṃ dṛṣṭim avaṣṭabhya naṣṭātmāno 'lpabuddhayaḥ|
prabhavanty ugrakarmāṇaḥ kṣayāya jagato 'hitāḥ|| 9||

काममाश्रित्य दुष्पूरं दम्भमानमदान्विताः।
मोहाद्गृहीत्वासद्ग्राहान्प्रवर्तन्ते ऽशुचिव्रताः॥ १०॥

kāmam āśritya duṣpūraṃ dambhamānamadānvitāḥ|
mohād gṛhītvāsadgrāhān pravartante 'śucivratāḥ|| 10||

चिन्तामपरिमेयां च प्रलयान्तामुपाश्रिताः।
कामोपभोगपरमा एतावदिति निश्चिताः॥ ११॥

cintām aparimeyāṃ ca pralayāntām upāśritāḥ|
kāmopabhogaparamā etāvad iti niścitāḥ|| 11||

आशापाशशतैर्बद्धाः कामक्रोधपरायणाः।
ईहन्ते कामभोगार्थमन्यायेनार्थसंचयान्॥ १२॥

āśāpāśaśatair baddhāḥ kāmakrodhaparāyaṇāḥ|
īhante kāmabhogārtham anyāyenārthasaṃcayān|| 12||

The people who demoniac are,
Nor action nor inaction know,[394]
Nor purity, nor rectitude,
Nor truth is ever found in them. 7

These people say that this world is
A truthless, baseless,[395] godless[396] thing,
The product merely and naught else,
Of carnal union caused by lust. 8

Holding this view, these ruined souls,
Small witted and of gruesome deeds,
As haters of the world appear
Upon its ruination bent. 9

Filled with desires unquenchable,
And passion, pride, hypocrisy,
Clinging to lies, delusion-lead,
They with intents unholy work. 10

Indulging in unmeasured thoughts,
That do not cease till death is reached,
To sate desire their only aim,
Convinced that this is all in all. 11

Bound by a hundred ties of hope,
Enchained by bonds of lust and wrath,
By means unjust they strive to gain,
For sensual pleasures, hoards of wealth. 12

[394] I.e., neither energy, nor right abstinence.
[395] Without moral basis.
[396] Without a God.

इदमद्य मया लब्धमिदं प्राप्स्ये मनोरथम्।
इदमस्तीदमपि मे भविष्यति पुनर्धनम्॥ १३॥

idam adya mayā labdham idaṃ prāpsye manoratham|
idam astīdam api me bhaviṣyati punar dhanam|| 13||

असौ मया हतः शत्रुर्हनिष्ये चापरानपि।
ईश्वरो ऽहमहं भोगी सिद्धो ऽहं बलवान्सुखी॥ १४॥

asau mayā hataḥ śatrur haniṣye cāparān api|
īśvaro 'ham ahaṃ bhogī siddho 'haṃ balavān sukhī|| 14||

आढ्यो ऽभिजनवानस्मि को ऽन्यो ऽस्ति सदृशो मया।
यक्ष्ये दास्यामि मोदिष्य इत्यज्ञानविमोहिताः॥ १५॥

āḍhyo 'bhijanavān asmi ko 'nyo 'sti sadṛśo mayā|
yakṣye dāsyāmi modiṣya ity ajñānavimohitāḥ|| 15||

अनेकचित्तविभ्रान्ता मोहजालसमावृताः।
प्रसक्ताः कामभोगेषु पतन्ति नरके ऽशुचौ॥ १६॥

anekacittavibhrāntā mohajālasamāvṛtāḥ|
prasaktāḥ kāmabhogeṣu patanti narake 'śucau|| 16||

आत्मसंभाविताः स्तब्धा धनमानमदान्विताः।
यजन्ते नामयज्ञैस्ते दम्भेनाविधिपूर्वकम्॥ १७॥

ātmasaṃbhāvitāḥ stabdhā dhanamānamadānvitāḥ|
yajante nāmayajñais te dambhenāvidhipūrvakam|| 17||

अहंकारं बलं दर्पं कामं क्रोधं च संश्रिताः।
मामात्मपरदेहेषु प्रद्विषन्तो ऽभ्यसूयकाः॥ १८॥

ahaṃkāraṃ balaṃ darpaṃ kāmaṃ krodhaṃ ca saṃśritāḥ|
mām ātmaparadeheṣu pradviṣanto 'bhyasūyakāḥ|| 18||

"I have today obtained this thing,
This wish I shall attain one day,
This wealth already I possess,
And that in future I shall have; 13

"This foe of mine I now have slain,
The others also I shall slay,
A lord am I, I please myself,
I perfect am, and happy, strong. 14

"Well born am I and rich withal,
Who else is there like unto me?
I'll sacrifice, give alms, rejoice."
So prate they by unwisdom fooled. 15

Distracted sore by many a thought,
Entangled in delusion's snare,
Enslaved by sensual pleasures, they
Fall headlong in a hell unclean. 16

Self-honored, stubborn, filled with pride,
Intoxicated by their wealth,
For show alone they sacrifice,
With no regard for ordinance. 17

Indulging in brute force and lust,
And vanity and arrogance,
In other selves, as in their own,
With malice filled, these men hate me. 18

तानहं द्विषतः क्रूरान्संसारेषु नराधमान्।
क्षिपाम्यजस्रमशुभानासुरीष्वेव योनिषु॥ १९॥

tān ahaṃ dviṣataḥ krūrān saṃsāreṣu narādhamān|
kṣipāmy ajasram aśubhān āsurīṣv eva yoniṣu|| 19||

आसुरीं योनिमापन्ना मूढा जन्मनि जन्मनि।
मामप्राप्यैव कौन्तेय ततो यान्त्यधमां गतिम्॥ २०॥

āsurīṃ yonim āpannā mūḍhā janmani janmani|
mām aprāpyaiva kaunteya tato yānty adhamāṃ gatim|| 20||

त्रिविधं नरकस्येदं द्वारं नाशनमात्मनः।
कामः क्रोधस्तथा लोभस्तस्मादेतत्त्रयं त्यजेत्॥ २१॥

trividhaṃ narakasyedaṃ dvāraṃ nāśanam ātmanaḥ|
kāmaḥ krodhas tathā lobhas tasmād etat trayaṃ tyajet|| 21||

एतैर्विमुक्तः कौन्तेय तमोद्वारैस्त्रिभिर्नरः।
आचरत्यात्मनः श्रेयस्ततो याति परां गतिम्॥ २२॥

etair vimuktaḥ kaunteya tamodvārais tribhir naraḥ|
ācaraty ātmanaḥ śreyas tato yāti parāṃ gatim|| 22||

यः शास्त्रविधिमुत्सृज्य वर्तते कामकारतः।
न स सिद्धिमवाप्नोति न सुखं न परां गतिम्॥ २३॥

yaḥ śāstravidhim utsṛjya vartate kāmakārataḥ|
na sa siddhim avāpnoti na sukhaṃ na parāṃ gatim|| 23||

तस्माच्छास्त्रं प्रमाणं ते कार्याकार्यव्यवस्थितौ।
ज्ञात्वा शास्त्रविधानोक्तं कर्म कर्तुमिहार्हसि॥ २४॥

tasmāc chāstraṃ pramāṇaṃ te kāryākāryavyavasthitau|
jñātvā śāstravidhānoktaṃ karma kartum ihārhasi|| 24||

These merciless and evil men,
These haters,[397] vilest of the vile,
Forever do I hurl them back,
In wombs demonic in the worlds.[398] 19

Deluded they from birth to birth,
Are born within demonic wombs,
Ne'er reaching me, O Kuntī's son,
They sink into the lowest depths. 20

The gates of hell, in number three,
Are lust, and wrath, and avarice,
Destructive of the self are these,
Therefore from them let men abstain. 21

The man who from these portals three,
Of darkness, is released, works out
His own salvation, Kuntī's son,
And thus attains the goal supreme. 22

Who scorning holy ordinance,
Doth act as bid by his desire,
Perfection gains not, nor yet joy,
Nor doth he reach the goal supreme. 23

Let scripture then decide for thee
What should be done or left undone,
Thus knowing what the law ordains,
In pious work thou shouldst engage. 24

---

[397]I.e., of God.
[398]Worlds: paths of life and death passing through many a hell.

Chapter Seventeen: The Yoga of the Three Faiths (श्रद्धात्रयविभागयोगः)

अर्जुन उवाच

ये शास्त्रविधिमुत्सृज्य यजन्ते श्रद्धयान्विताः।
तेषां निष्ठा तु का कृष्ण सत्त्वमाहो रजस्तमः॥ १॥

arjuna uvāca

ye śāstravidhim utsṛjya yajante śraddhayānvitāḥ|
teṣāṃ niṣṭhā tu kā kṛṣṇa sattvam āho rajas tamaḥ|| 1||

श्रीभगवानुवाच

त्रिविधा भवति श्रद्धा देहिनां सा स्वभावजा।
सात्त्विकी राजसी चैव तामसी चेति तां शृणु॥ २॥

śrībhagavān uvāca

trividhā bhavati śraddhā dehināṃ sā svabhāvajā|
sāttvikī rājasī caiva tāmasī ceti tāṃ śṛṇu|| 2||

सत्त्वानुरूपा सर्वस्य श्रद्धा भवति भारत।
श्रद्धामयो ऽयं पुरुषो यो यच्छ्रद्धः स एव सः॥ ३॥

sattvānurūpā sarvasya śraddhā bhavati bhārata|
śraddhāmayo 'yaṃ puruṣo yo yac chraddhaḥ sa eva saḥ|| 3||

यजन्ते सात्त्विका देवान्यक्षरक्षांसि राजसाः।
प्रेतान् भूतगणांश्चान्ये यजन्ते तामसा जनाः॥ ४॥

yajante sāttvikā devān yakṣarakṣāṃsi rājasāḥ|
pretān bhūtagaṇāṃś cānye yajante tāmasā janāḥ|| 4||

अशास्त्रविहितं घोरं तप्यन्ते ये तपो जनाः।
दम्भाहंकारसंयुक्ताः कामरागबलान्विताः॥ ५॥

aśāstravihitaṃ ghoraṃ tapyante ye tapo janāḥ|
dambhāhaṃkārasaṃyuktāḥ kāmarāgabalānvitāḥ|| 5||

कर्शयन्तः शरीरस्थं भूतग्राममचेतसः।
मां चैवान्तःशरीरस्थं तान्विद्ध्यासुरनिश्चयान्॥ ६॥

karśayantaḥ śarīrasthaṃ bhūtagrāmam acetasaḥ|
māṃ caivāntaḥśarīrasthaṃ tān viddhy āsuraniścayān|| 6||

Arjun said:

Who full of faith make sacrifice,
Discarding what the scriptures say,
What, Krishna, is the state of these,
Sāttvic, *rājasic* or *tāmasic*? 1

The Blessed Lord said:

Three-fold by nature is the faith
Inborn in all embodied souls;
Sāttvic, *rājasic* and *tāmasic*;
Of these three faiths now hear from me. 2

The faith of each, O Bharat's son,
Conforms itself to what he is;[399]
A man on earth is full of faith,[400]
Whate'er his faith so is the man. 3

The *sāttvic* men the gods adore,
The *rājasic* the fiends and jinns;[401]
The others, the *tāmasic* men,
Departed shades and goblin hosts.[402] 4

Who practice fierce austerities,
That are by scripture not enjoined;
The hypocrite, the egoists,
With strength of lust and passion filled, 5

The foolish ones who do torment
The organs in their bodies found,
Nay, me also who dwells within;
Know these to have demonic wills. 6

---

[399]I.e., to his own nature or heart.
[400]Faith is the dominant principle in man.
[401]*Yakṣas* and *Rākṣasas*.
[402]*Pretas* and *Bhūta*, the latter being nature-spirits resembling goblins.

आहारस्त्वपि सर्वस्य त्रिविधो भवति प्रियः।
यज्ञस्तपस्तथा दानं तेषां भेदमिमं शृणु॥ ७॥

āhāras tv api sarvasya trividho bhavati priyaḥ|
yajñas tapas tathā dānaṃ teṣāṃ bhedam imaṃ śṛṇu|| 7||

आयुःसत्त्वबलारोग्यसुखप्रीतिविवर्धनाः।
रस्याः स्निग्धाः स्थिरा हृद्या आहाराः सात्त्विकप्रियाः॥ ८॥

āyuḥsattvabalārogyasukhaprītivivardhanāḥ|
rasyāḥ snigdhāḥ sthirā hṛdyā āhārāḥ sāttvikapriyāḥ|| 8||

कट्वम्ललवणात्युष्णतीक्ष्णरूक्षविदाहिनः।
आहारा राजसस्येष्टा दुःखशोकामयप्रदाः॥ ९॥

kaṭvamlalavaṇātyuṣṇatīkṣṇarūkṣavidāhinaḥ|
āhārā rājasasyeṣṭā duḥkhaśokāmayapradāḥ|| 9||

यातयामं गतरसं पूति पर्युषितं च यत्।
उच्छिष्टमपि चामेध्यं भोजनं तामसप्रियम्॥ १०॥

yātayāmaṃ gatarasaṃ pūti paryuṣitaṃ ca yat|
ucchiṣṭam api cāmedhyaṃ bhojanaṃ tāmasapriyam|| 10||

अफलाकाङ्क्षिभिर्यज्ञो विधिदृष्टो य इज्यते।
यष्टव्यमेवेति मनः समाधाय स सात्त्विकः॥ ११॥

aphalākāṅkṣibhir yajño vidhidṛṣṭo ya ijyate|
yaṣṭavyam eveti manaḥ samādhāya sa sāttvikaḥ|| 11||

अभिसंधाय तु फलं दम्भार्थमपि चैव यत्।
इज्यते भरतश्रेष्ठ तं यज्ञं विद्धि राजसम्॥ १२॥

abhisaṃdhāya tu phalaṃ dambhārtham api caiva yat|
ijyate bharataśreṣṭha taṃ yajñaṃ viddhi rājasam|| 12||

The food also belov'd of each,
Is in its nature three-fold too,
And likewise worship, penance, gifts,
Of this distinction do thou hear. 7

The foods which energy augment,
And add to life, strength, health and joy,
Nutritious, oily, savory,
Delicious; these the *sāttvic* love. 8

The bitter, salty, heating, sour,
Astringent, pungent, over-hot,
Which sickness, pain and grief produce;
These by the *rājasic* are loved. 9

The food which is devoid of taste,
And stinking, putrid, stale, unclean,
Yea, leavings too; these are indeed
Loved always by the *tāmasic.* 10

That worship by the law enjoined,
Performed by men who seek no fruit,
Convinced that duty worship is,[403]
This kind of worship *sāttvic* is. 11

But worship offered for reward,
Or merely for the sake of show,
O best of all the Bhārats, know
Such worship to be *rājasic.* 12

[403]Lit. worship that must needs be performed.

विधिहीनमसृष्टान्नं मन्त्रहीनमदक्षिणम्।
श्रद्धाविरहितं यज्ञं तामसं परिचक्षते॥ १३॥

vidhihīnam asṛṣṭānnaṃ mantrahīnam adakṣiṇam|
śraddhāvirahitaṃ yajñaṃ tāmasaṃ paricakṣate|| 13||

देवद्विजगुरुप्राज्ञपूजनं शौचमार्जवम्।
ब्रह्मचर्यमहिंसा च शारीरं तप उच्यते॥१४॥

devadvijaguruprājñapūjanaṃ śaucam ārjavam|
brahmacaryam ahiṃsā ca śārīraṃ tapa ucyate||14||

अनुद्वेगकरं वाक्यं सत्यं प्रियहितं च यत्।
स्वाध्यायाभ्यसनं चैव वाङ्मयं तप उच्यते॥ १५॥

anudvegakaraṃ vākyaṃ satyaṃ priyahitaṃ ca yat|
svādhyāyābhyasanaṃ caiva vāṅmayaṃ tapa ucyate|| 15||

मनःप्रसादः सौम्यत्वं मौनमात्मविनिग्रहः।
भावसंशुद्धिरित्येतत्तपो मानसमुच्यते॥ १६॥

manaḥprasādaḥ saumyatvaṃ maunam ātmavinigrahaḥ|
bhāvasaṃśuddhir ity etat tapo mānasam ucyate|| 16||

श्रद्धया परया तप्तं तपस्तत्त्रिविधं नरैः।
अफलाकाङ्क्षिभिर्युक्तैः सात्त्विकं परिचक्षते॥ १७॥

śraddhayā parayā taptaṃ tapas tat trividhaṃ naraiḥ|
aphalākāṅkṣibhir yuktaiḥ sāttvikaṃ paricakṣate|| 17||

सत्कारमानपूजार्थं तपो दम्भेन चैव यत्।
क्रियते तदिह प्रोक्तं राजसं चलमध्रुवम्॥ १८॥

satkāramānapūjārthaṃ tapo dambhena caiva yat|
kriyate tad iha proktaṃ rājasaṃ calam adhruvam|| 18||

The worship which is 'gainst the law,
Devoid of chants and gifts and faith,
And also of the gifts of food,
Such worship *tāmasic* is called. 13

The worship of all twice-born men,
Of gods and teachers and the wise,
Lives pure and simple, continent,
And harmless; body penance this. 14

True speech which doth not stir up strife,
Which pleasant is and doeth good,
And study of the sacred texts,
The penance this of speech is called. 15

A tranquil mind, good heartedness,
Control of self, restraint of speech,
And purity of nature too,
As mental penance know thou this. 16

This three-fold penance if performed,
With perfect faith by men attuned,
Who are exempt from hope of fruit,
Is *sāttvic* penance rightly called. 17

The penance done for worship's sake,
For honor, welcome or reward,
Which fleeting and uncertain is,
Is here on earth deemed *rājasic*. 18

मूढग्राहेणात्मनो यत्पीडया क्रियते तपः।
परस्योत्सादनार्थं वा तत्तामसमुदाहृतम्॥ १९॥

mūḍhagrāheṇātmano yat pīḍayā kriyate tapaḥ|
parasyotsādanārthaṃ vā tat tāmasam udāhṛtam|| 19||

दातव्यमिति यद्दानं दीयतेऽनुपकारिणे।
देशे काले च पात्रे च तद्दानं सात्त्विकं स्मृतम्॥ २०॥

dātavyam iti yad dānaṃ dīyate 'nupakāriṇe|
deśe kāle ca pātre ca tad dānaṃ sāttvikaṃ smṛtam|| 20||

यत्तु प्रत्युपकारार्थं फलमुद्दिश्य वा पुनः।
दीयते च परिक्लिष्टं तद्दानं राजसं स्मृतम्॥ २१॥

yat tu pratyupakārārthaṃ phalam uddiśya vā punaḥ|
dīyate ca parikliṣṭaṃ tad dānaṃ rājasaṃ smṛtam|| 21||

अदेशकाले यद्दानमपात्रेभ्यश्च दीयते।
असत्कृतमवज्ञातं तत्तामसमुदाहृतम्॥ २२॥

adeśakāle yad dānam apātrebhyaś ca dīyate|
asatkṛtam avajñātaṃ tat tāmasam udāhṛtam|| 22||

ओं तत्सदिति निर्देशो ब्रह्मणस्त्रिविधः स्मृतः।
ब्राह्मणास्तेन वेदाश्च यज्ञाश्च विहिताः पुरा॥ २३॥

oṃ tat sad iti nirdeśo brahmaṇas trividhaḥ smṛtaḥ|
brāhmaṇās tena vedāś ca yajñāś ca vihitāḥ purā|| 23||

तस्मादोमित्युदाहृत्य यज्ञदानतपःक्रियाः।
प्रवर्तन्ते विधानोक्ताः सततं ब्रह्मवादिनाम्॥ २४॥

tasmād om ity udāhṛtya yajñadānatapaḥkriyāḥ|
pravartante vidhānoktāḥ satataṃ brahmavādinām|| 24||

The penance which is practiced
Under a notion that is false,
To torture self, or others hurt,[404]
Such penance is called *tāmasic*. 19

A gift for duty's sake bestowed
On one who cannot aught return,
Who's worthy, at a time and place
Both meet, is truly *sāttvic* gift. 20

But the gift that calls for due return,
Or that is made for some reward,
The gift that is not freely made,
Is deemed to be gift *rājasic*. 21

The gift to the unworthy given,
Which is mis-timed and out of place,
Without respect or with contempt,
Such gift's proclaimed as *tāmasic*. 22

It has been said that "*om tat sat*,"
This triple word denotes the Brahm;
By that[405] in days of yore were made
The brāhmaṇs, Veda and sacrifice. 23

Therefore whilst uttering "*om*" all acts
Of penance, gifts and sacrifice,
Enjoined by scripture are begun
By those who always know the Brahm. 24

---

[404]Lit. for the destruction of others.
[405]I.e., by Brahman (Śrīdhara).

तदित्यनभिसंधाय फलं यज्ञतपःक्रियाः।
दानक्रियाश्च विविधाः क्रियन्ते मोक्षकाङ्क्षिभिः॥ २५॥

tad ity anabhisaṃdhāya phalaṃ yajñatapaḥkriyāḥ|
dānakriyāś ca vividhāḥ kriyante mokṣakāṅkṣibhiḥ|| 25||

सद्भावे साधुभावे च सदित्येतत्प्रयुज्यते।
प्रशस्ते कर्मणि तथा सच्छब्दः पार्थ युज्यते॥ २६॥

sadbhāve sādhubhāve ca sad ity etat prayujyate|
praśaste karmaṇi tathā sacchabdaḥ pārtha yujyate|| 26||

यज्ञे तपसि दाने च स्थितिः सदिति चोच्यते।
कर्म चैव तदर्थीयं सदित्येवाभिधीयते॥ २७॥

yajñe tapasi dāne ca sthitiḥ sad iti cocyate|
karma caiva tadarthīyaṃ sad ity evābhidhīyate|| 27||

अश्रद्धया हुतं दत्तं तपस्तप्तं कृतं च यत्।
असदित्युच्यते पार्थ न च तत्प्रेत्य नो इह॥ २८॥

aśraddhayā hutaṃ dattaṃ tapas taptaṃ kṛtaṃ ca yat|
asad ity ucyate pārtha na ca tat pretya no iha|| 28||

With "*tat*," not aiming at reward,
All sacrificial acts are done,
And those of penance and of gifts,
By those who liberation seek. 25

And "*sat*" is used for all that is
Both good and real, O Pṛthā's son,
And "*sat*" likewise doth designate
All actions that auspicious are. 26

Steadfastness in austerity,
In sacrifices and in gifts,
And even acts for these performed,
Are fitly spoken of as "*sat.*" 27

Whate'er is wrought in want of faith
Of penance, gifts or sacrifice,
O Pṛthā's son, it is *asat.*
And naught both here and after death. 28

Chapter Eighteen: The Yoga of Liberation (मोक्षयोगः)

अर्जुन उवाच
संन्यासस्य महाबाहो तत्त्वमिच्छामि वेदितुम्।
त्यागस्य च हृषीकेश पृथक्केशिनिषूदन॥ १॥

arjuna uvāca

saṃnyāsasya mahābāho tattvamicchāmi veditum|
tyāgasya ca hṛṣīkeśa pṛthak keśiniṣūdana|| 1||

श्रीभगवानुवाच
काम्यानां कर्मणां न्यासं संन्यासं कवयो विदुः।
सर्वकर्मफलत्यागं प्राहुस्त्यागं विचक्षणाः॥ २॥

śrībhagavān uvāca

kāmyānāṃ karmaṇāṃ nyāsaṃ saṃnyāsaṃ kavayo viduḥ|
sarvakarmaphalatyāgaṃ prāhus tyāgaṃ vicakṣaṇāḥ|| 2||

त्याज्यं दोषवदित्येके कर्म प्राहुर्मनीषिणः।
यज्ञदानतपःकर्म न त्याज्यमिति चापरे॥ ३॥

tyājyaṃ doṣavad ity eke karma prāhur manīṣiṇaḥ|
yajñadānatapaḥkarma na tyājyam iti cāpare|| 3||

निश्चयं शृणु मे तत्र त्यागे भरतसत्तम।
त्यागो हि पुरुषव्याघ्र त्रिविधः संप्रकीर्तितः॥ ४॥

niścayaṃ śṛṇu me tatra tyāge bharatasattama|
tyāgo hi puruṣavyāghra trividhaḥ saṃprakīrtitaḥ|| 4||

यज्ञदानतपःकर्म न त्याज्यं कार्यमेव तत्।
यज्ञो दानं तपश्चैव पावनानि मनीषिणाम्॥ ५॥

yajñadānatapaḥkarma na tyājyaṃ kāryam eva tat|
yajño dānaṃ tapaś caiva pāvanāni manīṣiṇām|| 5||

Arjun said:

O mighty armed, I wish to know
The essence of *sannyās* and *tyāg*,[406]
O Keśi's[407] slayer, O Hṛṣīkeś!
The two considered as distinct. 1

The Blessed Lord said:

Renouncing work for greed[408] performed
Is by the sages called *sannyās*;
Renouncing the reward of work
Is by the learned known as *tyāg*. 2

Some sages say, as full of ill,
All action should abandoned be,
And some that acts of penance, gifts,
And sacrifice should not be shunned.[409] 3

O best among the Bhāratas, hear
The truth about this *tyāg* from me;
O tiger of mankind, 'tis said
Of three distinctive kinds is *tyāg*. 4

All acts of sacrifice and gifts
And penance should be practiced,
And not renounced, for these indeed
Are sanctifiers of the wise. 5

---

[406]*Sannyāsa* is literally "putting away." Both *sannyāsa* and *tyāga* mean "giving up," and "renunciation," "surrender." It is to be noted that the Lord, in his reply to Arjuna, declines to treat the two as separate virtues and deals with them as if they were identical.
[407]*Keśī*: a demon slain by Kṛṣṇa.
[408]I.e., for "fruits" sake.
[409]Lit. "abandoned."

एतान्यपि तु कर्माणि सङ्गं त्यक्त्वा फलानि च।
कर्तव्यानीति मे पार्थ निश्चितं मतमुत्तमम्॥ ६॥

etāny api tu karmāṇi saṅgaṃ tyaktvā phalāni ca|
kartavyānīti me pārtha niścitaṃ matam uttamam|| 6||

नियतस्य तु संन्यासः कर्मणो नोपपद्यते।
मोहात्तस्य परित्यागस्तामसः परिकीर्तितः॥ ७॥

niyatasya tu saṃnyāsaḥ karmaṇo nopapadyate|
mohāt tasya parityāgas tāmasaḥ parikīrtitaḥ|| 7||

दुःखमित्येव यत्कर्म कायक्लेशभयात्त्यजेत्।
स कृत्वा राजसं त्यागं नैव त्यागफलं लभेत्॥ ८॥

duḥkham ity eva yat karma kāyakleśabhayāt tyajet|
sa kṛtvā rājasaṃ tyāgaṃ naiva tyāgaphalaṃ labhet|| 8||

कार्यमित्येव यत्कर्म नियतं क्रियते ऽर्जुन।
सङ्गं त्यक्त्वा फलं चैव स त्यागः सात्त्विको मतः॥ ९॥

kāryam ity eva yat karma niyataṃ kriyate 'rjuna|
saṅgaṃ tyaktvā phalaṃ caiva sa tyāgaḥ sāttviko mataḥ|| 9||

न द्वेष्ट्यकुशलं कर्म कुशले नानुषज्जते।
त्यागी सत्त्वसमाविष्टो मेधावी छिन्नसंशयः॥ १०॥

na dveṣṭy akuśalaṃ karma kuśale nānuṣajjate|
tyāgī sattvasamāviṣṭo medhāvī chinnasaṃśayaḥ|| 10||

न हि देहभृता शक्यं त्यक्तुं कर्माण्यशेषतः।
यस्तु कर्मफलत्यागी स त्यागीत्यभिधीयते॥ ११॥

na hi dehabhṛtā śakyaṃ tyaktuṃ karmāṇy aśeṣataḥ|
yas tu karmaphalatyāgī sa tyāgīty abhidhīyate|| 11||

अनिष्टमिष्टं मिश्रं च त्रिविधं कर्मणः फलम्।
भवत्यत्यागिनां प्रेत्य न तु संन्यासिनां क्वचित्॥ १२॥

aniṣṭam iṣṭaṃ miśraṃ ca trividhaṃ karmaṇaḥ phalam|
bhavaty atyāginām pretya na tu saṃnyāsināṃ kvacit|| 12||

But even these should be performed
Without attachment, Pṛthā's son,
Forsaking also every fruit;
My best and final verdict this. 6

For verily it is not meet
To give up deeds that are ordained;
Renouncing these through ignorance,
Is said to be *tyāg* tāmasic. 7

Renouncing deeds that painful are,
From fear of bodily fatigue,
Is held to be *tyāg* rājasic,
And with it carries no reward. 8

A deed ordained that is performed
Solely because it should be done,
Attachment and all fruits forsworn,
Such *tyāg* is sāttvic deemed to be. 9

The *sattva*-filled renouncer who
Is talented and free from doubts,
Is not attached to pleasant deeds,
Nor doth he hate unpleasant ones. 10

For truly no embodied soul
Can ever wholy give up deeds;
But he is a renouncer called
Who doth abandon action's fruit. 11

The triple fruit, good, ill and mixed,
Of work awaits them hereafter,
Who non-renouncers are on earth,
But never those who have renounced. 12

पञ्चैतानि महाबाहो कारणानि निबोध मे।
सांख्ये कृतान्ते प्रोक्तानि सिद्धये सर्वकर्मणाम्॥ १३॥

pañcaitāni mahābāho kāraṇāni nibodha me|
sāṃkhye kṛtānte proktāni siddhaye sarvakarmaṇām|| 13||

अधिष्ठानं तथा कर्ता करणं च पृथग्विधम्।
विविधाश्च पृथक्चेष्टा दैवं चैवात्र पञ्चमम्॥ १४॥

adhiṣṭhānaṃ tathā kartā karaṇaṃ ca pṛthagvidham|
vividhāś ca pṛthakceṣṭā daivaṃ caivātra pañcamam|| 14||

शरीरवाङ्मनोभिर्यत्कर्म प्रारभते नरः।
न्याय्यं वा विपरीतं वा पञ्चैते तस्य हेतवः॥ १५॥

śarīravāṅmanobhir yat karma prārabhate naraḥ|
nyāyyaṃ vā viparītaṃ vā pañcaite tasya hetavaḥ|| 15||

तत्रैवं सति कर्तारमात्मानं केवलं तु यः।
पश्यत्यकृतबुद्धित्वान्न स पश्यति दुर्मतिः॥ १६॥

tatraivaṃ sati kartāram ātmānaṃ kevalaṃ tu yaḥ|
paśyaty akṛtabuddhitvān na sa paśyati durmatiḥ|| 16||

यस्य नाहंकृतो भावो बुद्धिर्यस्य न लिप्यते।
हत्वापि स इमाँल्लोकान्न हन्ति न निबध्यते॥ १७॥

yasya nāhaṃkṛto bhāvo buddhir yasya na lipyate|
hatvāpi sa imām̐l lokān na hanti na nibadhyate|| 17||

ज्ञानं ज्ञेयं परिज्ञाता त्रिविधा कर्मचोदना।
करणं कर्म कर्तेति त्रिविधः कर्मसंग्रहः॥ १८॥

jñānaṃ jñeyaṃ parijñātā trividhā karmacodanā|
karaṇaṃ karma karteti trividhaḥ karmasaṃgrahaḥ|| 18||

O mighty armed, learn thou from me,
The causes five by which alone
All actions are accomplished,
As in the *Sāṅkhya* creed set forth. 13

The body[410] first, the agent[411] then,
The various organs coming next,[412]
Activities of diverse kinds,[413]
And last of all the deities.[414] 14

Whatever deed a man performs
With body or with speech or mind,
It matters not if right or wrong,
These five indeed its causes are. 15

This being so, who verily,
From lack of knowledge, doth regard
Himself as the sole agent, he,
The foolish one, perceiveth not. 16

He who's free from ego sense,
Whose reason has no taint at all,[415]
He slayeth not, nor is he bound,
Although he may the people slay. 17

The knower,[416] knowledge,[417] object known,[418]
These, three-fold, give impulse to act;
The organ, agent and the act,
The triple base of action are. 18

[410]Lit. the *seat*, i.e., the body which is the sear of desire, aversion, etc.
[411]Actor, i.e., the person who considers himself as the doer of actions.
[412]The various organs, i.e., the sense organs, being the instruments of action.
[413]Activities such as movements of the fivefold vital air.
[414]The deities, i.e., the deities which preside over the eye and other organs, helping them to perform their functions.
[415]Untainted with the egoistic notion that "I am the doer."
[416]I.e., the person who has knowledge.
[417]Knowledge in general.
[418]Objects of knowledge in general.

ज्ञानं कर्म च कर्ता च त्रिधैव गुणभेदतः।
प्रोच्यते गुणसंख्याने यथावच्छृणु तान्यपि॥ १९॥

jñānaṃ karma ca kartā ca tridhaiva guṇabhedataḥ|
procyate guṇasaṃkhyāne yathāvac chṛṇu tāny api|| 19||

सर्वभूतेषु येनैकं भावमव्ययमीक्षते।
अविभक्तं विभक्तेषु तज्ज्ञानं विद्धि सात्त्विकम्॥ २०॥

sarvabhūteṣu yenaikaṃ bhāvam avyayam īkṣate|
avibhaktaṃ vibhakteṣu taj jñānaṃ viddhi sāttvikam|| 20||

पृथक्त्वेन तु यज्ज्ञानं नानाभावान्पृथग्विधान्।
वेत्ति सर्वेषु भूतेषु तज्ज्ञानं विद्धि राजसम्॥ २१॥

pṛthaktvena tu yaj jñānaṃ nānābhāvān pṛthagvidhān|
vetti sarveṣu bhūteṣu taj jñānaṃ viddhi rājasam|| 21||

यत्तु कृत्स्नवदेकस्मिन्कार्ये सक्तमहैतुकम्।
अतत्त्वार्थवदल्पं च तत्तामसमुदाहृतम्॥ २२॥

yat tu kṛtsnavad ekasmin kārye saktam ahaitukam|
atattvārthavad alpaṃ ca tat tāmasam udāhṛtam|| 22||

नियतं सङ्गरहितमरागद्वेषतः कृतम्।
अफलप्रेप्सुना कर्म यत्तत् सात्त्विकमुच्यते॥ २३॥

niyataṃ saṅgarahitam arāgadveṣataḥ kṛtam|
aphalaprepsunā karma yat tat sāttvikam ucyate|| 23||

यत्तु कामेप्सुना कर्म साहंकारेण वा पुनः।
क्रियते बहुलायासं तद्राजसमुदाहृतम्॥ २४॥

yat tu kāmepsunā karma sāhaṃkāreṇa vā punaḥ|
kriyate bahulāyāsaṃ tad rājasam udāhṛtam|| 24||

The science of the *guṇas*[419] holds
That agent, knowledge and the act,
As by the *guṇas* distinguished,
Are of three kinds; of this now hear. 19

Perception by which one perceives
The deathless[420] self in all that lives,
The partless 'midst divided ones,
As sāttvic knowledge know thou this. 20

Perception holding as distinct
The selves in various creature shapes,
Such knowledge do thou know to be
Rājasic knowledge doubtlessly. 21

Perception which doth blindly cling
To effects as the all in all,
Unreal,[421] narrow,[422] reasonless,[423]
Such knowledge is called tāmasic. 22

An act which is ordained,[424] when done
By one who seeketh no reward,
Without attachment, love or hate;
Such action sāttvic is declared. 23

The act which is performed by one
Who seeketh gain[425] for selfish ends,
Or which is wrought with weary toil,
Such act indeed is rājasic. 24

---

[419]Refers to Kapila's system of philosophy.
[420]Lit. indestructible.
[421]I.e., without truth.
[422]I.e., not comprehensive, insignificant.
[423]I.e., without any argument to support it.
[424]Refers to obligatory actions.
[425]Lit. by one longing for desires.

अनुबन्धं क्षयं हिंसामनपेक्ष्य च पौरुषम्।
मोहादारभ्यते कर्म यत्तत्तामसमुच्यते॥ २५॥

anubandhaṃ kṣayaṃ hiṃsām anapekṣya ca pauruṣam|
mohād ārabhyate karma yat tat tāmasam ucyate|| 25||

मुक्तसङ्गो ऽनहंवादी धृत्युत्साहसमन्वितः।
सिद्ध्यसिद्ध्योर्निर्विकारः कर्ता सात्त्विक उच्यते॥ २६॥

muktasaṅgo 'nahaṃvādī dhṛtyutsāhasamanvitaḥ|
siddhyasiddhyor nirvikāraḥ kartā sāttvika ucyate|| 26||

रागी कर्मफलप्रेप्सुर्लुब्धो हिंसात्मको ऽशुचिः।
हर्षशोकान्वितः कर्ता राजसः परिकीर्तितः॥ २७॥

rāgī karmaphalaprepsur lubdho hiṃsātmako 'śuciḥ|
harṣaśokānvitaḥ kartā rājasaḥ parikīrtitaḥ|| 27||

अयुक्तः प्राकृतः स्तब्धः शठो नैकृतिको ऽलसः।
विषादी दीर्घसूत्री च कर्ता तामस उच्यते॥ २८॥

ayuktaḥ prākṛtaḥ stabdhaḥ śaṭho naikṛtiko 'lasaḥ|
viṣādī dīrghasūtrī ca kartā tāmasa ucyate|| 28||

बुद्धेर्भेदं धृतेश्चैव गुणतस्त्रिविधं शृणु।
प्रोच्यमानमशेषेण पृथक्त्वेन धनंजय॥ २९॥

buddher bhedaṃ dhṛteś caiva guṇatas trividhaṃ śṛṇu|
procyamānam aśeṣeṇa pṛthaktvena dhanaṃjaya|| 29||

प्रवृत्तिं च निवृत्तिं च कार्याकार्ये भयाभये।
बन्धं मोक्षं च या वेत्ति बुद्धिः सा पार्थ सात्त्विकी॥ ३०॥

pravṛttiṃ ca nivṛttiṃ ca kāryākārye bhayābhaye|
bandhaṃ mokṣaṃ ca yā vetti buddhiḥ sā pārtha sāttvikī|| 30||

The act in ignorance[426] begun,
Without regard to consequence,
Capacity[427] or loss[428] or hurt,[429]
Such tāmasic is held to be. 25

Attachment free, without conceit,
Endued with firmness and with zeal,
Unmoved by failure or success,
Such agent sāttvic is declared. 26

Desiring fruits, and passionate,
Impure and cruel, full of greed,
The slave of sorrow and of joy,
Such agent is called rājasic. 27

Unsteady, vulgar, obstinate,
Deceitful, wicked, indolent,
Despondent, procrastinating oft,
Such agent is called tāmasic. 28

Of intellect[430] and determination now,
These *guṇa*-like of triple kind,
Of each I shall here fully speak,
Lend ear, O Dhanañjay, to me. 29

Which action and inaction knows,
What should be done, what should not be,
Fear, fearlessness, bondage, release,
Such intellect is sāttvic, Pārtha. 30

---

[426]*Moha*, which is more correctly delusion.

[427]I.e., the ability to carry out the work.

[428]I.e., of power or wealth resulting from an unfinished undertaking.

[429]I.e., injury to others.

[430]Intellect and courage: the former is the equivalent of *buddhi*, the latter of *dhṛti*, which is the firmness of *buddhi* (Telang).

यया धर्ममधर्मं च कार्यं चाकार्यमेव च।
अयथावत्प्रजानाति बुद्धिः सा पार्थ राजसी॥ ३१॥

yayā dharmam adharmaṃ ca kāryaṃ cākāryam eva ca|
ayathāvat prajānāti buddhiḥ sā pārtha rājasī|| 31||

अधर्मं धर्ममिति या मन्यते तमसावृता।
सर्वार्थान्विपरीतांश्च बुद्धिः सा पार्थ तामसी॥ ३२॥

adharmaṃ dharmam iti yā manyate tamasāvṛtā|
sarvārthān viparītāṃś ca buddhiḥ sā pārtha tāmasī|| 32||

धृत्या यया धारयते मनःप्राणेन्द्रियक्रियाः।
योगेनाव्यभिचारिण्या धृतिः सा पार्थ सात्त्विकी॥ ३३॥

dhṛtyā yayā dhārayate manaḥprāṇendriyakriyāḥ|
yogenāvyabhicāriṇyā dhṛtiḥ sā pārtha sāttvikī|| 33||

यया तु धर्मकामार्थान्धृत्या धारयते ऽर्जुन।
प्रसङ्गेन फलाकाङ्क्षी धृतिः सा पार्थ राजसी॥ ३४॥

yayā tu dharmakāmārthān dhṛtyā dhārayate 'rjuna|
prasaṅgena phalākāṅkṣī dhṛtiḥ sā pārtha rājasī|| 34||

यया स्वप्नं भयं शोकं विषादं मदमेव च।
न विमुञ्चति दुर्मेधा धृतिः सा पार्थ तामसी॥ ३५॥

yayā svapnaṃ bhayaṃ śokaṃ viṣādaṃ madam eva ca|
na vimuñcati durmedhā dhṛtiḥ sā pārtha tāmasī|| 35||

सुखं त्विदानीं त्रिविधं शृणु मे भरतर्षभ।
अभ्यासाद्रमते यत्र दुःखान्तं च निगच्छति॥ ३६॥

sukhaṃ tv idānīṃ trividhaṃ śṛṇu me bharatarṣabha|
abhyāsād ramate yatra duḥkhāntaṃ ca nigacchati|| 36||

By which one wrongly understands
The difference 'twixt right and wrong,[431]
What should be done, what should not be,
Such intellect is rājasic. 31

And which enshrouded is by gloom,
And therefore sees both right and wrong
And other things turned upside down,
Such intellect is tāmasic. 32

That determination which through *yoga*
Enables one to curb the mind,
The senses and the breaths of life,
Such determination, Pārtha, sāttvic is. 33

But that through which one clingeth fast
To piety[432] and lust and wrath,
And by attachment longs for fruit,
Such determination, Pārtha, is rājasic. 34

And that by which a foolish man
Doth not abandon fear and grief,
Nor sleep, despair, nor vanity, O Pārtha,
Is determination tāmasic. 35

And now about the three-fold joy
Hear thou, O chief of Bharata's race,
In which by habit one delights,
And which destroyeth every pain. 36

---

[431] *Dharma* and *adharma*.
[432] *Dharma*.

यत्तदग्रे विषमिव परिणामे ऽमृतोपमम्।
तत्सुखं सात्त्विकं प्रोक्तमात्मबुद्धिप्रसादजम्॥ ३७॥

yat tad agre viṣam iva pariṇāme 'mṛtopamam|
tat sukhaṃ sāttvikaṃ proktam ātmabuddhiprasādajam|| 37||

विषयेन्द्रियसंयोगाद्यत्तदग्रे ऽमृतोपमम्।
परिणामे विषमिव तत्सुखं राजसं स्मृतम्॥ ३८॥

viṣayendriyasaṃyogād yat tad agre 'mṛtopamam|
pariṇāme viṣam iva tat sukhaṃ rājasaṃ smṛtam|| 38||

यदग्रे चानुबन्धे च सुखं मोहनमात्मनः।
निद्रालस्यप्रमादोत्थं तत्तामसमुदाहृतम्॥ ३९॥

yad agre cānubandhe ca sukhaṃ mohanam ātmanaḥ|
nidrālasyapramādotthaṃ tat tāmasam udāhṛtam|| 39||

न तदस्ति पृथिव्यां वा दिवि देवेषु वा पुनः।
सत्त्वं प्रकृतिजैर्मुक्तं यदेभिः स्यात्त्रिभिर्गुणैः॥ ४०॥

na tad asti pṛthivyāṃ vā divi deveṣu vā punaḥ|
sattvaṃ prakṛtijair muktaṃ yad ebhiḥ syāt tribhir guṇaiḥ|| 40||

ब्राह्मणक्षत्रियविशां शूद्राणां च परंतप।
कर्माणि प्रविभक्तानि स्वभावप्रभवैर्गुणैः॥ ४१॥

brāhmaṇakṣatriyaviśāṃ śūdrāṇāṃ ca paraṃtapa|
karmāṇi pravibhaktāni svabhāvaprabhavair guṇaiḥ|| 41||

शमो दमस्तपः शौचं क्षान्तिरार्जवमेव च।
ज्ञानं विज्ञानमास्तिक्यं ब्रह्मकर्म स्वभावजम्॥ ४२॥

śamo damas tapaḥ śaucaṃ kṣāntir ārjavam eva ca|
jñānaṃ vijñānam āstikyaṃ brahmakarma svabhāvajam|| 42||

The joy which first like poison tastes,
But turns to nectar in the end,
Which cometh from heart's purity,[433]
Such joy is sāttvic joy indeed. 37

Which springeth from the bond between
The senses and their objects, tastes
As nectar first but poison last,
That joy is reckoned rājasic. 38

That which at first and afterwards
Deludes the self and springs from sleep,
And heedlessness, and indolence,
Such joy is counted tāmasic. 39

There does not live on earth below,
Or 'mongst the gods in heaven above,
A single being who is free
From these three *guṇas*, matter born. 40

The *brāhmiṇs*, *kṣatrīs*, *vaiśyas* too,
And *śūdras* also, Parantap,
Their various duties[434] are enjoined
In keeping with their nature's bent.[435] 41

Faith, self-restraint and peace of mind,
Forgiveness, patience, purity,
Uprightness, wisdom, knowledge too,
Are *brāhmiṇ* duties nature-born.[436] 42

---

[433]The original has also been rendered as "blissful knowledge of the Self."
[434]*Karmas.*
[435]Lit. according to the *guṇas* born of their own natures. Comp. Discourse IV, v. 13.
[436]I.e., are duties natural to *brāhmaṇas*.

शौर्यं तेजो धृतिर्दाक्ष्यं युद्धे चाप्यपलायनम्।
दानमीश्वरभावश्च क्षात्रं कर्म स्वभावजम्॥ ४३॥

śauryaṃ tejo dhṛtir dākṣyaṃ yuddhe cāpy apalāyanam|
dānam īśvarabhāvaś ca kṣātraṃ karma svabhāvajam|| 43||

कृषिगोरक्ष्यवाणिज्यं वैश्यकर्म स्वभावजम्।
परिचर्यात्मकं कर्म शूद्रस्यापि स्वभावजम्॥ ४४॥

kṛṣigorakṣyavāṇijyaṃ vaiśyakarma svabhāvajam|
paricaryātmakaṃ karma śūdrasyāpi svabhāvajam|| 44||

स्वे स्वे कर्मण्यभिरतः संसिद्धिं लभते नरः।
स्वकर्मनिरतः सिद्धिं यथा विन्दति तच्छृणु॥ ४५॥

sve sve karmaṇy abhirataḥ saṃsiddhiṃ labhate naraḥ|
svakarmanirataḥ siddhiṃ yathā vindati tac chṛṇu|| 45||

यतः प्रवृत्तिर्भूतानां येन सर्वमिदं ततम्।
स्वकर्मणा तमभ्यर्च्य सिद्धिं विन्दति मानवः॥ ४६॥

yataḥ pravṛttir bhūtānāṃ yena sarvam idaṃ tatam|
svakarmaṇā tam abhyarcya siddhiṃ vindati mānavaḥ|| 46||

श्रेयान्स्वधर्मो विगुणः परधर्मात्स्वनुष्ठितात्।
स्वभावनियतं कर्म कुर्वन्नाप्नोति किल्बिषम्॥ ४७॥

śreyān svadharmo viguṇaḥ paradharmāt svanuṣṭhitāt|
svabhāvaniyataṃ karma kurvan nāpnoti kilbiṣam|| 47||

सहजं कर्म कौन्तेय सदोषमपि न त्यजेत्।
सर्वारम्भा हि दोषेण धूमेनाग्निरिवावृताः॥ ४८॥

sahajaṃ karma kaunteya sadoṣam api na tyajet|
sarvārambhā hi doṣeṇa dhūmenāgnir ivāvṛtāḥ|| 48||

Prowess and glory, strength and skill,
Not turning from the foe away,
Benevolence and lordliness,
Are *kṣatrī* duties nature-born. 43

And cattle raising, ploughing, trade,
Are *vaiśya* duties nature-born,
Whilst menial service appertains
To *śūdra* duties nature-born. 44

Each on his special duty bent,
Man reaches thus the perfect state;
How he intent on his own work[437]
Attains perfection, learn from me. 45

From whom all beings are evolved,
By whom this world is filled all through,
His worship, wrought by one's own work,
Doth win for man the perfect state. 46

One's own work is, though meritless,
Better than another's work well done;
Who does the tasks[438] by nature set,[439]
Thereby incurs no sin at all. 47

His innate duty,[440] Kuntī's son,
Let no man shun, though full of faults,
For all man's undertakings are
With faults enwrapped, as fire by smoke. 48

---

[437]*Karma* ("action arising from the nature furnished by past thoughts and desires," Mrs. Besant).
[438]*Karma*.
[439]I.e., by his own nature.
[440]I.e., born with his nature.

असक्तबुद्धिः सर्वत्र जितात्मा विगतस्पृहः।
नैष्कर्म्यसिद्धिं परमां संन्यासेनाधिगच्छति॥ ४९॥

asaktabuddhiḥ sarvatra jitātmā vigataspṛhaḥ|
naiṣkarmyasiddhiṃ paramāṃ saṃnyāsenādhigacchati|| 49||

सिद्धिं प्राप्तो यथा ब्रह्म तथाप्नोति निबोध मे।
समासेनैव कौन्तेय निष्ठा ज्ञानस्य या परा॥ ५०॥

siddhiṃ prāpto yathā brahma tathāpnoti nibodha me|
samāsenaiva kaunteya niṣṭhā jñānasya yā parā|| 50||

बुद्ध्या विशुद्धया युक्तो धृत्यात्मानं नियम्य च।
शब्दादीन्विषयांस्त्यक्त्वा रागद्वेषौ व्युदस्य च॥ ५१॥

buddhyā viśuddhayā yukto dhṛtyātmānaṃ niyamya ca|
śabdādīn viṣayāṃs tyaktvā rāgadveṣau vyudasya ca|| 51||

विविक्तसेवी लघ्वाशी यतवाक्कायमानसः।
ध्यानयोगपरो नित्यं वैराग्यं समुपाश्रितः॥ ५२॥

viviktasevī laghvāśī yatavākkāyamānasaḥ|
dhyānayogaparo nityaṃ vairāgyaṃ samupāśritaḥ|| 52||

अहंकारं बलं दर्पं कामं क्रोधं परिग्रहम्।
विमुच्य निर्ममः शान्तो ब्रह्मभूयाय कल्पते॥ ५३॥

ahaṃkāraṃ balaṃ darpaṃ kāmaṃ krodhaṃ parigraham|
vimucya nirmamaḥ śānto brahmabhūyāya kalpate|| 53||

ब्रह्मभूतः प्रसन्नात्मा न शोचति न काङ्क्षति।
समः सर्वेषु भूतेषु मद्भक्तिं लभते पराम्॥ ५४॥

brahmabhūtaḥ prasannātmā na śocati na kāṅkṣati|
samaḥ sarveṣu bhūteṣu madbhaktiṃ labhate parām|| 54||

Whose reason is nowhere attached,
Who's self-subdued, to longings[441] dead,
He by renunciation wins,
The perfect state of actlessness.[442] 49

How he who has perfection gained
Attains to Brahm, the goal supreme
Of knowledge, O thou Kuntī's son,
Of this now briefly hear from me. 50

Endued with reason purified,
With firmness mastering the self,
Discarding things of sense, like sound,[443]
And giving up all loves and hates, 51

Abstemious, dwelling all alone,
Speech, body, mind all well controlled,
On *yoga* of contemplation bent,[444]
And fortified with unconcern,[445] 52

And casting off all egoism,[446]
Possessions, power, pride, wrath and lust;
The man who's selfless,[447] full of peace,
Is fit to be transformed to Brahm. 53

Becoming Brahm, with self serene,
He grieveth not nor longs for aught,
And treating all alike he gains
Supreme devotion unto me. 54

---

[441] I.e., desires.
[442] Lit. the supreme perfection of freedom from action.
[443] Lit. discarding sound and other objects of sense.
[444] *Dyāna-yoga.*
[445] I.e., indifference to worldly things.
[446] *Ahaṅkāra.*
[447] Lit. free from the idea of "my-ness."

भक्त्या मामभिजानाति यावान्यश्चास्मि तत्त्वतः।
ततो मां तत्त्वतो ज्ञात्वा विशते तदनन्तरम्॥ ५५॥

bhaktyā mām abhijānāti yāvān yaś cāsmi tattvataḥ|
tato māṃ tattvato jñātvā viśate tadanantaram|| 55||

सर्वकर्माण्यपि सदा कुर्वाणो मद्व्यपाश्रयः।
मत्प्रसादादवाप्नोति शाश्वतं पदमव्ययम्॥ ५६॥

sarvakarmāṇy api sadā kurvāṇo madvyapāśrayaḥ|
matprasādād avāpnoti śāśvataṃ padam avyayam|| 56||

चेतसा सर्वकर्माणि मयि संन्यस्य मत्परः।
बुद्धियोगमुपाश्रित्य मच्चित्तः सततं भव॥ ५७॥

cetasā sarvakarmāṇi mayi saṃnyasya matparaḥ|
buddhiyogam upāśritya maccittaḥ satataṃ bhava|| 57||

मच्चित्तः सर्वदुर्गाणि मत्प्रसादात्तरिष्यसि।
अथ चेत्त्वमहंकारान्न श्रोष्यसि विनङ्क्ष्यसि॥ ५८॥

maccittaḥ sarvadurgāṇi matprasādāt tariṣyasi|
atha cet tvam ahaṃkārān na śroṣyasi vinaṅkṣyasi|| 58||

यदहंकारमाश्रित्य न योत्स्य इति मन्यसे।
मिथ्यैष व्यवसायस्ते प्रकृतिस्त्वां नियोक्ष्यति॥ ५९॥

yad ahaṃkāram āśritya na yotsya iti manyase|
mithyaiṣa vyavasāyas te prakṛtis tvāṃ niyokṣyati|| 59||

स्वभावजेन कौन्तेय निबद्धः स्वेन कर्मणा।
कर्तुं नेच्छसि यन्मोहात्करिष्यस्यवशो ऽपि तत्॥ ६०॥

svabhāvajena kaunteya nibaddhaḥ svena karmaṇā|
kartuṃ necchasi yan mohāt kariṣyasy avaśo 'pi tat|| 60||

By such devotion such an one
Knows who and what I am in truth,
And knowing me in truth, he then
Finds entrance into me forthwith. 55

Who has in me a shelter found,
Though in all actions e'er engaged,
He by my grace attains at last
That state which knows nor end nor wane. 56

Resigning all thy acts by mind[448]
To me, on me alone intent,
Having recourse to *buddhi-yoga*,
Let e'er thy thoughts be fixed on me. 57

Intent on me thou, by my grace,
All obstacles shalt overcome;
But if through ego sense, thou wilt
Not listen, thou shalt be destroyed. 58

If thou in ego sense entrenched,
To thyself say that "I'll not fight,",
Thy resolution will be vain,
For thine own nature[449] will compel. 59

Bound as thou art, O Kuntī's son,
By thine own actions, nature born,
What thou, deluded, will not do,
That must thou do, though 'gainst thy will. 60

[448]I.e., mentally, or in thought, dedicating all actions to me.
[449]Thy nature as a *kṣatriya*.

ईश्वरः सर्वभूतानां हृद्देशे ऽर्जुन तिष्ठति।
भ्रामयन्सर्वभूतानि यन्त्रारूढानि मायया॥ ६१॥

īśvaraḥ sarvabhūtānāṃ hṛddeśe 'rjuna tiṣṭhati|
bhrāmayan sarvabhūtāni yantrārūḍhāni māyayā|| 61||

तमेव शरणं गच्छ सर्वभावेन भारत।
तत्प्रसादात्परां शान्तिं स्थानं प्राप्स्यसि शाश्वतम्॥ ६२॥

tam eva śaraṇaṃ gaccha sarvabhāvena bhārata|
tatprasādāt parāṃ śāntiṃ sthānaṃ prāpsyasi śāśvatam|| 62||

इति ते ज्ञानमाख्यातं गुह्याद्गुह्यतरं मया।
विमृश्यैतदशेषेण यथेच्छसि तथा कुरु॥ ६३॥

iti te jñānam ākhyātaṃ guhyād guhyataraṃ mayā|
vimṛśyaitad aśeṣeṇa yathecchasi tathā kuru|| 63||

सर्वगुह्यतमं भूयः शृणु मे परमं वचः।
इष्टो ऽसि मे दृढमिति ततो वक्ष्यामि ते हितम्॥ ६४॥

sarvaguhyatamaṃ bhūyaḥ śṛṇu me paramaṃ vacaḥ|
iṣṭo 'si me dṛḍham iti tato vakṣyāmi te hitam|| 64||

मन्मना भव मद्भक्तो मद्याजी मां नमस्कुरु।
मामेवैष्यसि सत्यं ते प्रतिजाने प्रियो ऽसि मे॥ ६५॥

manmanā bhava madbhakto madyājī māṃ namaskuru|
mām evaiṣyasi satyaṃ te pratijāne priyo 'si me|| 65||

सर्वधर्मान्परित्यज्य मामेकं शरणं व्रज।
अहं त्वा सर्वपापेभ्यो मोक्षयिष्यामि मा शुचः॥ ६६॥

sarvadharmān parityajya mām ekaṃ śaraṇaṃ vraja|
ahaṃ tvā sarvapāpebhyo mokṣayiṣyāmi mā śucaḥ|| 66||

The lord, O Arjun, dwells within
The hearts of all created things,
And by his *māyā*, whirls around
All beings on his spinning wheel. 61

With all thy being, Bharat's son,
Fly unto him for shelter now,
For by his grace thou shalt attain
To peace supreme, th'eternal home. 62

More hid than any mystery,
This wisdom has been shown to thee;
In all its fullness think on it,
And then take action as thou wilt. 63

Give ear unto my word supreme,
The greatest secret, once again,
Because thou art my dearest friend,
I speak of what is good for thee. 64

Thy mind, thy love, bestow on me,
Thy homage and thy worship too;
Thou'lt come to me, I pledge my word,
For thou art very dear to me. 65

Renouncing every duty then,
Seek shelter thou in me alone,
For I will truly set thee free
From all thy sins; hence, do not grieve. 66

इदं ते नातपस्काय नाभक्ताय कदाचन।
न चाशुश्रूषवे वाच्यं न च मां यो ऽभ्यसूयति॥ ६७॥

idaṃ te nātapaskāya nābhaktāya kadā cana|
na cāśuśrūṣave vācyaṃ na ca māṃ yo 'bhyasūyati|| 67||

य इदं परमं गुह्यं मद्भक्तेष्वभिधास्यति।
भक्तिं मयि परां कृत्वा मामेवैष्यत्यसंशयः॥ ६८॥

ya idaṃ paramaṃ guhyaṃ madbhakteṣv abhidhāsyati|
bhaktiṃ mayi parāṃ kṛtvā mām evaiṣyaty asaṃśayaḥ|| 68||

न च तस्मान्मनुष्येषु कश्चिन्मे प्रियकृत्तमः।
भविता न च मे तस्मादन्यः प्रियतरो भुवि॥ ६९॥

na ca tasmān manuṣyeṣu kaścin me priyakṛttamaḥ|
bhavitā na ca me tasmād anyaḥ priyataro bhuvi|| 69||

अध्येष्यते च य इमं धर्म्यं संवादमावयोः।
ज्ञानयज्ञेन तेनाहमिष्टः स्यामिति मे मतिः॥ ७०॥

adhyeṣyate ca ya imaṃ dharmyaṃ saṃvādam āvayoḥ|
jñānayajñena tenāham iṣṭaḥ syām iti me matiḥ|| 70||

श्रद्धावाननसूयश्च शृणुयादपि यो नरः।
सो ऽपि मुक्तः शुभाँल्लोकान् प्राप्नुयात्पुण्यकर्मणाम्॥ ७१॥

śraddhāvān anasūyaś ca śṛṇuyād api yo naraḥ|
so 'pi muktaḥ śubhā̐l lokān prāpnuyāt puṇyakarmaṇām|| 71||

कच्चिदेतच्छ्रुतं पार्थ त्वयैकाग्रेण चेतसा।
कच्चिदज्ञानसंमोहः प्रनष्टस्ते धनंजय॥ ७२॥

kaccid etac chrutaṃ pārtha tvayaikāgreṇa cetasā|
kaccid ajñānasaṃmohaḥ pranaṣṭas te dhanaṃjaya|| 72||

Tell not this word of mine to one
Who penance and devotion lacks,
Nor unto one who'd fain not hear,
Nor him who speaketh ill of me. 67

Whoso with love supreme for me
Amongst my lovers shall proclaim
This highest secret; he shall come,
Without the slightest doubt, to me. 68

Nor is there one amongst mankind
Who dearer service does than he;
Therefore none other here on earth
Shall be more dearly loved by me. 69

And who this holy dialogue
Of ours shall study earnestly,
By doing so he worships me
By wisdom sacrifice,[450] I deem. 70

And he also who full of faith,
Without reviling heareth this,
Released from sin shall enter in
The radiant world of righteous men. 71

And, Pṛthā's son, has this been heard
By thee with single pointed mind?
Hast thy delusion, Dhanañjay,
Unwisdom-bred, been now dispelled? 72

[450] Which is the highest form of sacrifice.

अर्जुन उवाच

नष्टो मोहः स्मृतिर्लब्धा त्वत्प्रसादान्मयाच्युत।
स्थितो ऽस्मि गतसंदेहः करिष्ये वचनं तव॥ ७३॥

arjuna uvāca

naṣṭo mohaḥ smṛtir labdhā tvatprasādān mayācyuta|
sthito 'smi gatasaṃdehaḥ kariṣye vacanaṃ tava|| 73||

संजय उवाच

इत्यहं वासुदेवस्य पार्थस्य च महात्मनः।
संवादमिममश्रौषमद्भुतं रोमहर्षणम्॥ ७४॥

saṃjaya uvāca

ity ahaṃ vāsudevasya pārthasya ca mahātmanaḥ|
saṃvādam imam aśrauṣam adbhutaṃ romaharṣaṇam|| 74||

व्यासप्रसादाच्छ्रुतवानेतद्गुह्यमहं परम्।
योगं योगेश्वरात्कृष्णात्साक्षात्कथयतः स्वयम्॥ ७५॥

vyāsaprasādāc chrutavān etad guhyam ahaṃ param|
yogaṃ yogeśvarāt kṛṣṇāt sākṣāt kathayataḥ svayam|| 75||

राजन्संस्मृत्य संस्मृत्य संवादमिममद्भुतम्।
केशवार्जुनयोः पुण्यं हृष्यामि च मुहुर्मुहुः॥ ७६॥

rājan saṃsmṛtya saṃsmṛtya saṃvādam imam adbhutam|
keśavārjunayoḥ puṇyaṃ hṛṣyāmi ca muhur muhuḥ|| 76||

तच्च संस्मृत्य संस्मृत्य रूपमत्यद्भुतं हरेः।
विस्मयो मे महान्राजन्हृष्यामि च पुनः पुनः॥ ७७॥

tac ca saṃsmṛtya saṃsmṛtya rūpam atyadbhutaṃ hareḥ|
vismayo me mahān rājan hṛṣyāmi ca punaḥ punaḥ|| 77||

Arjun said:

My stupor,[451] changeless lord,[452] is fled,
And by thy grace I've wisdom[453] gained;
No doubts[454] have I, I am convinced,
What thou dost bid, that I will do. 73

Sanjay said:

Thus did I hear, O mighty king,
This dialogue most wonderful,
That made my hair to stand on end,
'Tween Vāsudeva and noble Pārtha. 74

Through Vyāsa's favor did I hear
This highest and most secret *yoga*,
By Krishna's lips divine proclaimed,
Yea, by the Lord of Yoga himself. 75

Rememb'ring o'er and o'er again
This holy dialogue, O king,
Of Keśav with prince Arjun, I
Rejoice again and yet again. 76

Rememb'ring o'er and o'er again
That wondrous form of Hari too,
Great is my wonder, king, and I
Rejoice again and yet again. 77

---

[451]*Moha*: delusion or infatuation. The delusion arising from ignorance.

[452]*Acyuta*.

[453]*Smṛti*: wisdom, enlightenment, or recognition. Arjuna means to say that he has now realized the true nature of the self—in other words, that he has gained self-knowledge.

[454]Doubts which ignorance had produced in my mind as to the propriety of my engaging in this war.

यत्र योगेश्वरः कृष्णो यत्र पार्थो धनुर्धरः।
तत्र श्रीर्विजयो भूतिर्ध्रुवा नीतिर्मतिर्मम॥ ७८॥

yatra yogeśvaraḥ kṛṣṇo yatra pārtho dhanurdharaḥ|
tatra śrīr vijayo bhūtir dhruvā nītir matir mama|| 78||

Where'er is Krishna, Lord of Yoga,
Where'er the archer Arjun is,
There I deem doth fortune dwell,
And vict'ry, pow'r and righteousness. 78

Appendix: Traditional Summaries of the Gītā

Gītā-bhāṣyopakramaṇikā of Śaṅkara

ओं नारायणः परो ऽव्यक्तादण्डमव्यक्तसम्भवम्।
अण्डस्यान्तस्त्विमे लोकाः सप्तद्वीपा च मेदिनी॥

स भगवान् सृष्ट्वेदं जगत् तस्य च स्थितिं चिकीर्षुर्मरीच्यादीनग्रे सृष्ट्वा प्रजापतीन्प्रवृत्तिलक्षणं धर्मं ग्राहयामास वेदोक्तम्। ततो ऽन्यांश्च सनकसनन्दनादीनुत्पाद्य निवृत्तिलक्षणं धर्मं ज्ञानवैराग्यलक्षणं ग्राहयामास। द्विविधो हि वेदोक्तो धर्मः प्रवृत्तिलक्षणो निवृत्तिलक्षणश्च। जगतः स्थितिकारणं प्राणिनां साक्षादभ्युदयनिःश्रेयसहेतुर्यः स धर्मो ब्राह्मणाद्यैर्वर्णिभिराश्रमिभिश्च श्रेयो ऽर्थिभिरनुष्ठीयमानः।

The Introduction of Śaṅkara's Commentary on the *Gītā*

[Śaṅkarācārya (650?-720? C.E.) was one of the greatest exponents of the non-dualist (advaita) school of Vedānta philosophy. His writings set the standard high for philosophical and religious discussion in India. The brilliance of his work eclipsed the works of the writers who preceded him and influenced just about all of the writers who came after him, in one way or another. Recent scholarship (Hacker, Nakamura, Thrasher) has established his dates to be earlier by more than a century than was traditionally believed and his actual works to be far fewer than those attributed to him (only those commented on by his immediate disciples are accepted as his). Within Hindusim he was a Vaiṣṇava, not a Śākta, and probably not a māyāvādin as the following passage demonstrates. He may have been a follower of the Yoga school before becoming a Vedāntin.]

Nārāyaṇa is beyond the Unmanifest.
The world[1] is born of the Unmanifest.
Within the world are these worlds.
and the Earth with seven islands.

The Lord created this world and then he, desiring its preservation, created first the progenitors, Marīci and the rest, and taught them the *dharma* of involvement in it (pravṛtii) as described in the Veda. Then he created others, Sanaka and Sanandana and the rest, and taught them the *dharma* of cessation (*nivṛtti*) from it, characterized by knowledge and renunciation. Thus the Vedic *dharma* has two aspects, one defined by involvement and the other by cessation of involvement, and it is the cause of the preservation of the world. That *dharma*, which is the direct cause of the progress and salvation of living beings, is being performed by the class members, headed by the *brāhmaṇas*, in the various stages of life who desire the best for themselves and others.

[1]Literally, egg, aṇḍa.

दीर्घेण कालेनानुष्ठातृणां कामोद्भवाद्धीयमानविवेकविज्ञानहेतुकेनाधर्मेणाभिभूयमाने धर्मे, प्रवर्धमाने चाधर्मे, जगतः स्थितिं परिपिपालयिषुः स आदिकर्ता नारायणाख्यो विष्णुर्भौमस्य ब्रह्मणो ब्राह्मणत्वस्य रक्षणार्थं देवक्यां वसुदेवादंशेन कृष्णः किल सम्बभूव। ब्राह्मणत्वस्य हि रक्षणेन रक्षितः स्याद्वैदिको धर्मः तदधीनत्वाद्वर्णाश्रमभेदानाम्।

स च भगवान् ज्ञानैश्वर्यशक्तिबलवीर्यतेजोभिः सदा सम्पन्नस्त्रिगुणात्मिकां वैष्णवीं स्वां मायां मूलप्रकृतिं वशीकृत्य अजो ऽव्ययो भूतानामीश्वरो नित्यशुद्धबुद्धमुक्तस्वभावो ऽपि सन्स्वमायया देहवानिव जात इव च लोकानुग्रहं कुर्वन्निव लक्ष्यते। स्वप्रयोजनाभावे ऽपि भूतानुजिघृक्षया वैदिकं हि धर्मद्वयमर्जुनाय शोकमोहमहोदधौ निमग्नाय उपदिदेश, गुणाधिकैर्हि गृहीतो ऽनुष्ठीयमानश्च धर्मः प्रचयं गमिष्यतीति। तं धर्मं भगवता यथोपदिष्टं वेदव्यासः सर्वज्ञो भगवान् गीताख्यैः सप्तभिः श्लोकशतैरुपनिबबन्ध।

तदिदं गीताशास्त्रं समस्तवेदार्थसारसङ्ग्रहभूतं दुर्विज्ञेयार्थं। तदर्थाविष्करणाय अनेकैर्विवृतपदपदार्थवाक्यवाक्यार्थन्यायमपि अत्यन्तविरुद्धानेकार्थत्वेन लौकिकैर्गृह्यमाणमुपलभ्याहं विवेकतो ऽर्थनिर्धारणार्थं संक्षेपतो विवरणं करिष्यामि।

तस्यास्य गीताशास्त्रस्य संक्षेपतः प्रयोजनं परं निःश्रेयसं सहेतुकस्य संसारस्य अत्यन्तोपरमलक्षणम्। तच्च सर्वकर्मसन्न्यासपूर्वकादात्मज्ञाननिष्ठारूपाद्धर्माद्भवति। तथेममेव गीतार्थधर्ममुद्दिश्य भगवतैवोक्तम्—

When that *dharma* is overcome by *adharma* which is caused by a weakening of discrimination and knowledge resulting from the appearance of desire (kāma) in the performers of *dharma* over a long period of time and when *adharma* increases, the First Agent, Viṣṇu known also as Nārāyaṇa, wishing to maintain the stability of the world, in order to protect the brāhmaṇa-hood of the earthly Brahman, is born with a portion as Kṛṣṇa[2] from Vasudeva in the womb of Devakī. Once brāhmaṇa-hood is protected Vedic *dharma* is protected and, because they depend on that, the various classes and stages [are protected], too.

The Lord (*Bhagavān*), too, is always possessed of knowledge, sovereignty, power, strength, valor, and splendour. Bringing under his control the root-nature, which is his own illusory power composed of the three strands (*guṇa*), that unborn and undiminishing one, the controller of beings, although by nature eternally pure, awakended, and liberated, through his own illusory power is seen as if he is born and as if he possesses a body acting for the benefit of the world. Though he has no purpose of his own, out of a desire to benefit living beings he teaches the twofold Vedic *dharma* to Arjuna who is submerged in the ocean of lamentation and delusion. That *dharma* being accepted and performed by those with good qualities will increase. Vedavyāsa, the all-knowing and lordly one, expressed that *dharma* as taught by the Lord in seven hundred verses called the Gītā.

This Gītā scripture, which is a gathering together of the essence of the meanings of all the Vedas, is very difficult to understand. It is interpreted by many men as having many contradictory meanings even though they have discussed the words and their meanings, the sentences and their meanings, and its logic in order to uncover its meaning. Seeing this, I will undertake a brief explanation in order to bring out its meaning with discrimination.

Briefly speaking, the purpose of this Gītā scripture is the highest well-being which is defined as the final cessation of the cycle of rebirths along with its causes. And that occurs as a result of *dharma* in the form of being firmly established in knowledge of the self preceded by renunciation of all actions. Thus it is said by the Lord himself with respect to the *dharma* that is the meaning of the Gītā:

---

[2]This idea of being born "with a portion" is often understood to mean that Kṛṣṇa is but a portion or a part of Viṣṇu. That is, only a part of Viṣṇu descended and became Kṛṣṇa. The Bhāgavata Purāṇa reverses this relationship and recognizes Kṛṣṇa as the complete Godhead and Viṣṇu as the mere part. The Caitanyite Vaiṣṇava tradition takes this "with a portion" to mean that when Kṛṣṇa appeared he came along *with* a portion of himself, manifested separately, in the form of Baladeva, his brother and theologically speaking his "facilitator."

स हि धर्मः सुपर्याप्तो ब्रह्मणः पदवेदने (म. भा. १४.१६.१२) इत्यनुगीतासु।
तत्रैव चोक्तं
नैव धर्मी न चाधर्मी न चैव हि शुभाशुभी (म. भा. १४.१९.७)।
यः स्यादेकासने लीनस्तूष्णीं किंचिदचिन्तयन् (म. भा. १४.१९.१)।
ज्ञानं संन्यासलक्षणम् (म. भा. १४.४३.२६) इति च।
इहापि चान्ते उक्तमर्जुनाय
सर्वधर्मान्परित्यज्य मामेकं शरणं व्रज (गीता १८.६६) इति।

अभ्युदयार्थो ऽपि यः प्रवृत्तिलक्षणो धर्मो वर्णाश्रमांश्चोद्दिश्य विहितः, स देवादिस्थानप्राप्तिहेतुरपि सन्, ईश्वरार्पणबुद्ध्यानुष्ठीयमानः सत्त्वशुद्धये भवति फलाभिसन्धिवर्जितः। शुद्धसत्त्वस्य च ज्ञाननिष्ठायोग्यताप्राप्तिद्वारेण ज्ञानोत्पत्तिहेतुत्वेन च निःश्रेयसहेतुत्वमपि प्रतिपद्यते। तथा चेममेवार्थमभिसन्धाय वक्ष्यति

ब्रह्मण्याधाय कर्माणि यतचित्ता जितेन्द्रियाः (गीता ५.१०)।
योगिनः कर्म कुर्वन्ति सङ्गं त्यक्त्वात्मशुद्धये (गीता ५.११) इति।

इमं द्विप्रकारं धर्मं निःश्रेयसप्रयोजनं परमार्थतत्त्वं च वासुदेवाख्यं परब्रह्मा ऽभिधेयभूतं विशेषतो ऽभिव्यञ्जयद्विशिष्टप्रयोजनसम्बन्धाभिधेयवद्गीताशास्त्रम्। यतस्तदर्थविज्ञानेन समस्तपुरुषार्थसिद्धिरिति, अतस्तद्विवरणे यत्नः क्रियते मया॥

> That *dharma* is fully sufficient to procure the state or abode of Brahman.[3]

This is said in the Anugītā, and again it is said there:

> Neither following *dharma* nor *adharma*. pursuing neither the auspicious nor the inauspicious ... [4]
>
> One should remain seated on one seat, silent, not thinking about anything.[5]
>
> Knowledge is characterized by renunciation.[6]

and so forth.

And here too (in the Gītā) it is said to Arjuna at the end:

> Rejecting all *dharmas*, come to me alone for shelter.[7]

The *dharma* of involvement, though done for the purpose of worldly prosperity, is enjoined for the classes and stages and though it is the cause of attaining the abodes of the gods and so forth, when it is carried out as an offering to the Lord, free from desire for results, it brings about a purification of the mind. Purification of the mind, by providing the qualification for being established in knowledge, becomes the cause of the production of knowledge and by that, the cause of the highest good [liberation], too. Thus, presenting that very meaning he will say: "Placing one's actions in Brahman."[8] "the yogins perform work, having rejected attachment, for the purification of the mind."[9]

This Gītā scripture has a specialized purpose, relationship, and meaning since it reveals in detail this twofold *dharma* which has as its purpose the highest good [liberation] and the ultimate truth, known as Vāsudeva, which is the very meaning of the highest Brahman. Since in knowing that meaning all of the goals of human life are achieved, I apply myself to explaining it.

---

[3]Mahābhārata, Aśva, 16.12.
[4]ibid., 19.7.
[5]ibid., 19.1.
[6]ibid., 43.25.
[7]Bg., 18.66.
[8]Bg., 5.10.
[9]Bg., 5.11.

Gītārthasaṅgraha by Yamunā Muni

स्वधर्मज्ञानवैराग्यसाध्यभक्त्येकगोचरः।
नारायणः परं ब्रह्म गीताशास्त्रे समीरितः॥ १॥

ज्ञानकर्मात्मके योगलक्ष्ये सुसंस्कृते।
आत्मानुभूतिसिद्ध्यर्थे पूर्वषट्केन चोदिते॥ २॥

मध्यमे भगवत्तत्त्वयाथात्म्यावाप्तिसिद्धये।
ज्ञानकर्माभिनिर्वर्त्यो भक्तियोगः प्रकीर्तितः॥ ३॥

प्रधानपुरुषव्यक्तसर्वेश्वरविवेचनम्।
कर्मधीर्भक्तिरित्यादिः पूर्वशेषो ऽन्तिमोदितः॥ ४॥

अस्थानस्नेहकारुण्यधर्माधर्मधियाकुलम्।
पार्थं प्रपन्नमुद्दिश्य शास्त्रावतरणं कृतम्॥ ५॥

नित्यात्मासङ्गकर्मेहागोचरा साङ्ख्ययोगधीः।
द्वितीये स्थितधीलक्षा प्रोक्ता तन्मोहशान्तये॥ ६॥

असक्त्या लोकरक्षायै गुणेष्वारोप्य कर्तृताम्।
सर्वेश्वरे वा न्यस्योक्ता तृतीये कर्मकार्यता॥ ७॥

प्रसङ्गात्स्वस्वभावोक्तिः कर्मणो ऽकर्मतास्य च।
भेदा ज्ञानस्य माहात्म्यं चतुर्थाध्याय उच्यते॥ ८॥

कर्मयोगस्य सौकर्यं शैघ्र्यं काश्चन तद्विधाः।
ब्रह्मज्ञानप्रकारश्च पञ्चमाध्याय उच्यते॥ ९॥

Collected Teachings of the *Gītā*

[*Yamunā Muni, also known as Alavandar, is the author of this summary. He was born in the 10th century C.E. at Madurai in southern state of India now called Tamil Nadu. He was one of the earliest writers in Sanskrit in support of the Śrī Vaiṣṇava tradition and thus its first ācārya or exemplary teacher. He is said to have been the grandson of Nāthamuni who collected together the songs of the Alvar saints called the Divya-prabandham and made it part of the liturgy at the Śrīraṅga Temple.*]

The supreme Brahman, Nārāyaṇa, who is the sole object of *bhakti*, which *bhakti* is the goal of one's own *dharma*, knowledge, and detachment, is invoked in the *Gītā*. (1)

Knowledge and Action, regarded as yogas and well-refined are urged for the achievement of direct perception of the self in the first sextet. (2)

In the middle sextet, *bhakti-yoga*, which is produced by knowledge and action, is praised for the success in the actual attainment of the truth of Bhagavān. (3)

Distinguishing between *pradhāna*, *puruṣa*, the manifest, and the controller of all, as well as intelligence in action, *bhakti*, and so forth, whatever was left over from before, are described in the final [sextet]. (4)

The unfolding of the scripture to the surrendered Pārtha (Arjuna) who was troubled by his understanding of *dharma* and *adharma* and of compassion and affection improperly directed is done [in the first chapter]. (5)

In the second chapter, in order to ease his confusion, the understanding [mind-set] of Sāṅkhya-yoga, which is beyond the scope of the desire for any action unrelated to the eternal self, and which is characteristic of those with steady minds, is described. (6)

In order to protect the world by detachment, agency is attributed to the *guṇas* or to the controller of all, and the necessity of performing action is described in the third chapter. (7)

In the fourth chapter is an incidental statement of his (Kṛṣṇa's) own true nature, and described is the actionlessness of his actions, along with the varieties and greatness of knowledge. (8)

The easiness and quickness of *karma-yoga* and some of is varieties as well as the nature of knowledge of Brahman are described in the fifth chapter. (9)

योगाभ्यासविधिर्योगी चतुर्धा योगसाधनम् ।
योगसिद्धिः स्वयोगस्य पारम्यं षष्ठ उच्यते ॥१०॥

स्वयाथात्म्यं प्रकृत्यास्य तिरोधिः शरणागतिः।
भक्तभेदः प्रबुद्धस्य श्रैष्ठ्यं सप्तम उच्यते॥ ११॥

ऐश्वर्याक्षरयाथात्म्यभगवच्छरणार्थिनाम्।
वेद्योपादेयभावानामष्टमे भेद उच्यते॥ १२॥

स्वमाहात्म्यं मनुष्यत्वे परत्वं च महात्मनाम्।
विशेषो नवमे योगो भक्तिरूपः प्रकीर्तितः॥ १३॥

स्वकल्याणगुणानन्त्यकृत्स्नस्वाधीनतामतिः।
भक्त्युत्पत्तिविवृद्ध्यर्था विस्तीर्णा दशमोदिता॥ १४॥

एकादशे स्वयाथात्म्यसाक्षात्कारावलोकनम्।
दत्तमुक्तं विदिप्राप्त्योर्भक्त्येकोपायता तथा॥ १५॥

भक्तेः श्रैष्ठ्यमुपायोक्तिरशक्तस्यात्मनिष्ठता।
तत्प्रकारास्त्वतिप्रीतिर्भक्ते द्वादश उच्यते॥ १६॥

देवस्वरूपमात्माप्तिहेतुरात्मविशोधनम्।
बन्धहेतुर्विवेकश्च त्रयोदश उदीर्यते॥ १७॥

गुणबन्धविधा तेषां कर्तृत्वं तन्निवर्तनम्।
गतित्रयस्वमूलत्वं चतुर्दश उदीर्यते॥ १८॥

अचिन्मिश्राद्विशुद्धाच्च चेतनात्पुरुषोत्तमः।
व्यापनाद्भरणात्स्वाम्यादन्यः पञ्चदशोदितः॥ १९॥

देवासुरविभागोक्तिपूर्विका शास्त्रवश्यता।
तत्त्वानुष्ठानविज्ञानस्थेम्ने षोडश उच्यते॥ २०॥

The regulations for *yoga*, the four kinds of *yogī*, the cultivation of *yoga*, the completion of *yoga*, and the supremacy of his own *yoga* are described in chapter six. (10)

His own real nature with *prakṛti*, his disappearance, coming to shelter with him, different kinds of *bhaktas* and the superiority of the fully awakened one are described in the seventh chapter. (11)

In the eighth chapter various things of use to and to be known by those interested in surrending to Bhagavān, in his real, imperishable nature, full of his godly opulence, are described. (12)

His own greatness, the superiority of being human, and the special *yoga* of the great souls in the form of *bhakti* are praised in the ninth chapter. (13)

An expanded understanding of the limitlessness of his own auspicious qualities and of his own complete supremacy for the purpose of creating and increasing *bhakti* is the subject of the tenth chapter. (14)

In the eleventh are the viewing of the direct revelation of his real nature, liberation bestowed as well as *bhakti*'s being the only way of attaining him. (15)

The superiority of *bhakti*, a statement of the way, the standing in the self of one who is not attached and the varieties of that as well as his great pleasure in the *bhakta*, these are stated in the twelfth chapter. (16)

The true nature of deity, the cause of attaining the self, purification of the self, the cause of bondage, and discrimination are all raised in the thirteenth chapter. (17)

Types of bondage to the *guṇas*, their (the *guṇas'*) agency and their cessation and the rootedness in him of the three goals are discussed in the fourteenth chapter. (18)

That the supreme person (*puruṣottama*) is other than consciousness, whether mixed with unconscious matter or pure, and beyond pervading, supporting, and controlling [the world] is stated in the fifteenth chapter. (19)

After describing the divisions of the gods and demons, obedience to scripture is taught for firmness in learning the truth, religious performance, and specialized knowledge in the sixteenth chapter. (20)

अशास्त्रमासुरं कृत्स्नं शास्त्रीयं गुणतः पृथक्।
लक्षणं शास्त्रसिद्धस्य त्रिधा सप्तदशोदितम्॥ २१॥

ईश्वरे कर्तृताबुद्धिः सत्त्वोपादेयतान्तिमे।
स्वकर्मपरिणामश्च शास्त्रसारार्थ उच्यते॥ २२॥

कर्मयोगस्तपस्तीर्थदानयज्ञादिसेवनम्।
ज्ञानयोगो जितस्वान्तैः परिशुद्धात्मनि स्थितिः॥ २३॥

भक्तियोगः परैकान्तप्रीत्या ध्यानादिषु स्थितिः।
त्रयाणामपि योगानां त्रिभिरन्योन्यसङ्गमः॥ २४॥

नित्यनैमित्तिकानां च पराराधनरूपिणाम्।
आत्मदृष्टेस्त्रयो ऽप्येते योगद्वारेण साधकाः॥ २५॥

निरस्तनिखिलाज्ञानो दृष्ट्वात्मानं परानुगम्।
प्रतिलभ्य परां भक्तिं तथैवाप्नोति तत्पदम्॥ २६॥

भक्तियोगस्तदर्थी चेत्समग्रैश्वर्यसाधकः।
आत्मार्थी चेत्त्रयो ऽप्येते तत्कैवल्यस्य साधकाः॥ २७॥

ऐकान्त्यं भगवत्येषां समानमधिकारिणाम्।
यावत्प्राप्ति परार्थी चेत्तदेवात्यन्तमश्नुते॥ २८॥

ज्ञानी तु परमैकान्तो तदायत्तात्मजीवनः।
तत्संश्लेषवियोगैकसुखदुःखस्तदेकधीः॥ २९॥

भगवद्ध्यानयोगोक्तिवन्दनस्तुतिकीर्तनैः।
लब्धात्मा तद्गतप्राणमनोबुद्धीन्द्रियक्रियः॥ ३०॥

What is contrary to scripture is demonic; the scriptural, which is according to the *guṇas*, is completely separate. The threefold characteristics of that established by scripture is described in the seventeenth chapter. (21)

In the final chapter, awareness of the Controller as the agent, acceptance of the *guṇa* of clarity (*sattva*), and transformation of one's own actions are described as the core meaning of the scripture. (22)

Karma-yoga is serving through austerity, pilgrimage, charity, sacrifice and so forth. *Jñāna-yoga* is being situated in the purified self with one's emotions conquered. (23)

Bhakti-yoga is being situated in meditation and so forth with an exclusive love (*prīti*) for the supreme. The three *yogas* even conjoin with one another and also with the regular and occasional rites which are forms of the worship of the supreme. Thus these three are, by means of yoga, accomplishers of percption of the self. (24-25)

One whose ignorance is thoroughly vanquished, after seeing the self following the supreme, attains the highest *bhakti* and then gains his abode. (26)

If one wants it, *bhakti-yoga* accomplishes complete godly opulence; if one wants the Self then those three accomplish absolute unity with that. (27)

The single-mindedness towards the Lord is the same for all these *adhikārīs*. If they desire the supreme until it is achieved then that becomes final. (28)

But the knower [gnostic] who is the most single-minded, whose self and life rest on him, whose only happiness and misery are connection with or separation from him, whose only thought is him, (29)

who has gained the self by meditation on, applying himself for, speaking of, praising, eulogizing, and spreading the fame of Bhagavān, whose breath, mind, intellect, senses, and acts are given over to him, (30)

निजकर्मादिभक्त्यन्तं कुर्यात्प्रीत्यैव कारितः।
उपायतां परित्यज्य न्यस्येद्देवे तु तामभीः॥ ३१॥

एकान्तात्यन्तदास्यैकरतिस्तत्पदमाप्नुयात्।
तत्प्रधानम् इदं शास्त्रमिति गीतार्थसङ्ग्रहः॥ ३२॥

performs everything beginning from his own work up to and including *bhakti* impelled by love alone, should give up the sense of expedience and fearlessly place it on the Lord. (31)

With single-minded, unending servitude as one's only love, one reaches his abode. This scripture has this as its primary teaching. Thus ends the *Collection of the Teachings of the Gītā.* (32)

Introduction to the *Rāmānuja-bhāṣya* of Rāmānuja

हरिः ॐ

यत्पदाम्भोरुहध्यानविध्वस्ताशेषकल्मषः।
वस्तुतामुपयातोऽहं यामुनेयं नमामि तम्॥

श्रियः पतिः निखिलहेयप्रत्यनीककल्याणैकतानः स्वेतरसमस्तवस्तुविलक्षणानन्तज्ञानानन्दैकस्वरूपः स्वाभाविकानवधिकातिशयज्ञानबलैश्वर्यवीर्यशक्तितेजःप्रभृत्यसंख्येयकल्याणगुणगणमहोदधिः स्वाभिमतानुरूपैकरूपाचिन्त्यदिव्याद्भुतनित्यनिरवद्यनिरतिशयौज्ज्वल्यसौगन्ध्यसौन्दर्यसौकुमार्यलावण्ययौवनाद्यनन्तगुणनिधिदिव्यरूपः स्वोचितविविधविचित्रानन्ताश्चर्यनित्यनिरवद्यापरिमितदिव्यभूषणः स्वानुरूपासंख्येयाचिन्त्यशक्तिनित्यनिरवद्यनिरतिशयकल्याणदिव्यायुधः

Introduction of the Commentary on the *Gītā*

[Śrī Rāmānuja was one of the first of a long line of great teachers in the South Indian Vaiṣṇava community called the Śrīsampradāya. Scholarly opinion sets his dates at 1077–1157 C.E, though traditionally he was assigned to the years 1017-1120 C.E. Ramanuja was born Ilaya Perumal in a Brahmin family in the village of Perumbudur, Tamil Nadu, India. His father was Asuri Keshava Somayaji Deekshitar and his mother was Kanthimathi. His teacher during his childhood was Kañcipūrṇam, a disciple of Yamunā Muni, another early teacher of the Śrīsampradāya and the author of the previous summary of teachings of the Gītā. When Rāmānuja was older he studied Vedānta with a scholar named Yādavaprakāśa in nearby Kancipuram. Yādavaprakāśa was a teacher of a non-dualistic form of Vedānta and Rāmānuja had several disagreements with him which led to their eventual break with each other. On the suggestion of his childhood teacher, Rāmānuja went to visit the aging Yamunā Muni, but arrived shortly after his death. He nevertheless studied the teachings of Yamunā Muni through his disciples and became a great exponent of his tradition.]

Hari Oṃ!

Purified of countless impurities
by meditation on his lotus-like feet,
I am led to the truth of things,
I thus bow to the teaching of Yamunā.

The consort of Śrī is wholly auspicious and antagonistic to all that is evil. His essential nature consists purely of limitless knowledge and bliss and thus stands distinct from all other entities. He is a great ocean of countless, auspicious attributes, both inherent in him and beyond all limitation in excellence, attributes such as knowledge, power, lordship, energy, potency and splendour.[10] He has a divine form, which is both agreeable and worthy of him—inconceivably divine, wondrous, eternal and flawless, a treasury of limitless perfections such as radiance, beauty, fragrance, tenderness, pervasive sweetness and eternal youth. He is adorned with divine ornaments appropriate to him, manifold, variegated, infinite, wondrous, eternal, flawless, unlimited, and divine. He is equiped with divine weapons suited to him, countless, of wondrous powers, eternal, impeccable and surpassingly auspicious.

[10]This six traits said to constitute the one called Bhagavān.

स्वाभिमतानुरूपनित्यनिरवद्यस्वरूपरूपगुणविभवैश्वर्यशीलाद्यनवधिकातिशयासंख्येयकल्याणगुणगणश्रीवल्लभः

स्वसंकल्पानुविधायिस्वरूपस्थितिप्रवृत्तिभेदाशेषशेषतैकरतिरूपनित्यनिरवद्यनिरतिशयज्ञानक्रियैश्वर्याद्यनन्तगुणगणापमितसूरिभिरनवरताभिष्टुतचरणयुगलः

वाङ्मनसापरिच्छेद्यस्वरूपस्वभावः

स्वोचितविविधविचित्रानन्तभोग्यभोगोपकरणभोगस्थानसमृद्धानन्ताश्चर्यानन्तमहाविभवानन्तपरिमाणनित्यनिरवद्याक्षरपरमव्योमनिलयः विविधविचित्रानन्तभोग्यभोक्तिवर्गपरिपूर्णानिखिलजगदुदयविभवलयलीलः परं ब्रह्म पुरुषोत्तमो नारायणो

He is beloved of Śrī, whose eternal and impeccable nature, attributes, glory, sovereignty and virtues, unsurpassed and countless, are all agreeable and worthy of him. His feet are incessantly praised by countless numbers of perfected devotees whose nature, existence and activities are in accordance with his will and whose countless qualities such as knowledge, action and glory are eternal, impeccable and unsurpassed, all functioning joyously in complete subservience to him.

His nature and qualities transcend all thought and words. He dwells in the divine and imperishable supreme heaven which abounds in manifold, wonderful and countless objects, means and places of enjoyment. It is an abode appropriate to him and is infinite in its wondrous glory and magnitude. His sportive delight brings about the origination, preservation and dissolution of the entire cosmos, replete the with multifarious, variegated and innumerable objects and subjects of ordinary existence. Such is he, the supreme Brahman, the supreme person, Nārāyaṇa.

ब्रह्मादिस्थावरन्तमखिलं जगत्सृष्ट्वा स्वेन रूपेणावस्थितः ब्रह्मादिदेवमनुष्याणां ध्यानारधनाद्यगोचरोऽप्यपारकारुण्यसौशील्यवात्सल्यौदार्यमहोदधिः स्वमेव रूपं तत्तत्स्वजातीयसंस्थानमजहदेव कुर्वन् तेषु तेषु लोकेष्ववतीर्य अवतीर्य तैः तैराराधितस्तत्तदिष्टानुरूपं धर्मार्थकाममोक्षाख्यं फलं प्रयच्छन् भूभारावतारणापदेशेन अस्मादीनामपि समाश्रयणियत्वाय अवतीर्य उर्व्यां सकलमनुजनयनविषयतां गतः परावरनिखिलजनमनोनयनहारिदिव्यचेष्टितानि कुर्वन् पूतनाशकटयमलार्जुनारिष्टप्रलम्बधेनुककालियकेशिकुवलयापीडचाणुरमुष्टिकतोसलकंसादीन्निहत्य अनवधिकदयासौहार्दानुरागगर्भविलोकनालापामृतैर्विश्वमाप्ययन्निरतिशयसौन्दर्यसौशील्यादिगुणगणाविष्कारेणाक्रूरमालाकारादीन् परमभागवतान् कृत्वा पाण्डुतनययुधप्रोत्साहनव्याजेन परमपुरुषार्थलक्षणमोक्षसाधनतया वेदान्तोदितं ज्ञानकर्मानुगृहीतं भक्तियोगमवतारयामास।

तत्र पाण्डवानां कुरूणां च युधे प्रारब्धे स भगवान् पुरुषोत्तमः सर्वेश्वरेश्वरो जगदुपकृतिमर्त्य आश्रितवात्सल्यविवशः पार्थं रथिमात्मानं च सारथिं सर्वलोकसाक्षिकं चकार। एवमर्जुनस्य उत्कर्ष ज्ञात्वापि सर्वात्मनान्धो धृतराष्ट्रः सुयोधनविजयबुभुत्सया संजयं पप्रच्छ।

After creating the entire world, beginning from Brahma down to immobile things, he, being inaccessible in his transcendent form to the meditation of all creatures from Brahmā down to gods, men and so forth, and being also a shoreless ocean of compassion and loving condescension, paternal affection and generosity, he shaped his own figure into the likeness of the various kinds of creatures without giving up his own supreme nature, and thus he manifested his incarnation in the worlds of creatures and received their worship and granted them their lives' fulfilments comprising *dharma* (virtue), *artha* (gain), *kāma* (love) and *mokṣa* (release), in accordance with their desire. Under the pretext of relieving the Earth of her burdens but really in order to make himself available for us to take refuge in him, he incarnated on the earth as Śrī Kṛṣṇa. He thus became the visible object for the sight of all, and did divine actions that captivated the minds and eyes of all, high and low. He vanquished the wicked such as Pūtanā, Sakaṭa, the two Arjuna trees, Ariṣṭa, Pralamba, Dhenuka, Kāliya, Keśin, Kuvalayāpīḍa, Cāṇura, Muṣṭika, Tosala and Kaṃsa. He spread soothing happiness over the entire world with the ambrosia of his glances and speech, conveying his boundless compassion, friendliness and love. He made Akrūra, Mālākāra and others the most ardent devotees by manifestation of his unsurpassed qualities such as beauty and loving compassion. With the ostensible intention of imparting to the son of Pāṇḍu the martial spirit, he brought about the descent of the yoga of *bhakti* directed to himself, promoted with the aid of *jñāna* and *karma*—the *yoga* which has been promulgated by the Vedānta as the pathway to the supreme goal of release.

When war broke out between the Pāṇḍavas and the Kauravas, he, the lord, the supreme person, the god of gods, who had assumed mortal human form to help the world, overwhelmed by his love for those devotees who have taken refuge in him, that supreme person made Arjuna the master of the chariot and himself the driver, so that he could be seen by all the people. Even knowing that Krsna was the supreme being, Dhṛtarāṣṭra, who was blind in every way, wanted to hear about the victory of his son Suyodhana and thus questioned Sañjaya.

The *Gūḍhārtha-dīpikā* of Madhusūdana Sarasvatī

भगवत्पादभाष्यार्थमालोच्यातिप्रयत्नतः।
प्रायः प्रत्यक्षरं कुर्वे गीतागूढार्थदीपिकाम्॥ १॥

सहेतुकस्य संसारस्यात्यन्तोपरमात्मकम्॥
परं निःश्रेयसं गीताशास्त्रस्योक्तं प्रयोजनम्॥ २॥

सच्चिदानन्दरूपं तत्पूर्णं विष्णोः परं पदम्।
यत्प्राप्तये समारब्धा वेदाः काण्डत्रयात्मकाः॥ ३॥
कर्मोपास्तिस्तथा ज्ञानमिति काण्डत्रयं क्रमात्।
तद्रूपाष्टादशाध्यायैर्गीता काण्डत्रयात्मिका॥ ४॥

एकमेकेन षट्केन काण्डमत्रोपलक्षयेत्।
कर्मनिष्ठाज्ञाननिष्ठे कथिते प्रथमान्त्ययोः॥ ५॥
यतः समुच्चयो नास्ति तयोरतिविरोधतः।
भगवद्भक्तिनिष्ठा तु मध्यमे परिकीर्तिता॥ ६॥
उभयानुगता सा हि सर्वविघ्नापनोदिनी॥
कर्ममिश्रा च शुद्धा च ज्ञानमिश्रा च सा त्रिधा॥ ७॥
तत्र तु प्रथमे काण्डे कर्म तत्त्यागवर्त्मना॥
त्वंपदार्थो विशुद्धात्मा सोपपत्तिर्निरूप्यते॥ ८॥

Lamp on the Hidden Meanings

[*Madhusūdana Sarasvatī (c.1540–1640 C.E.) was an Indian philosopher in the Non-dualistic (Advaita) Vedānta tradition. Born in Bengal, in the District of Pharidpur, he is said to have studied Neo-logic in Navadvīpa before traveling to Vārānasī to study Vedānta. There he became a disciple of Viśveśvara Sarasvatī and Mādhava Sarasvatī and eventually became one of the most celebrated names in the history of the great debate between the dualist and non-dualist schools of Vedānta. His opus magnum is the Establishment of Non-dualism (Advaitasiddhi), and most non-dualistic teachers maintain that he more than sufficiently answered all the logical issues raised by the Dvaita school of Ānandatīrtha (Madhvācārya).*]

After studying the meaning of the commentary of Bhagavatpāda Śrī Śaṅkara with great care I write the *Lamp on the Hidden Meanings of the Gītā* on practically every syllable. (1)

The stated purpose of the *Gītā* is the highest good which is the final cessation of the cycle of births and deaths (*saṃsāra*) along with its causes. (2)

The highest realm of Viṣṇu, which is formed of being, consciousness, and bliss and which is full, is that for which the Vedas with their three divisions are started. (3)

Ritual action, worship, and knowledge are the three divisions in order. In that way the Gītā with its eighteen chapters also has three divisions. (4)

One division with each unit of six chapters is here observed. In the first and the last the conditions of action and knowledge are described. (5)

Since there is no combination of those two because of their being highly incompatible, the condition of *bhakti* for Bhagavān is proclaimed in the middle six. (6)

Since that [*bhakti*] indeed follows both, it eliminates all obstacles. It is of three kinds: mixed with action, pure and mixed with knowledge. (7)

But there in the first section, action through the path of its renunciation and the pure self, the meaning of the word "you" (*tvam*), along its justification, are described. (8)

द्वितीये भगवद्भक्तिनिष्ठावर्णनवर्त्मना।
भगवान् परमानन्दस्तत्पदार्थो ऽवधार्यते॥ ९॥

तृतीये तु तयोरैक्यं वाक्यार्थो वर्ण्यते स्फुटम्।
एवमप्यत्र काण्डानां सम्बन्धो ऽस्ति परस्परम्॥ १०॥

प्रत्यध्यायं विशेषस्तु तत्र तत्रैव वक्ष्यते।
मुक्तिसाधनपर्वेदं शास्त्रार्थत्वेन कथ्यते॥ ११॥

निष्कामकर्मानुष्ठानं त्यागात्काम्यनिषिधयोः।
तत्रापि परमो धर्मो जपस्तुत्यादिकं हरेः॥ १२॥

क्षीणपापस्य चित्तस्य विवेके योग्यता यदा।
नित्यानित्यविवेकस्तु जायते सुदृढस्तदा॥ १३॥

इहामुत्रार्थवैराग्यं वशीकाराभिधं क्रमात्।
ततः शमादिसम्पत्त्या संन्यासो निष्ठितो भवेत्॥ १४॥

एवं सर्वपरित्यागान्मुमुक्षा जायते दृढा।
ततो गुरूपसदनमुपदेशग्रहस्ततः॥ १५॥

ततः सन्देहहानाय वेदान्तश्रवणादिकम्।
सर्वमुत्तरमीमांसाशास्त्रमत्रोपयुज्यते॥ १६॥

ततस्तत्परिपाकेन निदिध्यासननिष्ठता।
योगशास्त्रस्तु सम्पूर्णमुपक्षीणं भवेदिह॥ १७॥

क्षीणदोषे ततश्चित्ते वाक्यात्तत्त्वमतिर्भवेत्।
साक्षात्कारो निर्विकल्पः शब्दादेवोपजायते॥ १८॥

In the second by the path of the description of the stance of *bhakti* Bhagavān, the highest bliss, the meaning of the word "that" (*tat*), is ascertained. (9)

But in the third section, their [self and Bhagavān's] oneness, the meaning of the statement [*tat tvam asi*] is clearly described. Thus, too, here there is a mutual relationship between the sections. (10)

The details of each chapter, however, will be discussed in those various places. This segmentation of the practices for liberation is said to be the meaning of this scripture. (11)

One should perform desireless action after rejecting actions that are done for some gain and that are forbidden. In that, too, the highest pious acts are mantra recitation (*japa*), hymns of praise (*stuti*), and so forth for Hari. (12)

When the capacity for discrimination appears in a mind whose sins have become diminished, then firm discrimination between what is eternal and what is not eternal is born. (13)

Gradually, detachment, named "bringing under control," from things here and in the next life appears; then, through the accomplishments of self-control, and the rest, renunciation becomes established. (14)

Thus, from the renunciation of all things the firm desire for liberation is born, and then approaching a teacher, and following that accepting instruction. (15)

After that there is hearing and so forth of the Vedānta to destroy one's doubts. The entire textual corpus of the *Uttara-mīmāṃsā*[11] is useful here. (16)

Then, with the maturing of that, one becomes established in meditation. The complete textual resources of *yoga* are exhausted here. (17)

Then, when the mind's flaws are destroyed, from statement an understanding of the truth occurs and from sound, direct experience, free from all doubt, is born. (18)

[11]This set of texts and commentaries reflecting on the meaning and interrelations of the Upaniṣads.

अविद्याविनिवृत्तिस्तु तत्त्वज्ञानोदये भवेत्।
तत आवरणे क्षीणे क्षीयेते भ्रमसंसयौ॥ १९॥

अनारब्धान्नि कर्माणि नश्यन्त्येव समन्ततः।
न त्वागामीनि जायन्ते तत्त्वज्ञानप्रभावतः॥ २०॥

प्रारब्धकर्मविक्षेपाद्वासना तु न नश्यति।
सा सर्वतो बलवता संयमेनोपशाम्यति॥ २१॥

संयमो धारणा ध्यानं समाधिरिति यत्त्रिकम्।
यमादिपञ्चकं पूर्वं तदर्थमुपयुज्यते॥ २२॥

ईश्वरप्रणिधानात्तु समाधिः सिध्यति द्रुतम्।
ततो भवेन्मनोनाशो वासनाक्षय एव च॥ २३॥

तत्त्वज्ञानं मनोनाशो वासनाक्षय इत्यपि।
युगपत्त्रितयाभ्यासाज्जीवन्मुक्तिर्दृढा भवेत्॥ २४॥

विद्वत्सन्न्यासकथनमेतदर्थं श्रुतौ कृतम्।
प्रागसिद्धो य एवांशो यत्नः स्यात्तस्य साधने॥ २५॥

निरुद्धे चेतसि पुरा सविकल्पसमाधिना।
निर्विकल्पसमाधिस्तु भवेदत्र त्रिभूमिकः॥ २६॥

व्युत्तिष्ठते स्वतस्त्वाद्ये द्वितीये परबोधितः।
अन्ते व्युत्तिष्ठते नैव सदा भवति तन्मयः॥ २७॥

एवम्भूतो ब्राह्मणः स्याद्वरिष्ठो ब्रह्मवादिनाम्।
गुणातीतः स्थितप्रज्ञो विष्णुभक्तश्च कथ्यते॥ २८॥

With the rising of knowledge of the truth, ignorance ceases. Then when the covering is destroyed error and doubt are destroyed. (19)

Action seeds that have not yet begun are destroyed completely and future ones are not born because of the power of knowledge of the truth. (20)

Because of the projection of actions that have already begun, the subconscious impulse is not destroyed, however. That is pacified by powerful self-control. (21)

Self-control, the triplet: keeping in memory, meditation, contemplation, preceded by the pentad beginning with the restraints (*yama*),[12] are used for that [pacifying the subconscious impulse]. (22)

Because of meditation on the controller (God), however, contemplation is accomplished quickly and then the mind is destroyed and the subconscious impulse (*vāsanā*) is too. (23)

Knowledge of the truth, destruction of the mind, and removal of the subconscious traces—from the simultaneous repeated practice of those, liberation-while-living becomes strong. (24)

Discussion of renunciation of the possesser of knowledge for this reason included in *śruti* (the revelatory texts of the Vedas). Effort should be made in practicing the part [of those three] that is not completed before. (25)

When the mind is stopped before by trance with distinction (*savikalpa-samādhi*), trance without distinction (*nirvikalpa-samādhi*), consisting of three stages, arises at that point. (26)

In the first stage one returns to normal consciousness by oneself, in the second stage one is awakened by another, and in the final stage one does not return, but stays absorbed in it forever. (27)

This kind of *brāhmaṇa* would be the finest of the tellers of Brahman, beyond the qualities, of steady consciousness, and a *bhakta* of Viṣṇu. (28)

---

[12]The five meant here are the first five practices of the classical eight-limbed yoga or *aṣṭāṅga-yoga*: *yama*, *niyama*, *āsana*, *prāṇāyāma*, and *pratyāhāra*.

अतिवर्णाश्रमी जीवन्मुक्त आत्मरतिस्तथा।
एतस्य कृतकृत्यत्वात् शास्त्रमस्मान्निवर्तते॥ २९॥

यस्य देवे परा भक्तिर्यथा देवे तथा गुरौ।
तस्यैते कथिता ह्यर्थाः प्रकाशन्ते महात्मनः॥ ३०॥

इत्यादिश्रुतिमानेन कायेन मनसा गिरा।
सर्वावस्थासु भगवद्भक्तिरत्रोपयुज्यते॥ ३१॥

पूर्वभूमौ कृत्वा भक्तिरुत्तमां भूमिमानयेत्।
अन्यथा विघ्नबाहुल्यात्फलसिद्धिः सुदुर्लभा॥ ३२॥

पूर्वाभ्यासेन तेनैव ह्रियते ह्यवशो ऽपि सः।
अनेकजन्मसंसिद्ध इत्यादि च वचो हरेः॥ ३३॥

यदि प्राग्भवसंस्कारस्याचिन्त्यत्वात्तु कश्चन।
प्रागेव कृतकृत्यः स्यादाकाशफलपातवत्॥ ३४॥

न तं प्रति कृतार्थत्वाच्छास्त्रमारब्धुमिष्यते।
प्राक्सिद्धसाधनाभ्यासाद्दुर्ज्ञेया भगवत्कृपा॥ ३५॥

एवं प्राग्भूमिसिद्धावप्युत्तरोत्तरभूमये।
विधेया भगवद्भक्तिस्तां विना सा न सिध्यति॥ ३६॥

जीवन्मुक्तिदशायान्तु न भक्तेः फलकल्पना।
अद्वेष्टृत्वादिवत्तेषां स्वभावो भजनं हरेः॥ ३७॥

आत्मारामाश्च मुनयो निर्ग्रन्था अप्युरुक्रमे।
कुर्वन्त्यहैतुकीं भक्तिमित्थम्भूतगुणो हरिः॥ ३८॥

One beyond caste, liberated-yet-alive, as well as attached to the Self, because he has accomplished the goal, scripture turns back from [does not apply to] him. (29)

"One who has the highest *bhakti* for God and just as for God for the guru, for such a great soul all these described blessings occur."[13] (30)

On the basis of the evidence of this scripture and others, in all conditions *bhakti* for Bhagavān, with body, mind, word, is to applied. (31)

Having performed *bhakti* on the previous stage one may be led to the highest stage, otherwise, because of a profusion of obstacles, accomplishment of the result is very rare. (32)

By prior practice one is drawn [to the path of mukti] even without control and such, too, is the statement of Hari: "accomplished after many births."[14] (33)

But if because of the unthinkable nature of impressions from previous existences, someone may have become accomplished previously, like the fall of a fruit from the sky, (34)

for him, because of having achieved the goal, it is not necessary to follow scripture. Because of that prior accomplishment, striving, and practice, the grace of Bhagavān is hard to know. (35)

Therefore when a prior stage has been completed, for the following stages *bhakti* for Bhagavān is enjoined. Without that, it is not achieved. (36)

But in the state of living liberation *bhakti* has no intended result. Like being without envy and so forth their nature is worshiping Hari. (37)

The self-satisfied sages, though free of knots, perform causeless *bhakti* to wide-stepping Hari. Hari is of such qualities.[15] (38)

---

[13] Śvetāśvatara Upaniṣad, 6.33.
[14] *Bhagavad-gītā*, 6.44.
[15] *Bhāg.*, 1.7.10.

तेषां ज्ञानी नित्ययुक्त एकभक्तिर्विशिष्यते।
इत्यादिवचनात्प्रेमभक्तो ऽयं मुख्य उच्यते॥ ३९॥

एतत्सर्वं भगवता गीताशास्त्रे प्रकाशितम्।
अतो व्याख्यातुमेतन्मे मन उत्सहते भृशम्॥ ४०॥

निष्कामकर्मानुष्ठानं मूलं मोक्षस्य कीर्तितम्।
शोकादिरासुरः पाप्मा तस्य च प्रतिबन्धकः॥ ४१॥

यतः स्वधर्मविभ्रंशः प्रतिषिद्धस्य सेवनम्।
फलाभिसन्धिपूर्वा वा साहङ्कारा क्रिया भवेत्॥ ४२॥

आविष्टः पुरुषो नित्यमेवमासुरपाप्मभिः।
पुमर्थलाभायोग्यः सन् लभते दुःखसन्ततिम्॥ ४३॥

दुःखं स्वभावतो द्वेष्यं सर्वेषां प्राणिनामिह।
अतस्तत्साधनं त्याज्यं शोकमोहादिकं सदा॥ ४४॥

अनादिभवसन्ताननिरूढं दुःखकारणम्।
दुस्त्यजं शोकमोहादि केनोपायेन हीयताम्॥ ४५॥

एवमाकाङ्क्ष्याविष्टं पुरुषार्थोन्मुखं नरम्।
बुबोधयिषुराहेदं भगवान् शास्त्रमुत्तमम्॥ ४६॥

From statements such as "Among them, the gnostic, who is ever yoked and whose bhakti is for one, is distinguished," this *bhakti* of love is proclaimed primary. (39)

All this is revealed by Bhagavān in the Gītā scripture. Therefore my mind is most enthusiastic to explain it. (40)

Performance of desireless action is praised as the root of liberation. Lamentation, and so forth, and the demonic sins, are its obstacles. (41)

From which may arise lapses in one's own *dharma*, performance of forbidden deeds and action done for the result or with arrogance. (42)

A person always filled thus by the demonic sins, becoming incapable of attaining the goals of human life, obtains a series of miseries. (43)

Misery is by nature hated by all living beings in this world. Therefore, the means to that, i.e., lamentation, delusion, and the rest, is forever to be rejected. (44)

"May the hard-to-leave root of the continuous flow existences without beginning, the cause of misery, that is, lamentation, delusion, and the rest, be in some way destroyed." (45)

Wishing to awaken human beings who are filled with that desire and who strive for the goal of human life, Bhagavān spoke this highest scripture. (46)

The *Sārārtha-varṣiṇī* of Viśvanātha Cakravartin

गौरांशुकः सत्कुमुदप्रमोदी स्वाभिख्यया गोस्तमसो निहन्ता।
श्रीकृष्णचैतन्यसुधानिधिर्मे मनोऽधितिष्ठन् स्वरतिं करोतु॥ १॥
प्राचीनवाचः सुविचार्य सोऽहमज्ञोऽपि गीतामृतलेशलिप्सुः।
यतेः प्रभोरेव मते तदत्र सन्तः क्षमध्वं शरणागतस्य॥ २॥

आत्मानात्मविवेकेन शोकमोहतमो नुदन्।
द्वितीये कृष्णचन्द्रोऽत्र प्रोचे मुक्तस्य लक्षणम्॥ ३॥

ज्ञानं कर्म च विस्पष्टमस्पष्टं भक्तिमुक्तवान्।
अतएवायमध्यायः श्रीगीतासूत्रमुच्यते॥ ४॥

निष्काममर्पितं कर्म तृतीये तु प्रपञ्च्यते।
कामक्रोधजिगीषायां विवेकोऽपि प्रदर्श्यते॥ ५॥

Raincloud of Essential Meaning

[*Viśvanātha Cakravartī was born in a Rāḍīya brāhmaṇa family in Devagrāma in the District of Nādiā in the middle of the sixteenth century of the Śaka Era.*[16] *The names of his mother and father are not known. Harivallabha was another name of Viśvanātha. In all of the songs that Viśvanātha wrote he used the name Harivallabha. While Viśvanātha was still a boy, but had finished his boyhood studies of grammar and other such basic subjects, he went to the village of Saiyadabad in the district of Murshidabad and studied bhakti scriptures such as the Śrīmad Bhāgavata. The sons of Rāmakṛṣṇa Ācārya, a disciple of Śrīla Narottama Ṭhākura, were the chief scholars in Saiyadabad at that time. Perhaps Viśvanātha studied the bhakti scriptures from one of them. Among all the books that Cakravartī Mahāśaya wrote, his Revealer of Essential Meaning (Sārārthadarśinī, his commentary on the Bhāgavata), is inferred to he his last. He finished that commentary in the month of Māgha (January-February) in 1626 Śakābda (1704 C.E.). If this conclusion is accepted as reasonable, then Viśvanātha wandered this earth from 1550 to at least 1630 Śakābda (1628 to 1708 C.E.).*[17] *He is the first commentator on the Gītā from the Caitanya Vaiṣṇava tradition and thus emphasizes the role of bhakti in the Gītā.*]

His golden radiance, pleasing to lily-like good folk, destroys by his own name the darkness of the earth. May the moon of Śrī Kṛṣṇacaitanya rule my mind and give me love for him. (1)

After considering carefully the words of the ancients, I, even though I am a fool, long for a little of the nectar of the *Gītā* in the view of the Master who was a renunciant. Therefore, let the holy forgive [the impertinence] of one who has sought shelter. (2)

Driving away the darkness of sorrow and delusion by distinguishing between the self and the non-self, in the second chapter Kṛṣṇacandra has described the characteristics of someone liberated. (3)

He describes knowledge and action distinctly and *bhakti* indistinctly. Therefore, this chapter is called the Śrī Gītā's aphoristic form. (4)

But desireless, dedicated action is expounded in the third chapter and discrimination in matters of lust, anger, and the desire to conquer is also demonstrated. (5)

---

[16]The Śaka Era began in 78 C.E. with the accession of Kanishkha to the throne. Thus, the beginning of the sixteenth century of the Śaka Era corresponds to 1578 C.E. and it lasts until 1678 C.E. The middle of the sixteenth century of that era would be, therefore, around 1628 C.E.

[17]From the introduction of *Bhakti-granthāvalī: five short works by Viśvanātha Cakravartin*, edited and translated into Bengali by Śrī Śyāmalāla Gosvāmin, English trans. by Neal Delmonico.

अध्यायेऽस्मिन् साधनस्य निष्कामस्यैव कर्मणः।
प्राधान्यमुचे तत्साध्यज्ञानस्य गुणतां वदन्॥ ६॥

तुर्ये स्वाविर्भावहेतोर्नित्यत्वं जन्मकर्मणोः।
स्वस्योक्तं ब्रह्मयज्ञादिज्ञानोत्कर्षप्रपञ्चनम्॥ ७॥

उक्तेषु मुक्त्युपायेषु ज्ञानमत्र प्रशस्यते।
ज्ञानोपायं तु कर्मैवेत्यध्यायार्थो निरूपितः॥ ८॥

प्रोक्तं ज्ञानादपि श्रेष्ठं कर्म तद्दार्ढ्यसिद्धये।
तत्पदार्थस्य च ज्ञानं साम्याद्या अपि पञ्चमे॥ ९॥

निष्कामकर्मणा ज्ञानी योगी चात्र विमुच्यते।
ज्ञात्वात्मपरमात्मानावित्यध्यायार्थ ईरितः॥ १०॥

षष्ठेषु योगिनो योगप्रकारविजितात्मनः।
मनसश्चञ्चलस्यापि नैश्चल्योपाय उच्यते॥ ११॥

अग्रिमाध्यायषट्कं यद्भक्तियोगनिरूपकम्।
तस्य सूत्रमयं श्लोको भक्तकण्ठविभूसणम्॥ १२॥

प्रथमेन कथासूत्रं गीताशास्त्रशिरोमणिः।
द्वितीयेन तृतीयेन तुर्येणाकामकर्म च॥ १३॥

ज्ञानञ्च पञ्चमेनोक्तं योगः षष्ठेन कीर्तितः।
प्राधान्येन तदप्येतत् षट्कं कर्मनिरूपकम्॥ १४॥

कदा सदानन्दभुवो महाप्रभोः
कृपामृताब्धेश्चरणौ श्रयामहे।
यथा तथा प्रोज्झितमुक्तितत्पथा
भक्ताध्वना प्रेमसुधामयामहे॥ १५॥

In this chapter the predominance of desireless action as a means is discussed while extolling the virtues of its result, knowledge. (6)

In the fourth chapter, the perpetual nature of the reason for his appearing as well as of his births and actions is stated and the superiority of knowledge of the Brahma sacrifices and so forth is revealed. (7)

Among the ways to liberation that have been described, knowledge is here recommended. But that action itself is the way to knowledge is recognized as the meaning of this chapter. (8)

It is stated in the fifth chapter that action is even better than knowledge for success in strengthening that [knowledge], as is knowledge of the that-category[18] and traits such as equanimity and so forth. (9)

Through desireless action the knower and the *yogī* are liberated after knowing the Self and the Super-self. This is proclaimed to be the meaning of the chapter. (10)

In the sixth is described the way to steady the unsteady mind of *yogīs* who have conquered themselves by some kind of *yoga*. (11)

This verse, an ornament for the throats of *bhaktas*, encapsulates the first group of the six chapters which gives shape to *bhakti-yoga*. (12)

With the first comes the thread of the story, the crown-jewel of the Gītā treatise. With the second, the third, and fourth comes desireless action. (13)

And knowledge is described in the fifth, yoga in the sixth. Therefore, this group of six primarily concerns action. (14)

Oh when will we seek shelter at the feet of that ocean of the nectar of grace, Mahāprabhu, ever a source of bliss. And like that so too by the path of the *bhakta*, a path liberated from liberation, may we attain the nectar of divine love (*preman*).[19] (15)

---

[18]Of the famous Upaniṣadic statement "That Thou Art!" (*tat tvam asi*). *Tat* refers to the absolute however it is conceived, i.e. as Brahman or as Supreme Person.

[19]This is the invocation that begins the second set of six chapters.

सप्तमे भजनीयस्य श्रीकृष्णैश्वर्यमुच्यते।
न भजन्ते भजन्ते ये ते चाप्युक्ताश्चतुर्विधाः॥ १६॥

भक्ता एव हरेस्तत्त्वविदो मायां तरन्ति।
ते चोक्ताः षड्विधाः अत्रेत्यध्यायार्थो निरूपितः॥ १७॥

पार्थप्रश्नोत्तरं योगं मिश्रां भक्तिं प्रसङ्गतः।
शुद्धाञ्च भक्तिं प्रोवाच द्वे गती अपि चाष्टमे॥ १८॥

भक्तानां सर्वतः श्रैष्ठ्यं पूर्वोक्तं तेष्वपि स्फुटम्।
अनन्यभक्तस्येत्यर्थोऽत्राध्याये व्यञ्जितोऽभवत्॥ १९॥

आराध्यत्वे प्रभोर्दासैरैश्वर्यं यदपेक्षितम्।
तत्शुद्धभक्तेरुत्कर्षश्चोच्यते नवमे स्फुटम्॥ २०॥

पात्रापात्राविचारित्वं स्वस्पर्शात्सर्वशोधनम्।
भक्तेरेवात्रैतदस्या राजगुह्यत्वमीक्ष्यते॥ २१॥

ऐश्वर्यं ज्ञापयित्वोचे भक्तिं यत्सप्तमादिषु।
सरहस्यं तदेवोक्तं दशमे सविभूतिकम्॥ २२॥

विश्वं श्रीकृष्ण एवातः सेव्यस्तद्दत्तया धिया।
स एवास्वाद्यमाधुर्य इत्यध्यायार्थ ईरितः॥ २३॥

एकादशे विश्वरूपं दृष्ट्वा संभ्रान्तधीः स्तुवन्।
पार्थ आनन्दितो दर्शयित्वा स्वं हरिणा पुनः॥ २४॥

कृष्णस्यैव महैश्वर्यं ममैवास्मिन् रणे जयः।
इत्यर्जुनो निश्चिकायेत्यध्यायार्थो निरूपितः॥ २५॥

In the seventh chapter the mighty power of Śrī Kṛṣṇa as the root of whatever is to be worshiped is proclaimed, and those who worship as well as those who do not worship are described in their four varieties. (16)

Bhaktas of Hari who know the truth cross over *māyā* and they are described here as of six types. This is the meaning of this chapter. (17)

Yoga, the answer to Arjuna's question, and, coincidentally, mixed *bhakti* and pure *bhakti* are discussed as well as the two destinations in the eighth chapter, (18)

The superiority of *bhaktas* in all respects is proclaimed first and then among them the clear superiority of the exclusive *bhakta*. This meaning is suggested in the chapter. (19)

The godly power which is depended upon in the worship of the lord by his servants and the superiority of pure *bhakti* for him are described clearly in the ninth chapter. (20)

Here are stated the absence of distinction between the worthy and unworthy recipients of *bhakti* and its ability to purify all by mere contact with it. This latter is regarded as its royal secret. (21)

Having communicated the divine opulence, he described *bhakti* in the seventh chapter and the rest, and then explained that (opulence) with its mystery and its manifestations in the tenth. (22)

Śrī Kṛṣṇa is the universe, therefore he is to be served with the intelligence given by him. He is the sweetness to be enjoyed. This is the teaching of the chapter. (23)

In the eleventh chapter, having viewed his cosmic form, Arjuna while praising him with a agitated mind becomes filled with joy after having Hari show his own form again. (24)

Arjuna is convinced of the super godly power of Kṛṣṇa and that he (Arjuna) will have victory in this war. Such is determined to be the teaching of this chapter. (25)

द्वादशे सर्वभक्तानां ज्ञानिभ्यः श्रैष्ठ्यमुच्यते।
भक्तेष्वपि प्रशस्यन्ते येऽद्वेषादिगुणान्विताः॥ २६॥

सर्वश्रेष्ठो सुखमयी सर्वसाध्यसुसाधिका।
भक्तिरेवाद्भुतगुणेत्यध्यायार्थो निरूपितः॥ २७॥

निम्बद्राक्षे इव ज्ञानभक्ती यद्यपि दर्शिते।
आदीयेते तदप्येते तत्तदास्वादलोभिभिः॥ २८॥

नमोऽस्तु भगवद्भक्त्यै कृपया सांशलेशतः।
ज्ञानादिष्वपि तिष्ठेत्तत्सार्थकीकरणाय या॥ २९॥

षट्के तृतीयेऽत्र भक्तिमिश्रं ज्ञानं निरूप्यते।
तन्मध्ये केवला भक्तिरपि भङ्ग्या प्रकृष्यते॥ ३०॥

त्रयोदशे शरीरञ्च जीवात्मपरमात्मनोः।
ज्ञानस्य साधनं जीवः प्रकृतिश्च विविच्यते॥ ३१॥

द्वयोः क्षेत्रज्ञयोर्मध्ये जीवात्मा क्षेत्रधर्मभाक्।
बध्यते मुच्यते ज्ञानादित्यध्यायार्थ ईरितः॥ ३२॥

गुणाः स्युर्बन्धकास्ते तु फलैर्ज्ञेयाश्चतुर्दशे।
गुणात्यये चिह्नततिर्हेतुर्भक्तिश्च वर्णिता॥ ३३॥

अनर्थ एव त्रैगुण्यं निस्त्रैगुण्यं कृताथता।
तच्च भक्त्यैव भवतीत्यध्यायार्थो निरूपितः॥ ३४॥

संसारच्छेदकोऽसङ्ग आत्मेशांशः क्षराक्षरात्।
उत्तमः पुरुषः कृष्ण इति पञ्चदशे कथा॥ ३५॥

In the twelfth chapter the superiority of all *bhaktas* to knowers is stated and those who are distinguished among *bhaktas* possess qualities like non-envy and such. (26)

The best of all, the happiest, the achiever of all goals, is *bhakti* which has amazing virtues. This is the teaching of the chapter. (27)

Although knowledge and *bhakti* are shown to be like neem leaves and grapes, they are nevertheless accepted by those who wish to taste them. (28)

Let me bow to the *bhakti* of Bhagavān—which if by grace it is present even a little in knowledge and so forth—causes them to be successful. (29)

In the third group of six chapters knowledge mixed with *bhakti* is outlined and in the middle of that singular *bhakti* is distinguished indirectly. (30)

In the thirteenth chapter the body of the self of living being and of the supreme self, the means to knowledge, the living being, and nature are distinguished. (31)

Between the two knowers of the field, the living being experiences the traits of the field, is bound and is liberated through knowledge. This is proclaimed the teaching of the chapter. (32)

The qualities (threads) are the binders, but they are known from their results in the fourteenth chapter. The set of indications in surpassing the qualities and *bhakti* is also described. (33)

Worthless is being of the three qualities and being free of the qualities is being successful. And that happens only by *bhakti*; such is the teaching of this chapter. (34)

Detachment is the cutter of cyclic existence, the self a part of the lord, and Kṛṣṇa the highest person beyond the perishable and the imperishable. Such is the narrative in the fifteenth chapter. (35)

जडचैतन्यवर्गाणां विवृतं कुर्वता कृतम्।
कृष्ण एव महोत्कर्ष इत्यध्यायार्थ ईरितः॥ ३६॥

षोडशे सम्पदं दैवीमासुरीमप्यवर्णयत्।
सर्गञ्च द्विविधं दैवमासुरं प्रभुरक्षयात्॥ ३७॥

आस्तिका एव विन्दन्ति सद्गतिं सन्त एव ते।
नास्तिका नरकं यान्तीत्यध्यायार्थो निरूपितः॥ ३८॥

अथ सप्तदशे वस्तु सात्त्विकं राजसं तथा।
तामसञ्च विविच्योक्तं पार्थप्रश्नोत्तरं यथा॥ ३९॥

उक्तेषु विविधेष्वेव सात्त्विकं श्रद्धया कृतम्।
यत्स्यात्तदेव मोक्षार्हमित्यधायार्थ ईरितः॥ ४०॥

सन्न्यासज्ञानकर्मादेस्त्रैविध्यं मुक्तिनिर्णयः।
गुह्यसारतमा भक्तिरित्यष्टादश उच्यते॥ ४१॥

सारार्थवर्षिणी विश्वजनीना भक्तचातकान्।
माधुरी धिनुतादस्या माधुरी भातु मे हृदि॥ ४२॥

The categories of the inanimate and the conscious, revealed by the actor, are completed and Kṛṣṇa alone is the most superior. Such is the teaching of the chapter. (36)

In the sixteenth chapter the Lord describes the fortunes of the godly and the demonic, and the twofold creation, godly and demonic, from the undecaying. (37)

The affimers (*āstika*) reach a good destination and they are good; the deniers (*nāstika*) go to hell. This is determined the meaning of the chapter. (38)

Thus in the seventeenth chapter, according to the questions of Arjuna and their answers, substance is distinguished into transparent, translucent, and opaque[20] and described. (39)

Among the various things described, only the transparent (*sāttvika*) that is performed with faith is worthy of liberation. This is proclaimed to be the meaning of this chapter. (40)

The threefold nature of renunciation, knowledge, and action, ascertainment of liberation, and the *bhakti* that is the highest essence of the esoteric are described in the eighteenth chapter. (41)

May the sweetness raining down as the [*Gītā*'s] essential meaning, giving life to all, nourish the *cātaka-bhaktas*,[21] and may its sweetness shine in my heart. (42)

[20] *Sāttvika*, *rājasika*, and *tāmasika*. These are often mistakenly translated, in my opinion, as goodness, passion, and darkness. For one thing *sattva* has nothing to do with goodness, nor does *rajas* passion. The metaphor underlying the three terms seems to be one of transparency to light.

[21] The *cātaka* is a mythical bird that draws all its nourishment the rain falling from rain-clouds.

The *Gītā-bhūṣaṇa-bhāṣya* of Baladeva Vidyābhūṣaṇa

सत्यानन्ताचिन्त्यशक्त्येकपक्षे
सर्वाध्यक्षे भक्तरक्षातिदक्षे।
श्रीगोविन्दे विश्वसर्गादिकन्दे
पूर्णानन्दे नित्यमास्तां मतिर्मे॥ १॥

The Ornament of the Gītā

[*Not much is known about Baladeva's early life. Several accounts*[22] *say that he was born in a vaiśya*[23] *family in a village called Remuna now in the Balesar subdivision of Orissa. Although his caste was not high, they report, he demonstrated himself to be an uncommonly gifted student and continued his studies in grammar, literary criticism, logic, Vedic studies, and Vedānta. At an early age he is supposed to have become a follower of the Mādhva tradition, a Vaiṣṇava tradition founded by the saint Madhva in South India in the 13th cent. C.E., and to have traveled to Mysore to study the Mādhva texts and commentaries. He later returned to his own state of Orissa and settled in the temple town of Jagannath Puri. There he met and had discussions with Rādhādāmodara, a brāhmaṇa from Kanyakubja who was a follower of the Caitanya tradition. He became attracted to the tradition and eventually became Rādhādāmodara's disciple. As a result he left Puri and went to Vṛndāvana where he studied the texts of the Caitanya tradition with the great scholar and commentator Viśvanātha Cakravartin and another scholar named Pītāmbara Dāsa.*]

May my mind forever rest on Śrī Govinda, on whose one side are true, unlimited, and unthinkable powers, the overseer of all, extremely clever at protecting *bhaktas*, the very root of the creation and so forth of the cosmos, full measure of bliss. (1)

---

[22]Sudesh Narang in *The Vaiṣṇava Philosophy according to Baladeva Vidyābhūṣaṇa* (Delhi: Nag Publishers, 1984), pp. 1-2. Michael Wright and Nancy Wright, "Baladeva Vidyābhūṣaṇa: the Gauḍīya Vedāntist" in the *Journal of Vaiṣṇava Studies*, Vol.1, No. 2 (Winter 1993), pp. 158-184. Bhaktivedanta Vaman Swami in his Bengali introduction to the *Siddhānta-ratnam* (Navadvīpa: Śrī Gauḍīya Vedānta Samiti, 1973), pp. v-vii.

[23]The *vaiśya* caste or *varṇa* is the third caste and is usually made up of agriculturalists, merchants, and artisans. Akṣaya Kumāra Śarmā, editor Baladeva's *Prameya-ratnāvalī*, criticizes the view that Baladeva was a *vaiśya* (Baladeva Vidyābhūṣaṇa, *Prameya-ratnāvalī*, edited, with his own commentary and the *Kānti-mālā* of Vedānta-vāgīśa, by Akṣaya Kumāra Śarmā Śāstrī. Calcutta: Sanskrit Sahitya Parishat, 1927, pp. x-xii.). Śarmā cites an unnamed person's view, possibly Bhaktisiddhānta's, that Baladeva was born in a *vaiśya* family and after being initiated by a Vaiṣṇava brāhmaṇa became a brāhmaṇa. Moreover, says this unnamed person, those who know the scriptures know that *brāhmaṇas* by birth are produced from *brāhmaṇas* by profession. Śarmā's response is that typical of a conservative *brāhmaṇa*. Such claims, he says, are to be rejected as the ravings of a mad man. No one is able to change to another caste in their current birth even with the greatest of austerities. Wherever there is the appearance of such a statement in the scriptures, it is to be understood as merely glorification of austerity (*tapas*). Citing some of the Hindu law texts, he says that no one is able to become a *brāhmaṇa* by assuming the occupation of one. One becomes a *brāhmaṇa* only by birth. Śarmā goes on to say that he has never heard of anyone who was not a *brāhmaṇa* receiving the honorific title of "preceptor" (*ācārya*) as Baladeva has.

अज्ञाननीरधिरुपैति यया विशोषं
भक्तिः परापि भजते परिपोषमुच्चैः।
तत्त्वं परं स्फुरति दुर्गमप्यजस्रम्
साड्गुण्यभृत् स्वरचितां प्रणमामि गीताम्॥ २॥

अहिंस्रस्यात्मजिज्ञासा दयार्द्रस्योपजायते।
तद्विरुद्धस्य नैवेति प्रथमादुपधारितम्॥ ३॥

द्वितीये जीवयाथात्म्यज्ञानं तत्साधनं हरिः।
निष्कामकर्म च प्रोचे स्थितप्रज्ञस्य लक्षणम्॥ ४॥

निष्कामकर्मभिर्ज्ञानी हरिमेव स्मरन् भवेत्।
अन्यथा विघ्न एवेति द्वितीयोऽध्यायनिर्णयः॥ ५॥

तृतीये कर्मनिष्कामं विस्तरेणोपवर्णितम्।
कामादेर्विजयोपायो दुर्जयस्यापि दर्शितः॥ ६॥

निष्कामं कर्म मुख्यं स्याद्गौणं ज्ञानं तदुद्भवम्।
जीवात्मदृष्टावित्येष तृतीयोऽध्यायनिर्णयः॥ ७॥

तुर्ये स्वाभिव्यक्तहेतुं स्वलीलानित्यत्वं सत्कर्मसु ज्ञानयोगम्।
ज्ञानस्यापि प्राग्यन्माहात्म्यमुच्चैः प्राख्यद्देवो देवकीनन्दनोऽसौ॥ ८॥

व्यंशकं धान्यवत्कर्म तुषांशादिव तण्डुलः।
श्रेष्ठं द्रव्यांशतो ज्ञानमिति तुर्यस्य निर्णयः॥ ९॥

ज्ञानतः कर्मणः श्रेष्ठ्यं सुकरत्वादिना हरिः।
शुद्धस्य तदकर्तृत्वं त्वित्यादि प्राह पञ्चमे॥ १०॥

निष्कामकर्मणा योगशिरस्केन विमुच्यते।
सनिष्ठो ज्ञानगर्भेणेत्येष पञ्चनिर्णयः॥ ११॥

To the *Gītā* do I bow down by which the ocean of ignorance is dried up, the highest *bhakti* becomes greatly nourished, and the highest truth, though difficult to understand, becomes forever manifest, bearer of true virtue composed by Him Himself. (2)

A desire to know about the Self arises for one who is harmless (i.e. not given to violence) and full of compassion, not for one who is the opposite of that. This is learned from the first chapter. (3)

In the second chapter Hari teaches knowledge of the real nature of the living being, the means to that knowledge, desireless action, and the characteristics of one whose intelligence is fixed. (4)

With desireless action the knower should remember Hari. Otherwise it (desireless action) only becomes an obstacle. This is the conclusion of the second chapter. (5)

In the third chapter freedom from desire in action is described at length and the way to beating desire, though hard to beat, is shown as well. (6)

Desireless action should be primary and the knowledge that is born of that secondary in perceiving the self of the living being. This is the conclusion of the third chapter. (7)

In the fourth chapter, the divine son of Devakī loudly proclaims the cause of his own appearance, the perpetuity of his sports, the discipline of knowledge in the actions of the good, and the greatness of knowledge in previous times. (8)

Action has two parts like a whole grain, a kernel separate from the chaff. Better than the substance-part (the chaff) is knowledge. This is the conclusion of the fourth chapter. (9)

Hari teaches in the fifth that action is better than knowledge because it is easier to perform and so forth, but for one who is pure it is performed without [a sense of] agency. (10)

By desireless action, with discipline (*yoga*) at its head and bearing within it knowledge, a person with firm conviction is liberated. This is the teaching of the fifth. (11)

षष्ठे योगविधिः कर्मशुद्धस्य विजितात्मनः।
स्थैर्योपायश्च मनसोऽस्थिरस्यापीति कीर्त्यते॥ १२॥

गीताकथासूत्रमवोचदाद्ये कर्म द्वितीयादिषु कामशून्यम्।
तत्पञ्चमे वेदनगर्भमाख्यन् षष्ठे तु योगोज्ज्वलितं मुकुन्दः॥ १३॥

सप्तमे भजनीयस्य स्वस्यैश्वर्यं प्रकीर्त्यते।
चातुर्विध्यञ्च भजतां तथैवाभजतामपि॥ १४॥

मां विदुस्तत्त्वतो भक्ता मन्मायामुत्तरन्ति ते।
ते पुनः पञ्चविधेत्येष सप्तमस्य विनिर्णयः॥ १५॥

उक्तान् पृष्टः क्रमाव्द्याख्यद्ब्रह्मादीन् हरिरष्टमे।
योगमिश्राञ्च शुद्धाञ्च भक्तिमार्गद्वयं तथा॥ १६॥

कृष्णांशः पुरुषो योगभक्त्या लभ्योऽर्च्चिरादिभिः।
कृष्णस्त्वनन्यभक्त्यैवेत्यष्टमस्य विनिर्णयः॥ १७॥

भक्त्युद्दीप्तिकरं स्वस्य पारमैश्वर्यमद्भुतम्।
स्वभक्तेश्च महोत्कर्षं नवमे हरिरूचिवान्॥ १८॥

पात्रापात्रधिया शून्या स्पर्शात्सर्वाघनाशिनी।
गङ्गेव भक्तिरेवेति राजगुह्यमिह स्मृता॥ १९॥

सप्तमादौ निजैश्वर्यं भक्तिहेतुं यदीरितम्।
विभूतिकथनेनात्र दशमे तत्प्रपुष्यते॥ २०॥

यच्छक्तिलेशात्सूर्याद्या भवन्त्युग्रतेजसः।
यदंशेन धृतं विश्वं स कृष्णो दशमेऽर्च्यते॥ २१॥

In the sixth are praised the use of yoga for one who has been purified by action and who has conquered himself and the way to stability of the mind even though it is unstable. (12)

In the first chapter Mukunda taught the thread of the story of the Gītā, in the second and the rest [i.e., third and fourth] action free of desire, in the fifth that [action] as the source of knowing, but in the sixth that [action] illumined by yoga. (13)

In the seventh the supreme might of the one to be worshiped is proclaimed and four types of worshiper as well as four types of non-worshiper. (14)

The *bhaktas* know me as I am and they cross beyond my *māyā*. They again are of five kinds. This is the conclusion of the seventh chapter. (15)

Asked, Hari explained in order Brahma and the rest as well as the two paths of *bhakti*, *bhakti* mixed with yoga and pure. (16)

The divine person (*puruṣa*) who is a portion of Kṛṣṇa is attainable by *bhakti* mixed with yoga along with offering flames and so forth, but Kṛṣṇa himself only by exclusive *bhakti*. This is the conclusion of the eighth chapter. (17)

Hari described in the ninth his own wonderful, supreme opulence which excites *bhakti* and the super supremacy of *bhakti* for him. (18)

Bhakti is free of consideration of worthy or unworthy recipient and by contact with it destroys all sins like the Gaṅgā. This is the royal secret here recalled. (19)

His supreme might, the cause of *bhakti*, that was proclaimed in the seventh chapter and the rest is further expanded here in the tenth with the description of his opulences. (20)

From just a little of whose power the sun and the rest, fiercely bright, arise and by a mere portion of whom the universe upheld, that Kṛṣṇa is honored in the tenth chapter. (21)

एकादशे विश्वरूपं विलोक्य त्रस्तधीः स्तुवन्।
दर्शयित्वा स्वकं रूपं हरिणा हर्षितोऽर्जुनः॥ २२॥

पूर्णः कृष्णोऽवतारित्वात्तद्भक्तानां जयो रणे।
भारते पाण्डुपुत्राणामित्येकादशनिर्णयः॥ २३॥

उपायेषु समस्तेषु शुद्धा भक्तिर्महाबला।
प्रापयेत्त्वरया यन्मामित्याह द्वादशे हरिः॥ २४॥

वशः स्वैकजुषां कृष्णः स्वभक्त्येकजुषां तु सः।
प्रीत्यैवातिवशः श्रीमानिति द्वादशनिर्णयः॥ २५॥

कथिताः पूर्वषट्काभ्यामर्थाज्जीवादयोऽत्र ये।
स्वरूपाणि विशोध्यन्ते तेषां षट्केऽन्तिमे स्फुटम्॥ २६॥

भक्तौ पूर्वोपदिष्टायां ज्ञानं द्वारं भवत्यतः।
देहजीवेशविज्ञानं तद्वक्तव्यं त्रयोदशे॥ २७॥

जीवेशौ देहमध्यस्थौ तत्राद्यो देहधर्मयुक्।
बध्यते मुच्यते बोधादिति ज्ञानं त्रयोदशात्॥ २८॥

गुणाः स्युर्बन्धकास्ते तु परिचेयाः फलैस्त्रयः।
मद्भक्त्या तन्निवृत्तिः स्यादिति प्रोक्तं चतुर्दशे॥ २९॥

संसारो गुणयोगः स्याद्विमोक्षस्तु गुणात्ययः।
तत्सिद्धिर्हरिभक्त्यैवेत्येतद्बुद्धं चतुर्दशात्॥ ३०॥

संसारच्छेदि वैराग्यं जीवो मेऽंशः सनातनः।
अहं सर्वोत्तमः श्रीमानिति पञ्चदशे स्मृतम्॥ ३१॥

In the eleventh chapter, after viewing his cosmic form, Arjuna while praising him with fearful heart caused him to reveal his own true form and was pleased by Hari. (22)

Kṛṣṇa is complete because he is the source of all descents and his *bhaktas*, the sons of Pāṇḍu, are victorious in the Bhārata battle. This is the lesson of the eleventh chapter. (23)

"Among all the different paths pure *bhakti* is the most powerful, since it can quickly bring one to me." This Hari says in the twelfth chapter. (24)

Kṛṣṇa is submissive to those devoted only to him but for those devoted only to his *bhakti* he, out of affection, is even more submissive. This is the lesson of the twelfth. (25)

The living beings and so forth which have been discussed in the previous two sextets from the point of view of utility, here, in the final sextet have their true natures clarified. (26)

In *bhakti* as previously taught knowledge is the doorway. Therefore, specialized knowledge of the body, the living being, and the Controller is his subject matter in the thirteenth. (27)

The living being and the controller are situated in the body. The first of those is linked to the characteristics of the body and is either bound or liberated through understanding. This is the teaching of the thirteenth. (28)

The three threads (qualities) are known as the bindings along with their results. Through *bhakti* for me those can be annulled. This is said in the fourteenth. (29)

Cyclic existence is connection with the threads and liberation is passing over the threads. That is accomplished by *bhakti* for Hari alone. This is learned from the fourteenth chapter. (30)

Dispassion cuts off cyclic existence; the living being is my eternal part; and I am the highest of all, the possessor of Śrī (Wealth, Opulence). These are recalled in the fifteenth chapter. (31)

बद्धान्मुक्ताच्च यः पुंशो भिन्नस्तद्धृत्तदुत्तमः।
स पुमान् हरिरेवेति प्राप्तं पञ्चदशादतः॥ ३२॥

दैवीं तथासुरीं कृष्णः सम्पदं षोडशेऽब्रवीत्।
उपादेयत्वहेयत्वे बोधयन् क्रमतस्तयोः॥ ३३॥

वेदार्थनैष्ठिका यन्ति स्वर्गं मोक्षञ्च शाश्वतम्।
वेदबाह्यास्तु नरकानिति षोडशनिर्णयः॥ ३४॥

सात्त्विकं राजसं वस्तु तामसञ्च विवेकतः।
कृष्णः सप्तदशेऽवादीत्पार्थप्रश्नानुसारतः॥ ३५॥

श्रद्धां स्वभावजां हित्वा शास्त्रजां तां समाश्रितः।
निःश्रेय्साधिकारी स्यादिति सप्तदशी स्थितिः॥ ३६॥

गीतार्थानिह संगृह्णन् हरिरष्टादशेऽखिलान्।
भक्तेस्तत्र प्रपत्तेश्च सोऽब्रवीदतिगोप्यताम्॥ ३७॥

उपाया बहवस्तेषु प्रपत्तिर्दास्यपूर्विका।
क्षिप्रं प्रसादनी विष्णोरित्यष्टादशतो मतम्॥ ३८॥

पीतं येन यशोदास्तन्यं नीतं पार्थसारथ्यम्।
स्फीतं सद्गुणवृन्दैस्तदत्र गीतं परं तत्त्वम्॥ ३९॥

यदिच्छातरिं प्राप्य गीतापयोधौ
न्यमज्जं गृहीतातिचित्रार्थरत्नम्।
न चोत्थातुमस्मि प्रभुर्हर्षयोगात्
स मे कौतुकी नन्दसूनुः प्रियस्तात्॥ ४०॥

श्रीमद्गीताभूषणं नाम भाष्यं
यत्नाद्विद्याभूषणेनोपचीर्णम्।
श्रीगोविन्दप्रेममाधुर्यलुब्धाः
कारुण्यार्द्राः साधवः शोधयध्वम्॥ ४१॥

The person who is different from both the bound and the liberated, who supports them and is the highest of them is Hari alone. This is learned from the fifteenth chapter. (32)

In the sixteenth Kṛṣṇa described the divine and demonic fortunes, making known the respective admirable and undesirable qualities of the two. (33)

Those who have firm regard for the values of the Vedas go to heaven and to eternal liberation. But those outside the Veda go to the hells. This is the teaching of the sixteenth. (34)

Kṛṣṇa discriminates between clear, translucent, and opaque substance in the seventeenth in response to the son of Pṛthā's[24] questions. (35)

One who rejects faith born of his own nature and depends on faith born of the scriptures is qualified for the highest good. This is the stance of the seventeenth chapter. (36)

Gathering together all the teachings of the *Gītā* in the eighteenth, Hari described there the great secrecy of the surrender of *bhakti*. (37)

There are many ways and among them surrender consequent on servitude is quickly pleasing to Viṣṇu. This is the view of the the eighteenth. (38)

That for which the breast milk of Yaśodā was drunk and the drivership of Arujun's chariot was accepted and which is swollen with true virtues, that is the ultimate truth sung here. (39)

Having found the boat of desire for whom, I dove into the ocean of the *Gītā* but am unable to fetch up the most wonderful gem of meaning that I found because of my exhileration; may he, the master, the Son of Nanda, most curious, be pleased with me. (40)

The commentary called the *Ornament of the Śrīmad Gītā* was built up with care by Vidyābhūṣaṇa. May the holy ones greedy for the sweetness of the love of Śrī Govinda, softened by compassion, correct it. (41)

---

[24]The son of Pṛthā is Arjuna.

Bibliography

Brahma, Nalinīkānta, ed. 1986. *Śrīmadbhagavadgītā.* 1st. Kalikātā, India: Navabhārata Pābliśārsa. In Sanskrit (Bengali script) with the commentary of Madhusūdana Sarasvatī with Bengali translation of text and commentary. Originally edited and translated by Bhūtanātha Saptatīrtha.

Bābā, Kṛṣṇadāsa, ed. 2023 Samvat (1955). *Śrīmadbhagavadgītā.* 1st. Kusumasarovara, Mathurā, India: Kṛṣṇadāsabābā. In Sanskrit (Devanāgarī) with the commentaries of Viśvanātha Cakravartin and Baladeva Vidyābhūṣaṇa.

Deutsch, Eliot, tr. 1968. *The Bhagavad Gita.* 1st. New York, Chicago, San Francisco: Holt, Rinehart and Winston.

Edgerton, Franklin, tr. 1972. *The Bhagavad Gītā.* 1st. Cambridge, Mass.: Harvard University Press. Fourth Printing.

Gosvāmin, Jīva. 1951. *Śrībhakti-śrīprīti-nāmaka-sandarbha-dvayam.* 1st. Edited by Purīdāsa. Vṛndāvana, India: Haridāsa Śarmā. In Sanskrit (Bengali Script).

———. 1967. *Tattvasandarbha.* 1st. Edited by Dr. Sitanath Goswami. Calcutta, India: Jadavpur Univerity. In Sanskrit (Devanāgarī) with the commentary of Baladeva Vidyābhūṣaṇa.

———. 1972a. *Bhagavatsandarbha.* 1st. Edited by Dr. Chinmayi Chatterjee. Calcutta, India: Jadavpur University. In Sanskrit (Devanāgarī).

———. 1972b. *Paramātmasandarbha.* 1st. Edited by Dr. Chinmayi Chatterjee. Calcutta, India: Jadavpur Univerity. In Sanskrit (Devanāgarī).

———. 1980. *Bhaktisandarbha.* 1st. Edited by Dr. Chinmayi Chatterjee. Calcutta, India: Jadavpur Univerity. In Sanskrit (Devanāgarī).

Gosvāmin, Rūpa. 495 [1981]. *Śrī Śrī Bhakti-rasāmṛtra-sindhuḥ.* 3rd. Mathurā, India: Śrī Kṛṣṇajanmasthāna. Edited with the commentaries of

Śrī Jīva, Mukundadāsa, and Viśvanātha Cakravartin and a Bengali translation by Haridāsa Dāsa. In Sanskrit and Bengali.

———. 2003. *The Bhakti-rasāmṛta-sindhu of Rūpa Gosvāmin.* 1st. New Delhi, India: Indira Gandhi Center for the Arts. Translated with introduction and notes by David L. Haberman.

Gosvāmin, Sanātana. G458 [1944]. *Bṛhad-bhāgavatāmṛta.* 1st. Edited by Purīdāsa. Mayamanasiṃha (now in Bangla Desh): Śacīnātharāya. In Sanskrit (Bengali script) with the author's own commentary.

Hacker, Paul. 1995. *Philology and Confrontation: Paul Hacker on Traditional and Modern Vedanta.* 1st. Edited by Wilhelm Halbfass. Albany, New York: State University of New York Press.

Minor, Robert N., tr. 1982. *Bhagavad-gītā: an exegetical commentary.* 1st. Columbia, Missouri: South Asia Books.

Prem, Sri Krishna. 2008. *The Yoga of the Bhagavad Gita.* 2nd. Sandpoint, Idaho: Morning Light Press.

Purīdāsa, ed. 1945. *Śrīmad-bhāgavatam.* 1st. Volume 1-3. Mayamanasiṃha, Bangla Desh: Śacīnātharāya-caturdhurīṇa. In Sanskrit (Bengali script) with verse index. No commentaries.

Puruṣottama. 1908. *Vedāntaratnamañjuṣā.* 1st. Edited by Ratnagopāla Bhaṭṭa. Benares, India: Chowkhamba Sanskrit Book Depot. In Sanskrit (Devanāgarī). This is a commentary on the Daśaślokī of Nimbārka.

Rāmānuja. 1968. *Vedārtha-saṅgraha of Śrī Rāmānujācārya.* 2nd. Edited by S. S. Raghavachar. Mysore, India: Sri Ramakrishna Ashrama. In Sanskrit (Devanāgarī) with English translation and introduction by S. S. Raghavachar, MA.

Sarasvatī, Madhusūdana. Sāla 1340 [1934]. *Bhaktirasāyanam.* 1st. Edited by Durgācaraṇa Sāṅkhya-Vedāntatīrtha. Kalikātā, India: Surendranātha Bhaṭṭācārya. In Sanskrit (Bengali script) with Bengali translation and commentary by Durgācaraṇa Sāṅkhya-Vedāntatīrtha.

Sargeant, Winthrop, tr. 1994. *The Bhagavad Gita.* 1st. Albany, New York: State University of New York Press. In Sanskrit (Devanāgarī and transliteration) and English.

Stcherbatsky, Th. 1965. *The Conception of Buddhist Nirvāṇa.* 2nd. The Hague: Mouton & Co. Indo-Iranian Reprints. Indo-Iranian Journal, VI. Originally published by the Academy of Sciences of the USSR, Leningrad, 1927.

Tarkabhūṣaṇa, Pramathanātha, ed. 2001. *Śrīmadbhagavadgītā.* 7th. Kalikātā, India: Deva Sāhitya Kuṭīra Prāibheṭa Limiṭiḍa. In Sanskrit (Bengali script) with the commentaries of Śaṅkara and Ānandagiri with Bengali translations of the text and Śaṅkara's commentary.

Tīrtha., Bhaktivilāsa, ed. 484 Gaurābda (1970). *Śrīmadbhagavadgītā.* 1st. Nadīyā, West Bengal, India: Śrī Gauḍīya Maṭha. In Sanskrit (Bengali script) and Bengali with the commentary of Viśvanātha Cakravartin.

van Buitenen, J. A. B., tr. 1981. *The Bhagavadgītā in the Mahābhārata: a Bilingual Edition.* 1st. Chicago: University of Chicago. In Sanskrit (transliteration) and English.

Vedavyāsa, Maharsi. 1986. *Viṣṇupurāṇam.* 1st. Edited by Thāneśacandra Upraiti. Dilli, India: Parimala Pablikeśansa. In Sanskrit (Devanāgarī) with the commentary of Śrīdhara Svāmin.

Vidyābhūṣaṇa, Baladeva. 1973. *Siddhāntaratnam.* 1st. Edited by Bhaktivedānta Vāmana Mahārāja. Nabadvīp, Nadīyā, India: Śrī Gauḍīya Samiti. In Sanskrit (Bengali script) with the autocommentary and Bengali translation.

Śaṅkara. 1949. *Upadeshasāhasrī of Śaṅkarāchārya.* 1st. Edited by Swāmi Jagadānanda. Mylapore, Madras: Sri Ramakrishna Math. In Sanskrit (Devanāgarī). English translation with notes by Swāmī Jagadānanda. Based on the commentary of Rāmatīrtha.

———. 1992. *A Thousand Teachings: the Upadeśasāhasrī of Śaṅkara.* 1st. Edited by Sengaku Mayeda. Albany, New York: State University of New York Press. English translation with long introduction by Sengaku Mayeda.

www.ingramcontent.com/pod-product-compliance
Lightning Source LLC
Chambersburg PA
CBHW031229290426
44109CB00012B/220
* 9 7 8 0 9 8 1 7 9 0 2 3 7 *